OAK ISLAND
Obsession

THE RESTALL STORY

OAK ISLAND
Obsession

LEE LAMB

THE DUNDURN GROUP
TORONTO

Copy-editor: Andrea Waters
Design: Jennifer Scott
Printer: University of Toronto Press

Library and Archives Canada Cataloguing in Publication

Lamb, Lee
    Oak Island obsession : the Restall story / Lee Lamb.

Includes bibliographical references.
ISBN-10: 1-55002-625-9
ISBN-13: 978-1-55002-625-2

    1. Oak Island treasure site (N.S.). 2. Restall family. 3. Treasure troves--Nova Scotia--Oak Island (Lunenburg). I. Title.

FC2345.O23Z49 2006   971.6'23   C2006-901339-X

1   2   3   4   5   10   09   08   07   06

Conseil des Arts du Canada   Canada Council for the Arts

Canada

ONTARIO ARTS COUNCIL
CONSEIL DES ARTS DE L'ONTARIO

We acknowledge the support of the **Canada Council for the Arts** and the **Ontario Arts Council** for our publishing program. We also acknowledge the financial support of the **Government of Canada** through the **Book Publishing Industry Development Program** and **The Association for the Export of Canadian Books**, and the **Government of Ontario** through the **Ontario Book Publishers Tax Credit program**, and the **Ontario Media Development Corporation**.

Care has been taken to trace the ownership of copyright material used in this book. The author and the publisher welcome any information enabling them to rectify any references or credits in subsequent editions.

J. Kirk Howard, President

Printed and bound in Canada.
Printed on recycled paper.

www.dundurn.com

Dundurn Press	Gazelle Book Services Limited	Dundurn Press
3 Church Street, Suite 500	White Cross Mills	2250 Military Road
Toronto, Ontario, Canada	High Town, Lancaster, England	Tonawanda, NY
M5E 1M2	LA1 4XS	U.S.A. 14150

Table of Contents

Introduction

Their lives were like no others.

All across Germany, Britain, Canada, and the United States, Bob and Mildred Restall amazed audiences with their death-defying feats on motorcycles inside a steel sphere known as the Globe of Death.

Then, at an age when they might have been expected to settle into a more conservative way of life, they embarked on a bold new adventure — one that would bring them recognition from around the world as television stations, magazines, and other news media chronicled the Restall search for treasure on Canada's famous Oak Island. That adventure would test them in every measure and would change them profoundly. Ultimately, it would end in unspeakable tragedy.

Bob and Mildred Restall were my parents. This is their story.

Note: Throughout this book, comments in square brackets within primary source material are mine. Comments in parentheses belong to the author of that particular piece. Original documents have been edited for clarity, spelling, and punctuation and have had extraneous content removed.

The Start of It All

CHAPTER 1

Although they were born on different continents, my parents' early years had much in common. Each started life in a family that struggled financially, each was forced to abandon formal schooling very early, and each chose a career in entertainment as the portal to adventure.

Once their lives intersected, my parents discovered they were a perfect match. They joined forces and set out, confident that their life together would be exciting and glamorous. Throughout the ensuing years, they encountered exhilarating highs and daunting lows, but true to their expectations, the life they shared proved to be a most extraordinary adventure.

My mother was English, born and bred, but Dad was a fourth-generation Canadian, born in Toronto.

Dad's parents, Ernest and Annie Restall, had three daughters and four sons. Shortly after the last child was born, Ernest moved the family to the United States in search of a better life. Ernest was a hard-working skilled tradesman, but he was also a heavy drinker. After only a few years in the United States, Ernest and Annie separated; alcohol was blamed.

Ernest returned to Canada, and Annie and the children remained in the United States. Ernest had taught his trade, plumbing, to his oldest son, my father. By the time his parents separated, Dad was already working to help the family financially. He had left school immediately after graduating from grade eight. His sisters Lillian and Margaret did the same, securing jobs with the Bell Telephone Company. In those days (around 1919), you could leave school before age sixteen if your family needed your assistance. So at the earliest opportunity, each of the Restall children left school to help support the family.

Dad, his siblings, and his mother lived in Yonkers, New York. Soon, the older boys in the family — Dad, Goldy, and Bill — discovered dirt track motorcycle racing and became local stars. The name Restall hardly conjures up visions of speed, so the boys adopted the surname Lee, after General Robert E. Lee. Dad took the name Speedy Bob Lee, Goldy became Goldy Lee or Curly Lee, and Bill became Wild Bill Lee or sometimes Billy Lee. Bill lost interest in riding motorcycles pretty quickly, but Dad and Goldy were hooked. As well as motorcycle racing, they began trick riding inside a motor drome and were so successful that they took their act to Britain.

A drome (sometimes called a wall) is a huge barrel-like structure. Motorcyclists ride around on the inside of the barrel walls. Spectators pay admission, climb a steep staircase, and stand on a platform that goes all around the top of the drome. Then they peer down into the barrel, watching the riders roar round and round, now riding with no hands, now steering with their feet, now crossing one leg over to ride sidesaddle, now standing with both feet on one pedal with hands in the air. Sometimes two riders on separate motorcycles race along the wall, criss-crossing each other's paths. Sometimes a car is driven inside the drome instead.

When my mother and father met, Mom was a dancer. She had been earning her own living, working with variety shows that played across England, from the time she was twelve years old. Mildred Shelley was born in Brackenhill, Ackworth R.D., England, in 1912 to Henrietta Shelley, née Greenwood, and Henry Shelley, a colliery banksman. Henry went overseas to serve in the First World War, leaving his wife and young daughter in England. In less than a year, Henry was killed in battle. Henrietta took little Mildred and returned to her parents' home. Her father owned two or three fish and chip shops and was also a gentleman farmer, keeping a few cows, pigs, and chickens. He was a stern man who expected each of his children to work long and hard in the service of the family in exchange for room, board, and a very small allowance. Henrietta toiled alongside her younger brothers and sisters. There were plenty of jobs, so even little Mildred was pressed into service.

My mother recalled no happiness in that household, no fun, no kindness, no compliments — only work. She and her mother slaved for the dour old man. When the family sat down together at mealtimes, his was the only voice allowed to be heard. It was fresh in Henrietta's mind why she had been in such a hurry to marry and leave home, but now she was a widow with a young daughter and few options.

Eventually Henrietta gathered enough money together for her escape, and she and Mildred were on their way. At that time in England, live theatre was flourishing. Comedies, dramas, musicals, and variety shows played in cities and towns all across the country. Henrietta had always dreamed of being an actress. Now she was determined to realize her dream. She proved to be a natural. With her commanding stage presence and magnificent speaking voice, it was not long before she was working in theatres across England and travelling to India, Japan, and other exotic countries for months at a time. Acting is an uncertain career, but Henrietta was almost never out of work.

While she was establishing herself as an actress, Henrietta sent my mother to live with her aunt and uncle in a rural seaside village in England. Mom told me that she doubted these people were really relatives, but they were warm, loving people who truly seemed to care about her. Life with them was idyllic.

Money was tight, but there was good solid food, the lovely seaside, and people who cared. Mom liked to recall the excitement when her mother sent money. Her aunt would take Mom on a shopping spree to buy beautiful new clothes. But many times during those years, my mother had only one school uniform, which she washed and ironed each evening. Sometimes she felt sorry for herself, wishing she had a vast wardrobe, but her aunt comforted her by saying, "Mildred, even if you wore a flour sack, you'd still be beautiful." Maybe it was there that Mom learned to carry herself proudly in spite of everything.

Those days with her aunt and uncle were the happiest of her childhood. When Henrietta returned from India one day and took Mom away, Mom and her aunt and uncle were heartbroken. But it was time for Mildred to earn her keep. She was twelve years old.

Henrietta enrolled my mother in a boarding school just outside London. There, girls from twelve to sixteen were schooled in the three Rs and taught to perform on stage. Their ballet teacher was Madame Kiesh, formerly a Russian prima ballerina. She claimed to have been a contemporary of Madame Pavlova. But the Dying Swan was choreographed for Pavlova, transporting her to fame and fortune, while

Madame Kiesh was left to spark the talent of troupes of bedraggled English schoolgirls.

No doubt the study of ballet helped these youngsters develop flexibility, economy of movement, and grace, useful attributes in any kind of stage performance. But they spent much more of their stage time performing tap dancing routines than they ever did executing ballet steps. In a succession of variety shows, they tap danced and acted out minor, non-speaking roles in dramas and comedies while travelling from one end of England to the other. For one particular run the girls even left Britain and appeared for a couple of months in Paris with the Folies Bergère. Imagine those statuesque beauties sharing the stage with a gaggle of tap dancing English schoolgirls whose average height was 5'3"! It must have been quite a sight. This Parisian run was definitely a high point for the little troupe and contributed to some very swelled heads.

The school kept all the proceeds from the theatre bookings. The girls received their lessons, room and board, and a very tiny allowance. A lot of petty nastiness took place among the dancers. My mother learned to rely solely on herself.

It was at this time that she developed a love of books, especially science fiction adventures. Ryder Haggard and Edward Rice Burroughs were favourite authors. Perhaps this is when she developed another of her lifelong traits. She was a very private person, and fiercely proud. She would have swallowed a poison pill before letting anyone see any trace of weakness or vulnerability, any reason for pity.

Life on the road consisted of tight friendships or acrimonious vendettas among troupe members, a stream of faceless boarding homes, furtive puffs on sneaked cigarettes, and, under the watchful eye of their ever-vigilant chaperone, cuddles and kisses from a series of star-struck beaus, soon to be abandoned as the girls criss-crossed the country plying their trade.

As soon as Mom was old enough to leave the troupe, she had publicity photos taken and struck out on her own.

When Henrietta remarried, she and her new husband, fellow actor William Newley, toured together, while my mother did her best to be employed, self-sufficient, and elsewhere. She would audition for jobs and enjoy several months of work until the tour ended, and then she'd inquire around, audition somewhere else, and repeat the whole process.

It was at one of these junctures that her life and my dad's intersected. He and his brother Goldy had enjoyed success as motorcycle performers in England. Now Dad wanted to use their drome act as a vehicle to see the world. Goldy, however, was ready for home. They agreed to part company. While Dad stayed on in Britain, Goldy undertook a short solo stint in Germany and Hungary and then returned to the U.S. for good. In 1932, he became Motorcycle Speed Racing Champion of the Eastern United States, dividing his time between motorcycle racing and motor drome work.

Dad continued with his plans for a tour of Germany. Thinking a woman at the Front of the drome would help bring in customers, he put the word out that he wanted to hire an attractive woman, preferably someone already in show business. Mom's tour was coming to an end and she was about to be jobless, so along with other troupe members, she trudged down to the fairgrounds to audition, and the job was hers.

Perhaps the term "the Front" needs an explanation. Whether they play parks, fairs, or carnivals, each show has a raised stage in front of it where performers with props, in this case motorcycles, give spectators a taste of what is inside the show. Huge canvases painted with show high-lights back the stage. One or two tall ticket booths with ticket sellers at the ready flank the stage, and an announcer with microphone in hand paces back and forth, entertaining the audience with elaborate descriptions of what they can expect to see once they pay their admission. He ends his spiel by urging on the crowd: "Step right up, ladies and gentle-men, and buy your tickets now."

On the drome Front, performers didn't just stand around like stat-ues. In centre stage, one motorcycle was on rollers; Dad or one of the crew members started it up and did tricks such as hands in the air or standing on the seat while the Harley drove surely and steadily to nowhere. (Harley Davidsons and Nortons were used on the Front, smaller motorcycles inside the drome, and French motorcycles inside the globe because they were even smaller in scale, and the globe's inte-rior was less than sixteen feet in diameter.)

When Mom was hired, the plan was that she would lend a female presence to the drome Front, but it was no time before she learned to ride a motorcycle, first on country roads and then inside the drome. Soon she was a full partner in the show, riding every bit as well as Dad did, taking turns on the microphone to encourage people to come in and see the show and talking knowledgeably with fans about laps, centrifugal force, and rpm's. She was billed as Mildred Lee, sister of Bob Lee. (These were the days when even movie stars did not admit they were married, for fear of killing the glamour they enjoyed as performers.)

As soon as Mom was competent on the motorbike, she and Dad took their act to Germany. Cupid's arrow must have found its mark swiftly, for just weeks after their arrival in Hamburg they were married. Throughout the next few years my parents travelled back and forth between Britain and Germany many times.

Among motorcycle enthusiasts in Germany, Bob and Mildred Lee were celebrities. Germans love high-performance machines, and they admire skill. Their appreciation of my parents bordered on adulation. And Mom found she had a knack for language; it was no time before she was using German phrases to chat with her new motorcycle fans.

In their early trips to Germany my parents performed in a drome. Later, they purchased the globe. The globe was a ball, nearly sixteen feet in diameter, held about five feet off the ground by steel poles. The ball was made of steel strips criss-crossed to give it strength and to provide a full view of what was going on inside. There were plenty of globes in Europe at the time; motorcyclists rode solo inside the ball, horizontally or vertically. My parents called their globe the Globe of Death, as did other globe owners. But it was their performance that was unique. The highlight of the show was their double act. Here is a description: *Dressed in their high-necked shirts, jodhpurs, and sleek riding boots, Bob and Mildred Lee step inside the Globe of Death, where two motorcycles stand waiting. Mildred climbs on her bike and starts it up; Bob puts his hand at the back of her seat and assists her to push off, then lets go as her machine starts to drive in circles near the bottom of the globe. Bob watches as Mildred's circles grow larger and larger until she is riding exactly horizontally at the mid-point of the globe. Bob climbs on his motorcycle, starts it up, and traces Mildred's path until he is riding right behind her. Now both of them are making horizontal laps. Then slowly Bob changes the angle of his laps until he is riding absolutely vertically in the globe, crossing Mildred's horizontal path. They ride like this at right angles to each other for several minutes. Standing on the ground inside the tent that encloses the globe, the audience stares, transfixed, as the riders and their motorcycles zoom by, defying gravity. First one motorcycle, horizontally, then the other, vertically, speed past, driving round and round in the steel cage. The globe shudders with the sheer force of the machines hurling themselves against its sides. All the while the mind-numbing rhythmic roar of engines created by those alternating laps engulfs the audience. It is mesmerizing. Then slowly Bob changes his path angle and gradually returns to Mildred's horizontal track; Mildred makes smaller and slower laps until she is down at the bottom of the globe, where she stops, still seated on her motorbike, watching as Bob begins his descent. His last laps become smaller as he slowly and tightly circles Mildred and brings his machine to a stop right beside hers. Then, switching off their motorcycles, in unison they step off, smile, and wave to the crowd.*

The act was breathtaking. It never failed to thrill the audience. Often people paid to watch again and again.

Another unique feature of their act was the automobile, a tiny car that Dad designed and constructed to drive in the globe. With Dad as the driver and Mom as his passenger, they sped around in the globe horizontally and then vertically, looping the loop in their automobile, as the announcer on the Front had promised. Men in the audience were especially fascinated by the little car and often excitedly waited after the show to examine it more closely and to ask questions about its construction. In Germany, Mom and Dad had an accident in that car. A fine dust had coated the globe and the little car skidded and crashed. Mom sustained a deep cut under her chin that, fortunately, left only a tiny scar; Dad received a broken arm. They considered themselves very lucky.

Dad was always very safety-conscious. He did his best to engineer accidents out of the equipment, machinery, and timing of their act. In their entire time performing together, they had only two accidents.

The longer they were in Germany the more popular they became. An avid photographer, Dad compiled album after album of photographs taken in Germany: photos of himself and Mom as young lovebirds walking in a park, feeding the swans, snuggled together in a drifting rowboat, and as celebrities among dozens of leather-jacketed fans on their own shiny motorcycles. There were photos taken in cabarets, in the lush countryside, and on fairgrounds jammed with spectators.

It was an exciting time for my parents, but it coincided with the time when the Nazis were coming into power in Germany. On the streets, convoys of trucks drove by, each with rows of soldiers sitting back to back, rifles pointing out into the street. On the fairgrounds, one day Mom and Dad stood horrified as a Nazi officer shot a teenage boy for no apparent reason. Bystanders rioted in response. Anxiety and fear were everywhere. Then one day my parents returned to their hotel room and found it had been ransacked. All of Dad's undeveloped films had been pulled from their canisters and strewn across the bed. They packed their bags and left for England immediately.

They found Britain much changed. Anticipation of war preoccupied the country, and money for entertainment was scarce. What little work my parents were able to get did not involve the Globe of Death. Instead they found themselves riding in dromes owned by others.

Engagements were sporadic and pay was paltry. For long spells they could get no work at all. At one point they were even reduced to selling cough drops to put food on the table.

Glory days were behind them. They were celebrities no more. Later, both Mom and Dad referred to this as the worst time in their lives.

It seemed a gift from heaven when at last Patty Conklin, of Conklin Bros. Shows, offered to pay their fare to Canada — and, more importantly, the fare of the globe — if they would join one of his cross-Canada carnivals. Dad would happily have worked anywhere, but to be back in his birth country was wonderful. He came over, signed the papers, then sent for my mother and me.

I had been born in England and was left in the care of a nurse in England while Mom and Dad went about their work in Germany. When they returned to Britain for good, the three of us travelled together, towing a tiny house trailer. By the time Mom and I boarded the SS *York* to follow Dad to Canada, I was two and a half years old.

The Conklin Bros. carnival consisted of rides, games, food concessions, and various shows, such as the girlie show, the Wild West show, the swim show, and the Ten-in-One (the carnival name for what some people call a freak show). The carnival played in cities across Canada for spots of from four days to ten days, with show people living on the show train throughout the season and equipment travelling in box cars at the back of the train.

I travelled with the show for a couple of years. When the show was set up, it was like living in a village. You knew everyone. Then suddenly everybody would pack up and move on to a new place where the village would reappear, but now the streets were in different locations. You had to search for your friends, but they were there.

When I was four, Dad and Mom and I went to Hawaii for nearly six months. They rode motorcycles as a free act in a drome in an amusement park. There was no tent, and no tickets were sold. People came down to see the free show and stayed to enjoy the paid attractions.

With only two shows a day, and none on Sunday, Mom and Dad had plenty of leisure time. Although I was only four, I have many fond memories of Hawaii. Among them are Dad patiently painting a big red toe in each of my sandals so I would know which shoe to put on which foot, and on another day in a seaside park showing me how the banyan tree puts down roots and becomes a totally new tree wherever its branches touch the ground. I can remember sitting with Mom, examining the intricate detail of the flower garden portrayed on her beautiful new cream and mauve Japanese silk kimono. While we were in Hawaii, she took lessons in dancing the hula, and then taught me the dance through a little Hawaiian song called "Manuella Boy."

When we returned to Canada, Mom hired five or six young women and trained them in the art of the hula. She created an authentic Hawaiian show to tour the carnival circuit along with the globe. The Hawaiian show presented, through dance, all of the moods of Hawaii, from the vigorous Hawaiian War Chant to the sensuous Aloha Oi. People of all ages enjoyed it.

Dressed in a green floral floor-length sarong, wearing a cluster of leis, Mom joined the Hawaiian show announcer inside the tent and, sharing the microphone, the two of them talked their way through a little skit that cast them as tour guides on a cruise ship that was bringing the "passengers," the audience, to Hawaii. Then, as the dancers began to weave their magic and the announcer guided the audience through the rest of the journey, Mom crept away to the small tent behind the shows, changed into her shirt and jodhpurs, and stepped on to the stage of the Globe of Death just in time to rev her motorcycle and do her loops. She dashed back and forth all afternoon and evening between the two shows.

Incidentally, while on the road Mom watched over her girls with laser-beam scrutiny, which, undoubtedly, she had learned from her own chaperone many years before.

Dancers in the Hawaiian show usually wore long grass skirts in a natural straw colour, although for some numbers their skirts were made of orange cellophane. You couldn't see through them, of course, as the skirts were densely packed with strands of cellophane, but each strand caught the light and shimmered as the dancers moved across the stage. Lelani, the star of the show, who really looked Hawaiian with her long, lustrous black hair and slow, smooth, undulating hula, wore a dark green cellophane skirt for her solo. She was magnificent.

I was part of the Hawaiian show until I realized that the laughter erupting from the audience each time we ended a particular dance was directed at me. Far too vain to be the butt of a joke, I walked away from my show business career forever.

The Hawaiian show lasted only one year. Not surprisingly, appearing in both the Hawaiian show and the Globe of Death was simply too much work for Mom.

Erecting and dismantling the globe at the beginning and end of every spot was extremely hard, heavy work. A crew of strong young men travelled with us, helping with set-up and tear-down, helping to maintain the motorcycles, and appearing on the Front. Some did solo rides inside the Globe of Death. Some of them remained life-long friends.

In 1941, when Bobby was born (and I was six years old), Mom and Dad decided that carnival life was not for their children. After that, we all lived together in a house in Hamilton, Ontario, in the off-season, and, in spring, when the carnival started up, Bobby and I were sent to live with Aunt Net, Uncle Bill, and Uncle George, Dad's uncles and aunt, in a grand three-storey house on Silverbirch Avenue in Toronto, two blocks from Balmy Beach. There, for four months of each year, Bobby and I immersed ourselves in the activities of our Toronto pals while Mom and Dad worked the carnival circuit by themselves.

Logical Connections

CHAPTER 2

Some find it difficult to imagine how my parents, who lived the carnival life and rode motorcycles, could end up digging for treasure. Yet it was a logical progression. Everything about them — their values, their skills, their strengths, and even their weaknesses — made them just the right candidates for the big adventure of Oak Island.

Let me give a clearer picture of our off-the-road life. My parents went with the carnival each spring, but in the fall, they came back, flush with money and eager to set about their other, very different lives.

In those days, the carnival was open from ten in the morning to after midnight six days a week. On Sundays the show train wound its way from city to city, while performers caught a break. But for the most part, travelling with the carnival meant four or five months of a relentless grind in sweltering heat, stormy wind, soaking rain, or cold so intense that fingers fumbled with tickets and money.

After the Canadian National Exhibition, which, except for Sundays, was a two-week stretch of eighteen-hour days, the show travelled through a series of fall fairs in towns such as Leamington, Ontario, or Trois-Rivières, Quebec, until heavy rain and bitter cold, the harbingers of winter, kept spectators away. Then the show wound its way back to storage in Brantford to hibernate until the following spring. Performers and concessionaires were exhausted. Many would head south for the winter or go to home bases across Canada.

Mom and Dad would come back from a summer on the road, tired and very thin, the result of having shaken pounds off all summer racing their motorcycles round and round inside the Globe of Death. For their efforts they would have a few extra thousand dollars to pay some bills and buy a big-ticket item or two, like a sewing machine, refrigerator, or new furnace. But no holiday was on their agenda. Instead, Dad immediately went to work as a plumber/steamfitter for Stelco, Hamilton's mammoth steel plant.

Our summer lives consisted of Mom and Dad on the road and Bobby and I living with our great-uncles and great-aunt. Our winter lives consisted of Dad working for Stelco, Mom running the household, and I (and later Bobby) attending Memorial Public School just two blocks away. Life, as far as I was concerned, was perfect. We had distinctly different summer and winter lives. We had a permanent home. Our lives were stable but far from dull. Something was going on all the time, and we all were happy partners in it.

Dad worked at Stelco full-time, but he always had other projects in the works that we all believed would someday make our lives better. We lived on the ground floor of a three-storey brick house in Hamilton; Dad worked on weekends and evenings to build two apartments above us to provide a bit of extra income. He also designed carnival rides and built them in the backyard. One was called the Ski Lift; it gave your heart a little lift each time you swooped down from the top. Several other adult rides and quite a number of kiddie rides followed.

Dad was great at figuring ways to use commonly available parts, like vehicle axles, gears, and sprockets, instead of expensive custom-made parts. Nevertheless, carnival rides were costly to construct, and any money that was realized from them was immediately plowed right back into whatever came next. Ideas for new rides came quicker than the money to finance them. I remember the dismay Bobby and I experienced after struggling valiantly to help Dad complete a ride, only to see him tighten the last nut, take pictures, then immediately set about tearing it down to cannibalize it and use the parts for his next ride, which he promised would be even better.

The whole family was involved in his enterprises. Using a steel brush, Bobby and I scrubbed the rust off of his latest ride and Mom climbed up and applied the silver undercoat, then the enamel final coat. Whatever the project, we were all in it together.

I'll never forget one winter when Dad spent all his spare time at a table in the corner of the living room, with pen and India ink, making meticulous drawings for patent applications; a folding boat was one project, some new kind of bathtub was another. Someone bumped the table and the India ink fell on the new living room rug. I expected an ear-splitting shriek from Mom, but not a sound. Then Dad quietly said, "Milk might work." Immediately all four of us were on our hands and knees with a big bowl full of milk, scrubbing the rug like mad. Not another word was uttered until the job was done. Then we shared a good laugh while admiring our handiwork.

When Dad was occupied with segments of projects that only he could work on, the rest of us kept busy in other ways. Mom played the piano or sewed while Bobby and I spent our time drawing, making models, or developing other skills for the fantastic futures we planned.

Dad's projects weren't hobbies. They were always something that, if successful, would free him from Stelco and benefit us all. It wasn't that he didn't like plumbing and steamfitting, but he felt a life working for others was a life wasted. Dad dreamed of being free of daily constraints so that he could devote himself totally to his inventions and projects.

I remember coming home one day and telling him I'd just met our next-door neighbour in the fabric store downtown, where she was working. She had told me that she didn't need the money, but now that she was a widow what else was there for her to do with her time. Dad looked at me sombrely and said, "Imagine having so little creativity that you have to get a job for excitement." We both shook our heads piously. Lack of creativity would never be our problem.

At home I learned that work can be fun and that it is great to always be working towards something. But Sundays were different. Sunday dinner, the best meal of our week, was served around noon, then the family piled into the car and away we went on a mystery tour. Dad kept the destination a secret, letting it slowly reveal itself as the journey progressed. Sometimes we visited Grimsby or Jordan to see the beautiful cherry blossoms, or to Hamilton's Rock Garden, or maybe Niagara Falls. Sometimes we carried our aluminum boat on the roof of the car and launched it in Lake Ontario at Van Wagner's Beach. Then we'd slowly putt along the shoreline for miles. Not having a lot of faith in our little craft, Mom, Bobby, and I nagged Dad to keep close to shore so we could swim in if anything went wrong. It never did. In winter we often went tobogganing or ice skating on the Back Bay. Whatever the adventure, at the end of the day, we always hurried home in time to huddle together in the dark, on the living room carpet, with a sandwich supper, sharing our once-a-week treat of Canada Dry ginger ale or Orange Crush, listening intently to Lamont Cranston and The Shadow on the radio.

We were a happy lot. Mealtimes were great times in my family; everyone shared hopes, dreams, and recitations of daily foibles. Conversations were cheerful, optimistic, and revolved exclusively around the present or the future. No crying over spilt milk, no gossip or negative talk. Not that we were all that virtuous; more likely we were so egocentric that the only topic of conversation that stood a chance was us. Ours was a family of laughter and high hopes, where the most precious thing of all was time. Dad was the one who set that tone.

But he didn't mind indulging in a bit of dreaming. Many times he would smile and begin, "When our ship comes in …," and then he'd spin some fantastic dream like "Your mother and I will have his and hers Cadillac convertibles" or "We'll throw away the old washing machine in the basement and send all our laundry out." Time after time he would draw us through these little imaginary journeys. We'd all listen, spellbound.

Mom always said that she would be satisfied with very little, and that it was Dad who had the grandiose plans for wealth. I believe that's true. But it always made her smile when he started his "When our ship comes in" talk.

We all believed that Dad was a genius. Time and again he proved he could put together whatever was needed out of the most unlikely everyday materials. He could fix anything structural or mechanical, any kind of engine. He took care of things for us, and he was always ready to help a friend. He knew working parts and he knew the principles behind them — hydraulics, magnets, generators.

Dad read a lot. He was unable to pass by a newspaper without reading at least a snippet of it. I remember waking on a school day one morning and being amazed to find Dad sitting at the kitchen table reading a newspaper.

"Aren't you going to work today?" I asked.

"Yes, but I was going to be ten minutes late and they dock you a half-hour, even if you're only late five minutes. I thought I'd just read a bit and go in on time for the half-an-hour late," he said. Some time later, when I began getting my breakfast ready, he was still there. "I was so engrossed in my reading I missed the half-hour, so I thought I'd just read a bit more and go in for the one-hour late," he explained. Half an hour later, on my way out the door to school, he was still in the kitchen but no longer reading; now he stood, noisily gathering his things together.

"Waiting for the hour-and-a-half late?" I asked innocently.

"No!" he retorted. "I'm going to work. If I keep reading, I'll never get to work at all."

Dad's interests were far-ranging. He owned the complete eight-volume set of Bernard McFadden's *Encyclopedia of Naturopathic Remedies*. Mention an ache or pain and Dad could suggest the cure. Talk about air travel and he could launch into the history of flight and finish with whatever exciting advancements were on the draw-ing boards now. He kept track of anthropological and archeological discoveries and developments in technology and mechanics. He read the newspaper from cover to cover every day; he read construction, mechanics, health, and science magazines, as well as anything else he could get his hands on. More importantly, he remembered every-thing he read. This was the early 1940s. There was no nuclear physics, stem cell research, or any of the myriad highly technical sci-entific specialties that now exist. Dad knew the answers to all the questions that touched our lives. As far as Mom, Bobby, or I were concerned, he knew everything.

Dad grew up in the era of the self-made man. Men like Henry Ford started with nothing but determination and ingenuity and became fabulous success stories. Ahearn, Bell, Howe, Marconi, and others who invented things or used their creativity to think of new ways to use existing things were setting themselves apart from the crowd. In fact, at that time most of Canada's new wealth was generated by inventors and entrepreneurs working alone. It was possible to go from having noth-ing to having it all, and you could do it solo. Dad saw himself in that league.

Dad's good nature was magnetic. The moment he came in the door each day after work, he would sing out "I'm home!" and everybody would run to say hello. He was such a cheerful, optimistic person, the room brightened whenever he entered.

Many of our car rides included a sing-along. In a good strong voice Dad would belt out a robust beginning to a song and we'd all join in, but before long the song would falter for lack of words. Just before it gave its last gasp, Dad would loop it back to the beginning, drawing us with him, and round we'd go again, with great gusto. In that way, one song lasted the duration of a trip. "I'll Take You Home Again, Kathleen" was a favourite. Dad sang it to alleviate Mom's yearning for England. At first that pleased her, but after years of the loop treatment, he needed only to sing the first line to elicit groans of despair from her.

I thought Dad was not only the smartest man alive, but also the most patient, kind, and all-round wonderful. He never lost his temper, never raised his voice except in laughter or song. He was not critical; he focused on the good. He was observant. If he noticed that you weren't happy he'd comment on it out loud, so everyone knew what everybody else was feeling. I remember one spring when Mom spent day after day pacing irritably back and forth in front of the living room window, concentrating deeply on thoughts she wasn't sharing, acting very much like a caged, angry animal. Bobby and I cringed. Finally Dad declared, "It's spring. Your mother has had enough of this home life. She's restless to get on the road again."

Of course he was right. Mom was a performer, an entertainer, a star. Domestic chores were always a struggle. Her Sunday roasts were magnificent, but weekday meals confounded her. Fried Spam or hamburger patties with boiled potatoes made frequent appearances at our table. She tried to be more adventurous, but those attempts yielded little success. Once she slaved away all afternoon over some "mock duck" concoction gleaned from a magazine: in reality it was hammered flank steak, tough as shoe leather, rolled around bread stuffing. Too polite to criticize, we feigned delight and struggled to saw our way through it.

Vegetables in my home were mashed potatoes, canned peas, canned corn, or canned lima beans. I learned to detest them all, save the potatoes. Dessert was always pudding or canned fruit. No cakes or cookies ever came out from Mom's oven. She never learned to bake.

But then, what would you expect from a dancer-cum-motorcyclist? Surely it was not a future of domestic bliss that attracted my mother to my father.

Anyway, my mother had lots of talents in other aspects of domestic life. She certainly was good at sewing. After she fought her way through her first project, living room drapes, there was no stopping her. She made all kinds of clothing, from cowboy shirts to tailored suits. And nothing looked homemade.

She played piano surprisingly well. She taught herself to read music, and eventually between hard work and her exceptional ear for music she was able play even complicated arrangements of popular or classical pieces. Rachmaninoff's Prelude, *Rustle of Spring*, *Deep Purple*, and the boogie-woogie version of *Flight of the Bumble-Bee* come to mind.

She read voraciously, mostly fiction, especially science fiction. And she was a great storyteller. I remember once leaving the house just as my friend Shirley arrived. I explained I was on my way out and Shirley said, "Oh, that's okay. I really came to visit your mother anyway. I was hoping she'd tell me one of her stories."

Mom was good at handling money. When they travelled with the globe she always managed to surreptitiously sneak some money aside. At the end of the year she would have quite a little nest egg. But it was not for herself. Sooner or later Dad would find himself in a financial bind, and, to his relief, out would pop the secret stash. In Hamilton, she ran the household on rents from the apartments upstairs, and she could always manage to accumulate a little private cache of money. Come some unforeseen expense, we would be rescued again.

Dad was quick to give Mom credit for her ability to come to our rescue. But he must have thought the money came by magic, for after they stopped using the globe and we no longer had rental apartments, Dad still came to her, hat in hand, for unexpected expenses like income tax, and he seemed mystified when she had nothing to give. Surely only my father would find income tax to be an unexpected expense year after year.

Mom was around seventeen when she met Dad; he was eight years older, handsome, and a world traveller. Mom was always his biggest fan. She could disagree vociferously with Dad, but if anyone else tried, she would spring to his defence. And you could see, day in and day out, how happy she was in her life with him. They constantly showed each other affection, laughed together a lot, and obviously preferred being in each other's company.

They talked everything over; Dad valued Mom's opinion. And always, throughout their lives, they arranged to do some things together. In Hamilton they had their own small street motorcycles, and on many evenings they would go for a spin together at dusk, purring down the quiet side streets of Hamilton. They cherished their time alone.

However, they were not always lovebirds. They had fierce arguments, but the fierceness was all on Mom's part. She had a fiery temper. When something displeased her, she'd rant and rave, while Dad, always the peace-maker, murmured in the background, "There, there Mildred." Suddenly she would announce that she was leaving, cram some clothes into a suitcase, and storm out of the house and down the street. Dad would follow, imploring her to return. Bobby and I would tremble. Eventually, they would return, silently unpack the suitcase, and spend some private time together. After that, peace and happiness would reign once more.

When I was an adult Mom once confided in me about these episodes. "I got sick and tired of packing. I knew I'd soon be unpacking again. Eventually I stopped packing altogether. I just left. Once I stormed out of the house, marched along Main Street, and got on a streetcar. The door closed and then Bob rushed up to the glass door and started rapping on it," she told me. "I urged the conductor, 'Don't let him on! Don't let him on!' Bob kept rapping. The poor conductor didn't know what to do. He said, 'Lady, I can't just ignore a customer. I've got to let him on.' Eventually I gave in, he let Bob on, then we got off the streetcar together and walked home, holding hands. I guess the people on the streetcar thought we were crazy."

Mom once told me another suitcase story. She and Dad were in a small Ontario town with the carnival one evening when one of their spats erupted. In a fury, Mom packed up, raged out of their hotel room, and marched resolutely down the street, suitcase in hand. A car driving down the street in her direction slowed beside her, and a man wound down his window and quietly called to her, "Five dollars for five minutes?" Stunned for a moment, she recovered and retorted, "Bugger off!" then sharply turned and marched back to the hotel and the safety of married life. That may have been the moment when she gave up packing.

With all that activity going on around our house — a married couple riding out on dual motorcycles, carnival rides being constructed in the backyard, the house assuming constantly changing dimensions — it's not surprising that our neighbours looked on us with a mixture of bewilderment and envy.

Occasionally I had friends whose parents wouldn't allow them to come to my house. It was the show business connection. When I told my mother, she exploded. "These people are nothing! We are infinitely superior to these small-minded bigots who have never even been out of their own country. We are cultured, knowledgeable, well-travelled, and well-read." Somewhat chastened, I tried to keep all of that in mind.

For the most part, we were impervious to what other people thought. They knew nothing. We never had visitors, other than show people, and then only once or twice a year. We never had company for dinner. Only once do I remember my parents attending a parent-teacher night for Bobby and me. We were completely insular.

One winter, Dad decided not to return to Stelco. He ran his own plumbing and heating business for about two years. Quickly it became clear that he was pretty good at getting work, very good at doing the work, and abysmal at collecting the money. And when he ran his own business, his evenings and weekends were totally absorbed by that. No time for inventions or for building carnival rides. He hated that. He felt more a prisoner of his own business than he ever had at Stelco. Around that time my parents also quit travelling with the carnival. They played only the Exhibition and fall fairs. Then they stopped even that.

Bobby was ten and I was sixteen in 1951 when Rick made his appearance. He might as well have had four parents. We all loved him to death. But by the time Rick was three, I was gone from the home, so I'm not part of his memories of childhood. And on top of that, when we try to compare notes, it is clear that the parents I recall from my early years bear no resemblance to the parents Rick had.

Priorities changed. I think I can even remember the turning point for Dad. One evening in Hamilton, in the winter that Rick was born, I was watching through our living room window to the street where a blizzard was raging and a man's car was stuck in the snow. He tried to drive forward; he tried to drive back; he tried to shovel; he tried to push. Nothing worked. Mom took a look too, and then Dad walked into the living room and stood beside us, looking out the window. I remarked that guy sure could use a push. Dad was silent for a while, then said, "Well, yes, he could use a push, but I've been thinking … that's the problem with me, I spend too much time giving pushes, and if I keep spending my time and energy giving a push here and there instead of concentrating on my own projects, I'll never get anywhere." Mom and I were incredulous. We flounced out of the room and didn't speak to Dad all evening.

It was a remarkable change. As time went by, Dad became ever more preoccupied with his projects. Our beautiful Sunday mystery tours faded into memory.

Shortly after Rick's birth, we sold the house in Hamilton so that Dad could build one in Stoney Creek. It was a beautiful, big, modern house with real ceramic tile in the bathroom and a basement with a walkout to ground level overlooking a ravine. Mom and I loved it. Dad kept saying, "Don't get attached to it. We're building it for sale." I think he had aspirations to become a full-time house builder.

In between work that kept food on the table, it took Dad about two years to complete that house. Or should I say, Mom and Dad? She held this while he hammered that. When it was time to paint the exterior, two stories front, three stories rear, Dad built a scaffold and Mom swung up and painted, ever the helpmate.

They barely got that house finished and sold before they decided to give the Globe of Death another try. They hadn't ridden in it for four years. It was during their first month back that they had their only other accident. Mom said she could hear Dad riding too fast; he was too close behind her. She went faster; Dad sped up. Mom went even faster; so did Dad. Mom said she couldn't figure out what was going on; it was as if he had lost his sense of timing. Finally Dad's motorcycle clipped Mom's rear wheel. Fortunately, she fell not into the centre of the globe but against the side. She slid down to the bottom, where her motorcycle lay waiting with wheels spinning. Although badly bruised and stiff for weeks, she fortunately sustained no serious injury.

They completed the year without further mishap. During the following season, Bobby, now sixteen, joined them, learning to ride a motorcycle for the Front. However, Mom and Dad found they no longer enjoyed carnival life. It was a grind.

Then they had a stroke of good fortune. In Quebec City, their last spot of the season, Sam Pollack of Pollack Brothers Circus caught their act and offered them star billing to tour the United States with the Globe of Death. They were thrilled. This would be the crowning achievement of their careers.

They had been riding motorcycles with the carnival for years, but carnivals and circuses are very different. A circus consists of a number of acts that appear together under one roof, or big top, with everyone under contract for so many months for so many dollars to circus proprietors. Circus management sets the standards and the tone for the entire show. On the other hand, a carnival is a travelling collection of rides, shows, and concessions, some owned by show management, others by independent operators who give a percentage of their take to show bosses.

One big difference between carnivals and circuses lies in the expertise of the performers. While one act or another in a carnival may require some skill, in the circus, all performers are highly trained. Top billing in a circus means you are the main attraction among many very accomplished acts, including high wire artists, tumblers, trapeze artists, jugglers, clowns, and animal trainers. These people spend their entire lives honing their skills.

In that era there was another significant difference between circuses and carnivals. Carnivals were, at that time, sometimes sleazy, containing acts like striptease shows. They also contained games of chance that were not always honest — rings in the ring toss that were too small to go over the good prizes, roulette wheels that were rigged to stop where the operator wanted. The circus, on the other hand, was innocent, wholesome good fun.

My parents were delighted by the offer to headline Pollack Brothers Circus and proudly accepted. Preparations began for their trek to California. I must admit, after all those years of dreams of the fun we'd have when we joined the circus, it broke my heart to see them set out without me. But by now I was married and had just given birth to my daughter.

Mom, Dad, Bobby, and Rick were on their way to their next great adventure. Mom pulled a house trailer behind the Packard. Dad drove a truck loaded with the globe and motorbikes, behind which was towed the globe's base mounted on wheels.

To get to where the circus opened in California, Mom and Dad had to drive across the United States, including over the mountains in California. Mom found that to be a daunting experience. Although they intended to drive in a convoy, road conditions and those old vehicles pulling such heavy loads precluded that, so Mom insisted that Bobby, by then seventeen years old, ride with her. More than once she gladly let Bobby take the wheel to spell her off. Later she told me that she had been absolutely terrified pulling the house trailer through the mountains. Several times she had to take a run at an incline to get underway, and she trembled as she drove through winding mountain roads edged by sheer drops.

In the meantime, Dad was having his own troubles getting through the mountains with his old five-ton truck and heavy load. The engine in the truck sputtered to a stop on several occasions. It took all of Dad's ingenuity to keep it going to their destination.

When they neared Oakland, California, where they were to first appear, they were met by a squadron of motorcycle police. They were so late that Pollack Brothers Circus had arranged for a police escort. With sirens blazing, lights flashing, and the roar of heavy-duty motorcycle engines engulfing them, they sped through the city, straight to the circus grounds, making an entrance worthy of their star status.

Mom told me that although she truly hated the harrowing drive to California and the trek between cities, she revelled in circus life. She easily made friends with other performers and enjoyed many good times with them. But it was a different story for Dad. He had no interest in developing friendships, and he soon tired of the laborious grind of setting up the Globe of Death, doing the shows, tearing down, then driving to the next spot. On the carnival show train he could rest as the train wound its way to the next town. With the circus there was no respite. At the end of their contract, they sent the Globe of Death into retirement.

Circus life must have been fantastic in the days when performers and equipment travelled together on long show trains, but my parents were a few years too late for that. The Globe was a monster to move. Lugging their own equipment around from city to city in their own vehicles took all the romance from it.

And it was at this moment that Oak Island came into their lives.

Enter Oak Island

CHAPTER 3

When Dad, Mom, and the boys returned from travelling with the circus, my husband and I expected Dad to go right back to work for Stelco, but he amazed us with the news that he was going to dig for treasure on Oak Island, and that Mom and the boys were going with him. It sounded utterly fantastic to me.

In 1959 I had never heard of Canada's famous "Treasure Island." For more than two hundred years, treasure hunters have come to the island, fortunes have been spent mounting recovery operations, and men have died, all for the belief that deep within Oak Island is locked a treasure so vast that it cannot be calculated. Some claim the treasure consists of gold, silver, and jewels; others believe that sacred documents or religious artifacts lie buried there.

Those beliefs are not inspired by the booty that has made its way to the surface during the years of searching, for no treasure has been recovered from Oak Island except for a few links of gold chain and a scrap of parchment bearing the letters "vi." What fires the imagination and spurs search after search is undeniable evidence that beneath the surface of Oak Island lies a subterranean network of shafts, pits, tunnels, and caverns that are man-made. When searchers dug into the first shaft in 1804, they found indications that it held a treasure. Ever since, that shaft has been referred to as the Money Pit. Each time anyone digs in or near the Money Pit, sea water surges in with such overwhelming force that it destroys the recovery work, thereby safeguarding the treasure of Oak Island. The elaborate underground system that creates this flood must have taken many men many years to construct. Its existence makes no sense at all unless it was designed to secure something of tremendous value. This incredible engineering feat, designed hundreds of years ago, remains unsurpassed and undefeated. That is what draws an endless procession of treasure hunters to Oak Island despite the lack of treasure found so far. Which of us will be the first to finally break through to that fantastic motherlode?

The discoveries made by each group of searchers act as a lure to the next. And that next group, armed now with even more tantalizing information, sets out confident that they will be the ones to at last unlock the treasure of Oak Island. And so it has gone for more than two centuries. During that time, much knowledge has been gained, but all at tremendous cost.

What kind of discoveries are so compelling that they act as the motivation for search after search when there is no material reward, not even any substantial proof of treasure? That is easier to understand if I take you on an imaginary walking tour of Oak Island. Throughout more than two hundred years of searching, each team of treasure hunters has made well-documented discoveries; as a result, we now have the benefit of considerable hindsight. Using information gained by those searchers, let's try to imagine Oak Island as it must have been in 1750, after the treasure was in the ground but before any treasure hunters disturbed it.

Oak Island is less than one mile long by half a mile wide and lies only three hundred feet from the small town of Western Shore on the east coast of Nova Scotia. Almost all of the work in searching for treasure has occurred at the south end of the island, furthest away from the mainland.

Imagine that we sail in from the Atlantic Ocean through Mahone Bay and land on the beautiful beach of Smith's Cove on the eastern coastline of Oak Island, almost at its southern tip. Walking inland on the sandy beach of Smith's Cove, we find that beyond the beach the land rises fairly steeply ahead of us from sea level up to a height of thirty-two feet. At that height there is a plateau about three hundred feet across. When we walk to the other side of the plateau, we see that the land drops sharply down to sea level in a cove on the western coastline of the island. This is South Shore Cove. By traversing the south end of the island from Smith's Cove up, across the plateau, and down to South

Shore Cove, we have covered all the parts of Oak Island that have fascinated treasure hunters since 1795.

If we stand in the centre of the plateau we see a tree with a block and tackle hanging from a lower limb, and under that a depression in the earth. Digging down, we uncover previously dug earth to a depth of ten feet. Under that we find planking made of tightly fitted logs. Surely treasure chests lie below. But no, under the logs we dig through ten more feet of earth, only to find beneath it another layer of logs. Again and again we uncover ten feet of previously dug earth, then a layer of logs. At ninety feet down we find a large inscribed stone that tells of a fortune buried below.

We realize that we have been digging in a man-made hole or shaft (the Money Pit) and that the layers of logs and earth must have been placed there to prevent settling of the earth so that no signs of excavation would be evident on the surface.

If we were able to remove the inscribed stone and to set a drilling rig on the earth beneath it, our drill might pass through oak chests filled with gold at a depth of 104 feet, we might feel the drill pass through a cavity in the earth that must surely be the entrance to a tunnel at 154 feet, and at a depth of 170 feet we might come to an iron plate that stops us from going further. Measuring from the surface of the plateau, we realize that our Money Pit is at least 170 feet deep, and all but the top 32 feet of it is below sea level.

But we will not be able to remove the inscribed stone and make those discoveries beneath it, for the Money Pit contains an ingenious booby trap. Once we have cleared the pit of earth and logs down to a depth of ninety feet, sea water floods in with a mighty force and fills the pit where we were digging up to sea level. This is because those who were responsible for burying the treasure protected it by constructing a tunnel system that causes water from Smith's Cove with many pounds of pressure behind it to burst in and obliterate any interference with the Money Pit. If we were to pump out the Money Pit, we would find that sea water continues to rush in at 450 gallons per minute.

To fully understand the magnitude of the sea water inlet tunnel, we need to go back to Smith's Cove, where we landed. Hidden under the water in the sandy bottom of the cove are five box-style drains. Those five drains are protected by layers of first tightly packed stones, then eel grass, then coconut fibre, then two feet, six inches of beach sand. The drains make their way inland under the beach and eventually converge into a single drain constructed in keystone formation. This travels 525 feet inland from Smith's Cove through the hard clay of the island, sloping downwards until it connects with the Money Pit at a depth of roughly 110 feet. Along its way, it changes from a single keystone drain to a tunnel four feet in diameter that is kept from collapsing by boulders placed within it. The drains and tunnel ensure that every time anyone digs down the Money Pit or digs a new hole near it, sea water breaks through and sweeps away their work. There is a sketch of a cross-section of the Money Pit and inlet tunnel (see Figure 1). Be aware that anything beneath 110 feet in the Money Pit is assumption. The layers of previously dug earth and log planking in the Money Pit, the stone with markings that purportedly tell of a treasure buried below, the connecting sea water inlet tunnel, the keystone drain, and the five box-style drains have all been seen by various treasure hunters since 1795 as they attempted to retrieve Oak Island's treasure. However, the chests of gold, walk-in tunnel, and iron plate may not exist; they have been deduced from drill core samples or from traces of wood, metal, or clay left on a drill bit.

The original work on Oak Island is ingenious. All that we know of it we learned through the efforts of a series of treasure hunters who, in their attempts to reach the treasure, laid bare parts of the original beach work in Smith's Cove as well as shafts and tunnels in the island. But

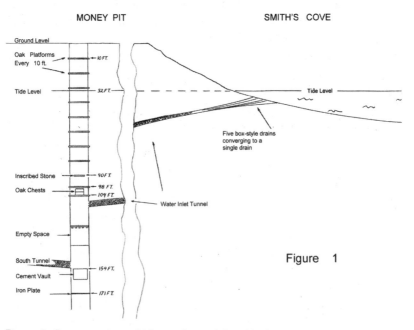

Figure 1: Cross-section of Money Pit and Smith's Cove.

South Shore Cove

Smith's Cove

OAK ISLAND

Aerial photograph courtesy
Service Nova Scotia and
Municipal Relations
NS Geomatics Centre
160 Willow St.
Amherst, NS
B4H 3W5

these searches by party after party have left the island honeycombed with shafts and tunnels. My brother Bobby wrote a summary of discoveries made by the various treasure hunting parties that came before the Restalls. His account appears in Chapter 13. Some readers may prefer to read that section now.

People often comment that surely with modern machinery and technological know-how, if there were a treasure it would have been raised by now. Perhaps when you read this you will appreciate the way that the brilliantly designed sea water inlet system, treasure hunters, and Mother Nature herself have inadvertently conspired to keep the treasure safe.

Anyone can dig for treasure. But to keep anything you find, you'll need a Treasure Trove Licence issued by the government. In Oak Island's case, that is the government of Nova Scotia. This licence gives you permission to keep 95 percent of what you find. The other 5 percent goes to the government. Of course, you will also need the permission of the person who owns the land you want to dig on. When my family got involved with Oak Island, the land was owned by Mel R. Chappell of Sydney, Nova Scotia, and he held the Treasure Trove Licence for Oak Island.

Dad had read about Oak Island in a *Popular Science* magazine back in 1939. It was a dazzling tale. Throughout the years, numerous magazine and newspaper articles appeared, serving to keep his interest alive. One day he decided the time had come to take action. He began to correspond with Chappell.

Chappell had already, with a partner, mounted his own search for treasure on Oak Island, as had his father and uncle before him. By the time Chappell's own search faltered, he no doubt reasoned that his family had sunk enough money into Oak Island. Now he was ready to let others shoulder the cost of recovery operations while he collected a share of whatever they found.

When my father got involved with Oak Island, Chappell was in his seventies, in poor health, and desperate to see the treasure raised within his lifetime. Chappell truly believed Oak Island held a vast treasure and he wanted it found — not only for its fabulous monetary value but also to vindicate his father, uncle, and himself for the huge financial sacrifices they had made during their own searches.

Chappell was besieged by would-be treasure hunters. My father was just one of many. I found Chappell's first letter to my father among the family papers.

November 7th, 1955
Dear Sir:

Your letter under date of October 31st received and the content is quite interesting to me.

I would gather that you have known of Oak Island and the Treasure Seeking there for some time.

You mentioned visiting the Island in October. I am wondering whether it was before Mr. Greene had ceased his operations for the season. He finished up his work for the Fall about ten days ago, the last three days being very dirty, miserable weather with snow, sleet, rain, hail, and high winds, and the following week, right up to the present has been very dirty, raw, cold weather.

The most intriguing part to me of your communication is that you feel that "now" is the time to start work. Practically every other person who has ever been interested in Oak Island has thought of starting early in the season and not working thru the late fall and winter months. You must have a different idea in mind than the rest of them have had.

In answer to your direct question, wherein you ask if I am free to enter into an agreement, at this time would say that I made an agreement with Mr. Greene last summer. He has at least carried out his end of it so far, to a certain degree. I will not be in a position to definitely answer your question until I hear further from him and we come to a definite understanding regarding further work. All he did this Fall was to put down four small drill holes.

It is evident to my mind that you have some kind of approach which is different to those who have been working there in the past, or any others with whom I have discussed the matter.

I am also wondering just how familiar you are with the actual true history of the Oak Island workings.

With a little further information as to your intention, I could then determine whether to deal with you further or whether to continue negotiations with some other parties who are very keenly interested.

I would appreciate hearing from you at your earliest convenience.

Thanking you

Yours very truly,

M.R. Chappell

Dad must have been pleased with that letter. But that was 1955. Letters went back and forth between Chappell and Dad at no great speed. Chappell's letter to Dad in October 1956 was brief and cordial, just keeping in touch, and mentioned he would visit the Island "if my health holds."

In a letter dated January 1, 1957, Chappell stated that he had not visited the island the previous fall due to a slow recovery from peritonitis. He went on to say, "I am anticipating developments there early in the Spring, and I am looking forward to developments that will be of interest to all who have, in the past, had anything to do with Oak Island." It sounds as if Chappell was hopeful that Greene, still working on the island, was on the brink of bringing up the treasure.

But at the end of the same month, Dad received a long letter from Chappell. This part is interesting:

> During the last several weeks I have had a great deal of correspondence regarding Oak Island.
>
> Since my experience with Mr. Greene has finalized and my agreement with him terminated, I am now free to deal with any other party, but before coming to any agreement, I must be definitely satisfied that the work will be carried on. I have lost approximately five years in connection with Oak Island recovery work, due to tying up with parties without investigating, or having a definite undertaking from them regarding the carrying out of the undertaking.
>
> From my angle I have the title to the property, the treasure trove rights, and a considerable amount of work already accomplished, not least of which would be the pumping sump pit which extends down to a depth of at least 150–155 feet. I am putting up these items, along with any other information I may have. The party with whom I make an agreement would carry out the actual work of recovery, which recovery would be divided on a fifty-fifty basis, or if that did not prove satisfactory to the party undertaking the recovery work, I will be willing to negotiate further in this connection. But the main point, and what must be decided first, is a definite knowledge that whoever undertakes the work will carry it through.

Dad must have been over the moon when he received that letter. Here is his reply:

> March 1st, 1957
> Dear Mr. Chappell:
> Thank-you for your most interesting letter of Jan. 28th, which so clearly sets out your position.
> At that time my backers were scattered and have only just returned to Ontario. It is good news that you

are now ready to enter into an agreement to recover the treasure buried on Oak Island. I completely understand that (because of past experience) you must be sure that there will be no delay in getting on with the job.

My position is this, while having no assurance of ever concluding an agreement with you, I arranged as best I could to interest several people in this venture. These people are sound and would stand any financial investigation, just as my knowledge and experience will stand any investigation.

I can now contract to do all the recovery work, including all material, labour, tools, equipment, and know-how. This at my expense. I will further undertake to work in an intelligent workman-like manner and proceed with all the speed consistent with safety, endeavouring to recover all the treasure to the best of my ability. That I agree not to damage the site in any manner with explosives.

You to provide the license and the site including all material on the site and all work done to the present. You also to provide all information in your possession. All of which I must return after a reasonable time for study.

In the event that I fail to seal the sea off from the shafts in six months you will have the right to terminate the agreement at that time.

He then listed terms that matched Greene's contract. Dad concluded with, "If I am to have the chance at recovery, an early start is to my advantage, to be there set up, and catch some early good weather before the water temperature rises much." It seemed as if it was time to get out the pens for signatures. But then Dad received the following letter from Chappell:

April 8th, 1957
Dear Mr. Restall:
I have been delayed in replying to your letter of March 1st, due partly to my being away from Sydney considerable of that time, and otherwise due to being extremely busy.

While I was in New York during March, I contacted an old friend of mine who has been interested in Oak Island for many years. He is an Engineer of high standing and has a number of friends who have decided to throw in their lot with him, and do work at Oak Island with a view to solving the mystery and recovering the treasure. He proposes to commence work as soon as the weather permits in the Spring.

We have had a very backward season and just how soon he will be able to get to work I do not know but anticipate it will be early in June. The party to whom I refer has spent some time on Oak Island and has investigated matters from the beginning and is thoroughly familiar with the situation there and what has been done in past years, the conditions he is up against, etc.

I am looking forward to him solving the mystery, but if anything should happen, through unforeseen circumstances such as sickness, or other cause beyond his control, and I am open to make further negotiations, will be glad to communicate with you.

Yours very truly

M.R. Chappell

It had slipped from Dad's grasp. But, as Mom always said, Dad had the persistence of a bloodhound. He kept on writing. On October 4, 1957, while responding to a letter from Dad, Chappell made no mention of those New York friends and cohorts, but this letter referred to two Ontario mining men finalizing their arrangements with him and proceeding with the search.

In a letter dated August 22, 1958, Chappell described difficulties with the work now in progress and indicated that he would be in touch with Dad if the present crew abandoned their work.

In February 1959 Dad wrote to Chappell again. He referred to a six-month interval between letters and mentioned that it was time for him to begin planning his season of travelling with the Globe of Death. In his letter Dad stated, "I would very much like to make the next attempt when the present agreement ends or if the brothers abandon it. There would be no running around for financing, I can guarantee to start within thirty days and give it my undivided attention."

What happened next is not among the papers I inherited (perhaps Chappell and Dad used the telephone, rather than writing), but suddenly Dad had his opportunity to search for treasure on Oak Island. His contract came not in spring, as he'd hoped, but in October 1959.

Just heading into winter, it was the worst possible time to undertake such an enterprise. But in his letters to Chappell, Dad had always declared he would be able to start immediately and had implied that winter was not a problem, so now he could scarcely suggest a delay. It had taken him four years of correspondence to get this opportunity, and he could be sure that if he failed to take action at once, Chappell would never give him another chance.

Mom, Dad, and Bobby, now eighteen years old, moved to Oak Island. Rick, just nine years old, stayed with me in Hamilton to continue school; the rest of the family would get settled before sending for him. They had no idea what hardships they might face through winter on the island, but Dad knew it was necessary to demonstrate to Chappell that they were prepared to work in all seasons and conditions. They arrived on the island on October 15, 1959, with all the equipment and savings that they could muster, a total value of $8,000.

Their Oak Island adventure had begun.

Facing Reality

CHAPTER 4

Earlier, I said that my parents were the ideal candidates for the adventure of Oak Island. They were already accustomed to unusual activities. They weren't tied into any one job or source of income. Mom and the boys were devoted to Dad and cheerfully followed whatever path he chose, accustomed to making sacrifices for his projects. The family was quite insular, not needing outsiders for companionship or approval. Dad was knowledgeable, a great innovator, could be relied upon to make something from nothing, could fix anything mechanical or structural, and always persisted until he completed whatever he set out to do.

Dad believed that once the treasure was raised, Oak Island, with its shafts, tunnels, and unique method of safeguarding the treasure, would take its rightful place alongside the Seven Wonders of the World. And he was the man who could make that happen.

On the island, Dad was in his element. It was as if his previous life had been no more than a warm-up for this great challenge. Bobby made an enthusiastic and dedicated co-worker. Yet living conditions were harsh beyond belief. Mom, who had always been 100 percent behind Dad, was a city girl. Their primitive existence on Oak Island was a difficult adjustment.

Their initial contract with Chappell granted them only three months on the island. Chappell promised that an extension would be forthcoming as long as there was progress, so Dad and Bobby set right to work. They began to dig a shaft on the beach at Smith's Cove, intending to intercept the inlet tunnel that brings sea water to the Money Pit, while Mom set about housekeeping in the minimalist fashion dictated by their circumstances: no electricity, no running water.

Luckily, right from the start she began to record her impressions of life on the island, a woman's take on this adventure. This is her account of her introduction to Oak Island.

The Reluctant Treasure Hunter: Part One
by Mildred Restall

Treasure hunting is strictly a man's game. Just mention the word treasure to some men and right away their eyes gleam, their hands start to twitch, and their breath goes a little faster. Tell them a tale of treasure hunting and there they sit, absolutely spellbound; but long before you get to the end of your story you will find that you have lost them. They have gone into a dream world of their own.

Fortunately for their family's sake, it remains just a dream. However, there is always the odd one who is not content just to dream. Such is my case.

One October day in 1955, my husband suggested that he and I take a little vacation alone. We left our two sons with our recently married daughter and took off, heading East from Hamilton, Ontario. It was to be one of those leisurely, meandering trips, stopping and going as we pleased. At least that was my understanding. Less than three days later and after covering nearly fourteen hundred miles, I found myself on a small fishing boat heading for Oak Island.

Oak Island is in Mahone Bay, Nova Scotia, opposite Western Shore, a small community about fifty miles down the coast from Halifax. Oak Island lies just off the mainland and runs on an angle, lengthwise, out into the bay.

It's an odd-shaped island; nearly a mile in length and half a mile at its widest point. At one end two fair-sized coves are almost opposite each other; a swamp running from coast to coast separates the length of the Island into two halves. At the extreme end of the outer half and facing East is a small, crescent-shaped beach known as Smith's Cove. It was here that we docked. We left the boat and walked across a sandy beach, then up through the woods to the top of a hill about thirty-five feet above sea level. Here we came to a large horseshoe-shaped clearing roughly 300 feet in diameter, ringed by spruce trees, and as we walked across to the far side of the clearing we saw the pits. We had been told that someone was working on the island, and there, by the pits were three men using a drilling rig.

Bob, my husband, talked with the man in charge while I looked around the area. I stood on one shaft that had been planked over and looked down another that was open; I could see water far below. I heard Bob asking questions. How deep was this pit, how deep that one, and who blew the big hole in the ground a couple of hundred feet away, and so on. I gazed around me; it all seemed so fantastic. Treasure hunting!

Bob and I next went to Halifax, where we spent some time in the library and newspaper morgue. Then on to the parliament buildings, where we learned more about the island and who the present owner was. We were treated with the utmost of courtesy as we shuffled from department to department. Everyone was very helpful, giving us all the information they could, even if at times I suspected a gleam of amusement in their eyes. I showed enthusiasm and keen interest; after all, if it weren't for Oak Island, where would I be right now? Certainly not on a vacation in Nova Scotia. Besides, I had nothing to worry about, I told myself, people don't just run off treasure hunting.

At last our vacation came to a pleasant end. Nearly four years elapsed, and to me Oak Island was a thing of the past. Although I was aware that there had been some correspondence between my husband and the owner, I thought it would all blow over in time.

Then out of the blue, my husband told me that he had decided to go treasure hunting and asked me if I was "with him." I stared at him dumbfounded. Treasure hunting! What did I want to go treasure hunting for? But suddenly the image of myself traipsing all over an island with a pick and shovel over my shoulder was too much. I started to laugh, I thought it was the funniest thing I had ever heard, and couldn't stop laughing.

I wasn't laughing a few weeks later when once again I found myself on the way down to Nova Scotia. This time, however, we were loaded to the limit. My husband and I drove one car, towing a box trailer crammed full with suitcases, shovels, picks, motors, and pumps. Our eldest son, Robert Jr., then eighteen years old, drove another car, towing a boat with an outboard motor, the inside of the boat filled with camping equipment and more tools. We made the trip in fine style. But several times I thought to myself, "Of all the cockeyed things we have ever done, this tops them all."

On October 15, 1959, the day after we arrived at Western Shore, we rented a boat to get over to the island. It was a raw, windy day and by the time we reached the Oak Island dock I was freezing. Just as I stepped onto the dock, my husband closed the throttle with a firm twist. It snapped clean off. "That's a good start," I thought. An omen? Well we were here, so off we went to see the pits.

It had been four years since I last saw the pits, and standing there looking down at them I was shocked at their condition. One pit had partially collapsed, leaving broken and twisted timbers around; you could no longer see the water. In the other, the larger of the two, rotting cribbing was visible, as all the deck planking had been ripped off, exposing it to the weather. Even my son's face fell momentarily. Looking across the slate grey sea at the black smudges of other islands, I felt utterly wretched. I don't think I have ever seen a place so bleak and lonely as that island, that day. I just wanted to go home.

Soon Bobby's eyes began to sparkle as he and his Dad walked around, talking. They walked here, they walked there, son asking questions, my husband answering ... all about the history of the place. I trailed after them, ignored and unnoticed. Finally Bob said it was time for us to go back. Catching sight of my face with its woebegone expression, he started to laugh. "Look," he said to Bobby, pointing to me, "the reluctant treasure hunter." They both thought that was hilarious and went off down the hill, roaring with laughter.

We launched our boat the next day, a 16-foot molded plywood boat with a 35hp motor. Then we began to haul lumber over to the island to build a construction shack for our equipment.

The shack was built between the pits and the edge of the clearing on the west side. It stood facing east, about 15 feet back from the pits. The floor was laid across a small ditch, giving us space underneath to store some of the heavier tools. We extended the floor 2 1/2 feet in front of the shack to give us a platform so we could walk across the ditch. Behind the building, two small hillocks gave shelter from the westerly winds, and the circle of trees protected the shack from the northern blasts and the western and southerly gales. It was too cold for camping on the island, so we stayed on the mainland, going to and from the island every day.

When the shack was near completion, needing only the workbench, lockers, and shelves, we gathered our tools, camping gear, and other things that we didn't need on the mainland, put them inside, and locked up. That night a storm blew up and for two days we couldn't get over to the island; our boat was too small to weather such rough seas. When we finally did get over, it was only to find that someone had broken into the shack and stolen an assortment of stuff. Blankets, car radio, tools, and more were gone. About $200 worth, altogether. That is when my husband decided that we should move onto the island to live.

It wasn't easy trying to get settled in an 8 foot by 12 foot construction shack, especially for me, but I suppose my years with Bob Restall had prepared me for this.

We bought a two-burner, propane gas plate for cooking (and for heating Bob's soldering iron!), and a small used space heater for warmth. Now we had what they call here "stiddy heat." For water, we had the big hole created when an earlier treasure hunter [Mel Chappell] used explosives. It was now a pond after years of seepage from the rains and snows. Drinking water was obtained by straining a pailful of water through cheesecloth and then boiling it. For groceries we went to the mainland once a week. And for the other necessity for civilized folk, Bob and Bobby built a traditional-sized dry water closet (outhouse) a little ways out back.

We made arrangements to leave our car with some people on the mainland with whom we had become friendly. Their property ran down to the shore where they had a small landing we could use. So when we went shopping, Bobby would take my husband and me over to their place, return to the island, and later pick us up at an arranged time. We never left the island unattended for more than a few minutes, ever again.

What landlubbers we were. Our brash eighteen-year-old took charge of navigation. After all, hadn't he been boating on the lakes up in Ontario one summer. As well as operating the motorboat, he had to row the skiff out to where the boat was moored and bring it in for us. We had a mooring just off the mainland and one in Smith's Cove at the island. Sometimes as he rowed from shore I wondered where on earth he was going. What with the breeze blowing one way and the pull of the tide another, he wouldn't seem to be heading any-where near the mooring.

How I hated those trips to and from the island in that small boat. Up to then, all my sea journeys had been aboard ocean liners. But that little thing bobbed and rocked at the slightest ripple. I would cling to the sides grimly while my son took away in a show-off swing that put the boat way over on its side (my side), expecting at any moment to get an earful of water. Sitting contentedly on the back seat, my husband invariably burst into song, "Ohhhh, a life on the ocean wave, la da de da da da." … Some life.

Having brought the best equipment he could find for the job of treasure hunting, Robert Senior and his Junior settled down into uninterrupted treasure hunting all the daylight hours, six (or more) days a week. Most nights were spent researching, planning, and just dreaming. For my two men, time could always be filled in some useful fashion. For me, things were different.

The days were endless. After breakfast the men vanished through the woods to work down at Smith's Cove, leaving me alone to fill in the mornings as best I could. By ten I had nothing to do; I couldn't whip up a batch of cookies or such — no oven. I had no sewing, no knitting, I didn't want to read — this I saved for the long evenings. I managed to fill in the time somehow until after the men had been in for lunch. Then began the long, draggy afternoons.

I never had been alone in a place amid acres and acres of space. At first I was afraid to leave the clearing — the surrounding forest frightened me, and the beach had such an air of desolation that it was more than I could bear. But as the days went by I gradually gathered courage and went exploring. Some days I went down to the beach behind our shack and poked among the rocks at low tide. Sometimes I went to see what the men were doing at Smith's Cove, but I wasn't especially interested in their doings; I found it rather boring.

By suppertime I'd be back at the shack to wait for my husband and son. Merely to pass the time I would walk around the clearing, look down the pits, walk around the clearing, look down the pits, and then look down the pits and walk around the clearing, just for a little variety.

After living in a bustling city and in the midst of enormous activity, the quiet and solitude of the island was too much. The only sounds to be heard were of a few birds, the rustling of the tall evergreens, and the lapping of the waves. Sometimes I wished the trees would stop rustling, the waves, lapping, then perhaps I could hear something. My ears were attuned to voices, autos, radios — all common noises that are part of living among people. After being in show business all my life with the crowds, music, lights, city noises, this quiet was overwhelming.

As the sun set each day a hush fell over everything. At night I couldn't sleep, for the silence was like a huge void. I found myself straining my ears, listening. For what? I didn't know. The drone of planes overhead on their way to and from the Halifax Airport made me feel even more lonely, and when we did have the occasional visitor, strangely, instead of wanting to greet them, I felt an urge to run away and hide.

There would be many days without a soul coming near, and when they did, they were usually armed to the teeth. Deer hunting season was on. I, who had never been at such close range to guns before, felt something close to panic at the sight of these men, casually hefting their deer rifles from side to side as they stood talking to my husband and son.

Such was the state of my nerves that each night, when I finally managed to fall asleep, the slightest sound would bring me alert, fully wide awake. One night a scuffling noise outside woke me up. I glanced up and there, through the window by the door, I could see the outline of a man's head. I thought of the robbery and of men prowling the island with guns. I was frightened sick. I nudged Bob, but he was dead to the world. The head disappeared and slowly the door started to open. I lay there watching, petrified with fear, trying to think of something clever, but nothing came. Oh, if only we had a gun under the pillow, I thought. Now the door was open.

In a flash of inspiration I decided I might be able to frighten the intruder away. I waited, holding my breath. Then, as he stepped quietly inside, I jabbed Bob hard with my elbow and at the same time screeched at the top of my voice. Startled, Bob grabbed the flashlight we kept by the bed, swung the beam over to the door, and there, leaning against the doorpost, white-faced and shaking, was … Bobby, just returning after having had to answer Nature's Call.

For days after this little episode, whenever I thought of it I had a fit of the giggles, but my son refused to see the humour of it, grumbling about how he nearly "got shot."

Towards the middle of November it started to rain. It teemed for three and four days at a stretch for nearly a month. This is when we found out how cramped we were for living space. After putting in a double and single bed, then space for cooking, shelves for food, also the heater, there wasn't enough room left for us all to be standing at the same time. To make matters worse, my two men tried to work, regardless of the weather. It was quite warm so they didn't mind getting wet. I managed to dry some of their clothes during the dry spells, but most of the time their things were hung inside the shack near the ceiling to dry. The saturated, dripping ones were hung over where there was a little floor space, and the ones that were just damp hung over the beds. Sometimes the humidity was more than we could stand, so we would leave the door open and the heater on full blast. I got very tired of pawing my way through wet clothes to do my work. And mold invaded all our books and papers.

The coast of Nova Scotia is very rugged. Boulders, large and small, line the coast, with sandy beaches dotted here and there. It was the same on the island, so one either left his boat moored out in deep water or made a skid to drag the boat up beyond high tide. I often worried about our boat being moored out, especially at night when while lying in bed I could clearly hear the wind and waves. But Smith's Cove is fairly well sheltered from the storms, except when one is blowing from the southeast, off the Atlantic.

A strong wind brought in big rollers at the cove one day. In what seemed only minutes, there was a roaring wind with teeming rain and huge waves pounding on the beach. Before long the mooring started to shift from the pull of the boat and the stern was getting closer to the rocks at the end of our wharf. The men tried to pull the boat in, but the lines were tangled and the boat remained fast to the mooring. The tide was falling and soon the boat would be smacking down hard on the rocks, so there was nothing else to do but to go into the water and cut the lines.

Bob went in, stumbling and slipping over the rocks, he pushed the back end of the boat out then worked his way to the nose and cut the lines. It seemed like hours before he was able to guide the boat around the end of the wharf and heading for shore. Time and time again the boat slammed down onto the water, just missing him by inches. With Bobby in up to his waist, hauling on the painter, and Bob pushing at the rear, they brought the boat close to the shore. The transom was full of water, and the boat grounded. I was assigned the job of bailing it out while they heaved and shoved, inching it out of the water. Every wave that came along helped to bring the boat in a little, at the same time pouring more water into the transom. We yelled instructions to each other, but they were ignored, for none of us could hear above that howling wind. Finally we got the boat out of the water and pushed it up the beach, rolling it along logs. This was backbreaking work and we were all exhausted and looked like drowned rats by the time the boat was safe and secure, high on the beach.

Ever after that, we always brought the boat right out of the water. We never left it moored out again.

One day, late in November the owner of the Island came to visit just to see how we were getting on. As we all sat in the shack, huddled around the heater, he told us of the many people who were interested in Oak Island, and how anxious they were to get permission to work on the island. We felt very lucky indeed to be the chosen ones. Without mentioning names, he also told us that a party from the West Coast was very eager to come treasure hunting, but the trouble was, this group wanted a three-year contract and that was not accept-able to Mr. Chappell. Silently, we were thankful.

The lobster season opened December 1st. We had-n't seen any boats around for a long time because of the bad weather. Now everything was calm and clear as if the weather were behaving itself to give the fishermen a break. December 1st came on Sunday that year, so the season couldn't open until Monday. The official open-ing time was set for 10:00 a.m. It was just as if a gun had been fired. Precisely at 10:00 on the dot, boats scooted out from the mainland in all directions — big boats, little boats, all piled high with lobster pots. They raced one another for locations, and jockeyed for position along the way. Some dropped their pots around the islands near shore and some on the shoals in between, while others headed further out to sea. One fellow we knew screamed and waved "Hello" as he shot by, while we stood on the beach, amazed by all the commotion.

For a few days activity was hectic. Boats were chug-ging around the bay from early morning to sunset, and sometimes in the middle of the night. We often specu-lated about those midnight runs, wondering Who was taking Who's lobsters. By the end of the first week the new enthusiasts had dropped out and only the regular fishermen remained. It was again raw and wet, and lob-stering is a cold, miserable job.

It was getting close to Christmas and I was anxious to get home to our other son, Ricky. On this initial move to the island, we had left him with my daughter and her family so that he wouldn't miss school. I was also homesick for people, lights, noise, anything but this deadly quiet. I tried to talk the others into leaving with me and coming back in the spring, figuring that once I got them off the island, that would be the end of this idiotic business, but they wouldn't hear of it. We knew that we couldn't leave our possessions on the island for there wouldn't be a thing left when we got back. We already had a hoist and motors set up at the pit head. They would be extremely attractive to looters. The shack was livable, so Bob decided that he and

Bobby could manage on the island for the winter and get some work done. [In December 1959, Chappell wrote Dad advising that he would extend Dad's original three-month contract on the island for all of 1960.]

So it was settled. My husband would take me back home and Bobby would stay behind to look after things until his dad returned. Our eighteen-year-old son lived alone on the island for five weeks.

Back in Hamilton, Bob collected more equipment and left for Nova Scotia at the end of January. I wondered how long it would be before they would miss me. Who would do the dishes, make the beds, do the cooking? How long before the loneliness would get on their nerves? I think I was the one who was lonely. I heard over the radio of the terrible winter Nova Scotia was having and I expected to hear any day that they were on their way home. But still they stayed. By the end of March I knew that they were determined to carry on with their treasure hunt.

Adjusting to life on an island wasn't difficult only for Mom; it presented challenges for Dad and Bobby too. Almost everything that had to be done was done by them. They built, maintained, and repaired equipment. They dug, they chopped, they heaved, and they hauled, side by side.

For Dad, there was much more to Oak Island than recovering gold or jewels. Of equal importance to him was discovering precisely how the treasure had been put down and how those who buried it had planned to bring it up. Dad and Bobby were determined to recover the treasure in such a way as to preserve the magnificent underground systems that for so long had confounded every recovery effort. After all, how could Oak Island become the Eighth Wonder of the World if evidence of this extraordinary engineering feat was destroyed in the lust for gold?

Before they'd arrived on the island, Dad had read countless articles and books on Oak Island. He knew the Money Pit as it would have been before anyone dug into it and discovered its first secrets. He also knew that little of the original work remained. Many years before, each layer of earth and logs in the Money Pit had been removed to see what lay beneath. Now the island was riddled with shafts, holes, and tunnels created not only by those who buried the treasure but also by the succession of treasure hunters who had sought to recover it.

In October, when Bobby and Dad set to work, there was no longer any sign of the original Money Pit. All that could be seen where it had been were two adjoining rectangular holes bordered by broken timbers, encircled by a rickety log fence.

Bobby and Dad started digging a shaft in Smith's Cove beach in an attempt to locate and block the sea water inlet tunnel. If they could stop the water, they would be able to search for treasure in the Money Pit area at their leisure. They spent each day in arduous physical labour, and at night they reviewed the day's progress, discussed options, and debated theories of what was meant by various findings. During the long, cold winter nights of their first six months, they carefully reread every publication on Oak Island that they could find. They compared the information in those sources each with each other and related them to the signs of earlier expeditions that were still visible on the island. In this way they were able to calculate what lay where underground. This informed the direction of their work on the island.

It was like detective work. Every time they encountered previously dug earth, marker stones, timbers, or other objects, they tried to determine if they were part of work done by other treasure hunters or by those who had buried the treasure. They hoped to find the original work because that could lead them more directly to the treasure. However, other searchers' work could be useful too; Dad and Bobby could add to that previous work or use it to calculate new directions for their own search. Conversely, whenever they encountered earth that had never been dug before, they knew they had gone beyond anything of interest.

Just living on an island presented special problems. They had neither electricity nor a telephone. They used propane lamps and stove; they rigged a battery charger, then charged a battery connected to an old car radio to listen to the news once a week. Obtaining food necessitated a trip to the mainland by boat, then a fifteen-minute car ride into Chester, where they kept a post office box and where the Shamrock Food Store supplied their groceries on a running tab, as it did for local fishermen. Phone calls for the family came in to a service station. Dad collected messages each time he went ashore. Return calls were made from a pay phone. Often letters or phone calls were of vital importance to their work. But whenever a call out was placed, it might be necessary to wait by the phone for the return call for long periods of time. Sometimes communications were missed. All of this was time-consuming and frustrating.

Large shipments of supplies were ferried to the island by a hired boat (usually Gerald Stevens's *Fury*), but smaller supplies of lumber, machine parts, gas, and oil were brought to the island in the family's outboard motorboat. Every journey to the mainland resulted in valuable time lost from what they considered to be their real work of searching for treasure. Once on the beach at Smith's Cove, supplies needed to be carried up the steep hill to the flat grassy plateau that held the Money Pit.

After the first six months on the island, Bobby began a daily journal of the work. Many of us would try to keep a journal in circumstances as extraordinary as these, but most of us would eventually miss a day or two, and then another, until gaps outnumbered entries and we finally gave up. But Bobby never gave up. There is a journal entry for every day from March 20, 1960, to August 17, 1965, the end of his search.

The rhythm of island life comes through clearly in Bobby's journals. The following entries were written that first winter, when my mother was in Ontario with Rick, and Dad and Bobby worked alone on the island.

Sunday, March 20, 1960

Gerald Stevens brought fuel oil and gasoline to island, and planks and barrels to Grandall's Point. Made barrel bungs tight.

Monday, March 21, 1960

Built raft in 2–3 hours with 12 barrels, 6 logs, 27 planks, wire and nails. Loaded Plymouth and it floated like an iceberg (sank to plank level) to Smith's Cove with speedboat. Very slow going. Towed it back to Grandall's Point and staked it down so it floats at high tide and is dry at low tide.

Tuesday, March 22, 1960

Got 8 more barrels from Mader and trucked them to Grandall's Point. Extra buoyancy needed for 5,000 lb. compressor. Did odds and ends rest of day.

Wednesday, March 23, 1960

Cleared everything out of compressor that wasn't nailed to the floor. Fixed barrel bungs to be watertight. Sudden wind and we beached boat and puttered around with odds and ends that needed attention.

Thursday, March 24, 1960

Rigged braces for hoist at beach. Took hoist car from main pits and mounted in beach hole. Pumped out hole and started clearing ice and snow. Made record run to Chester. Uncovered and launched boat, scooted 2 1/2 miles to Chester by water, got mail, some groceries, newspaper and pics at drugstore, roared back and pulled up and covered boat in 45 minutes flat.

Friday, March 25, 1960

Cleared out beach hole. Set up generators and charged batteries.

Saturday, March 26, 1960

Put eight barrels under raft. Went to Chester by boat. Nearly drowned and froze coming back in 4 to 6 foot waves. Cold today. Seawater froze to deck.

Sunday, March 27, 1960

Cut poles to crib beach hole. Took them to Smith's Cove.

Monday, March 28, 1960

Moved raft from Grandall's Pt. to Government Wharf in Western Shore. Stored planks for loading it in gas station by dock.

Tuesday, March 29, 1960

Loaded compressor and towed it over and unloaded at Smith's Cove. Took raft apart and stacked up barrels, planks, and logs.

Wednesday, March 30, 1960

Went to Chester and here and there. Got winch welded up. Rained all afternoon, got completely drenched coming back.

Thursday, March 31, 1960

Took barrels to Andy's. Built runway and platform over hole and cleared out three wheelbarrow loads of sand, using hoist and winch.

Friday, April 1, 1960

Cribbed one end of hole after cutting up poles and clearing sand and building loading platform in hole. Rained most of afternoon.

Saturday, April 2, 1960

Went to Chester and returned barrels. General running around used up the day.

Sunday, April 3, 1960

Cleared out stones and sand (about ten hoist loads) and cribbed far end of beach hole toward the point.

Monday, April 4, 1960

Dug hole 6" deeper for pump.

Tuesday, April 5, 1960

Fixed part of caved-in cribbing near pump. Briggs and Stratton got a seized valve and we fixed it (luckily). Found two old beams just seaward of our cribbing. They are vertical, about 6" or 8" by same. Very old and rotten. Apparently part of an old cribbing. Later noticed 8" x 1" boards in a square shape at least 5' long. Some kind of hollow post or trough.

Wednesday, April 6, 1960

Dug beach hole deeper. Went to Chester and wasted day getting Chappell [on phone].

Thursday, April 7, 1960

R.E. [Dad] went to Halifax to see Chappell. Met Harris [R.V. Harris, author of *The Oak Island Mystery*] and others.

Friday, April 8, 1960

Went to Chester. Learned a lot about the *Teazer*. One fellow will show us where it went down. Finished fixing cribbing.

Saturday, April 9, 1960

Deepened hole about 4". Checked pump in Chester and bought it. [This was a huge pump previously used on the island to pump water from the Money Pit.]

Sunday, April 10, 1960

Fixed carburetor on compressor and tested it. Fixed carburetor on Lawson mill. Dug out about 1 foot in hole. Found it will be necessary to crib at least part of hole. Added one tier of planks.

Monday, April 11, 1960

Added two tiers of plank cribbing to hole. Total depth 11 1/2 feet.

Tuesday, April 12, 1960

Reached 13 feet in hole. Had considerable sliding in. Will have to abandon horizontal method of cribbing sides.

Wednesday, April 13, 1960

Went to Chester and ordered planks and beams for cribbing vertically. Worked on sump pump for awhile.

Thursday, April 14, 1960

Got planks over. Went to Chester and dropped coupling into machine shop. Put cribbing into place and tacked frame in temporarily.

Friday, April 15, 1960

Hole is just over 14 feet deep. It is cribbed to the 13 1/2 foot level.

Sunday, April 17, 1960

Reached about 15 1/2 feet in hole. Still previously dug.

Monday, April 18, 1960

Put gas tank from Fargo on Chappell's pump. Went to Chester for flexible gas line. Went down about 1 foot in hole.

Tuesday, April 19, 1960

Reached total depth of 17 feet. Clay spongy. Encountering more rocks. We are roughly 6 feet below low tide.

A car was needed on the island because drums of gas and oil, lumber, and equipment of all kinds had to be transported from the beach, up thirty-two feet to the plateau, and across to the Money Pit area. With back seats removed, the car served as a truck and towing vehicle.

The compressor made the same journey across the bay on a raft. My husband, an excavating contractor in Hamilton, had sent down his air compressor and power tools so that Dad and Bobby could work in the frozen earth on the beach and deal with other heavy-duty digging.

Falling in Love

CHAPTER 5

According to Dad's contract with Chappell, once the treasure was recovered, and after the government received its 5 percent, Chappell and Dad would split the rest fifty-fifty. Dad was confident that he could wrap up the work on the island in short order. To finance the recovery operation, he had $8,000 in equipment and cash, and an investor waiting in the wings.

Fred Sparham and Dad had known each other for years. Not only were they both in the plumbing and heating trade, they were also good friends. They talked shop together and helped each other out.

In December 1959, Chappell had extended Dad's contract for all of 1960. On January 19, 1960, Dad and Fred signed a contract in which Fred agreed to provide Dad with $6,000 in exchange for 25 percent of Dad's share of the treasure. This seemed completely reasonable to both men. Dad thought he could intercept the sea water tunnel, bring up the treasure, and be on his way in a matter of months. He believed he could manage it easily with his own investment and Fred's $6,000. That was a lot of money in 1960, and Fred was not a wealthy man. He was a successful, conservative businessman of modest means. It's a testament to his belief in the existence of a treasure on Oak Island and to his faith in Dad that he would risk so much.

Aside from this initial investment, over time Fred helped the recovery operation in many ways. Dad was accustomed to working in Hamilton, which, with its steel mills and related secondary industries, was a cornucopia of mechanical and electrical parts and equipment. My father did not have time to learn where to find specific equipment or parts down east, nor did he have time to drive the sixty miles to Halifax to pick them up. Consequently, there were many distress calls to Fred. He would locate whatever was needed, and his son, Eddie, would pack and ship it.

As the search stretched into years, it became necessary to bring in other investors to finance the operation. But there were many times when absolutely no fresh capital came in, and it was Fred who sent along $50 or $100 to keep food on the Restall table. Whenever operating funds were low, Fred would gather together a group of people who had a bit of money and Dad would make a quick trip to Ontario, give a little talk, and show slides of his work on the island in hopes of generating investment capital.

But we're getting ahead of ourselves. In January 1960, Fred came in. And he and Dad both thought that Fred would be the only investor ever needed.

In the spring of 1960 Dad had the opportunity to purchase the big pump that previous searchers had used to pump out the Money Pit. In a letter dated April 9, he tells Fred that he has bought the pump for $1,000. It was capable of pumping the sea water out as fast as it came into the Money Pit area. In the following letter he related the difficulties of getting the pump to the island.

> June 5th, 1960
> Dear Fred:
> Received your letter with cheque on Thursday, June 2nd, and it just arrived right. Had arranged to get the big pump, a load of planks and four barrels of gas over on Saturday (4th), which we did. Had to load the boat and unload in the pouring rain.
> The fellow who brought the load to the Island had to go to the mainland near the Island to pick up the casing for the pump. We had trucked it down the week before. It took us so long getting the first load loaded, over and unloaded that the tide was falling fast when we went to get the casing. It is a shallow spot and with the load on we had a devil of a job getting the boat off the bottom. Anyway, when he pulled into his own dock

he had no reverse and almost tore the dock away.

We now have all of the big pump on the Island and have the bridge over the shaft almost complete. This week we have to cart the equal of three boat loads up the hill and across the Island. We will then be able to set up the pump and try it out. It sure is a big piece of equipment. The whole thing is coated with grease which was thick fish oil when put on. It will take some time to clean up properly.

Am pleased to hear that you are coming down with your wife, and if you can bring Mildred and Ricky as well, that would be fine. It appears that you will be coming down just at the time Mildred can get Ricky out of school. Things generally don't work out like that.

Very pleased that you have got a fridge and stove as the weather turned so that nothing will keep except canned goods without a fridge.

We want to start putting the pump together about Thursday if we can. The copper gaskets haven't shown up. Will you phone them and if they haven't been sent, get them to send them right away. We can't afford to take the pump apart again to put these gaskets in, and using cotton or string isn't satisfactory as this casing is the drive shaft casing and mounts all the shaft bearings, and seals the oiling system from the sea water being pumped out.

Drop me a line re the gaskets and when the fridge and stove are shipped. Send them by Smiths to R.E. Restall c/o Gerald Stevens, Back Harbour, Chester Nova Scotia, VIA HALIFAX.

We had the mosquitoes very bad a week ago but by oiling about 18 shafts and ponds we got rid of them overnight.

We have lots of black ants here and right now they are flying. Another week, I am told, and their flying season is over. The natives say they bite off all their wings. I sure hope they are right as the darned things are an inch and a quarter long. They claim these big black ants killed all the Oak trees. How can that be? Give my regards to all. Will be seeing you soon.

Bob

During the third week in June, Mom arrived back on the island with Rick to find Dad and Bobby busy assembling the pump. Business commitments kept Fred in Hamilton.

Here is the rest of that first piece Mom wrote about her introduction to Oak Island:

The Reluctant Treasure Hunter: Part Two
by Mildred Restall

When school closed for the summer holidays, I took Ricky, then nine years old, down to Nova Scotia. He thoroughly enjoyed the train trip to Halifax and was quite excited at the prospect of living on an island for the summer. As for myself, I wasn't as enthusiastic. "Anyway, it's only for a couple of months," I told myself.

My husband met us in Halifax, and the three of us drove down to the island.

What a difference. The island was a riot of colour. The magnificent firs a rich green. The grass a thick carpet. And up in a clear blue sky, the sun shone bright and golden. Sailboats were gliding over a sparkling sea and small craft skimmed around the bay. The air was fragrant with the perfume of wild roses that grew in abundance all over the island. Standing on the beach and looking out over Mahone Bay, with emerald islands dotted here and there, I thought that never, anywhere, had I seen a place more beautiful.

Ricky and I quickly settled down to island living. For Ricky, it was a long summer of swimming, boating, exploring, and all the fascinating things a 9-year-old boy can find to do on an island of his own. As for myself, I soon settled into routine. Forgotten were the miseries of the fall before.

During the winter months the men had built another shack down near the beach. It was 8 feet by 12 feet, big enough to hold two or three barrels of gas as well as the tools. We emptied the shack and constructed two bunks for the boys. This gave us more room in the shack on the hill and some privacy.

They had also made a cradle for the boat. It was a plywood platform, slightly V-shaped, long enough and wide enough to hold a sixteen-foot boat. It rested on two axles with wheels, and a tongue at the front allowed for easy steering in and out of the water, as needed. The old car that Bobby had driven down to Nova Scotia was used to pull the float, as we called it, out of the water and up the slope of the beach. It was quite easy to wheel the float down into the water using only manpower.

While I was away the car had been towed behind our boat to the island on a raft made of planks and gas barrels. A compressor was brought over in this manner too. Bob told me that they nearly lost the whole works when they were loading them at the mainland. The car came in very handy on the Island for transporting barrels of gas, groceries, lumber, etc. from the beach up the hill to the Pit area.

Across the big pit, on an angle, a forty-foot span had been erected. This was to hold a huge pump and motor. The pump was on the island ready to be fitted together and put into place. Along the side of the span, against the end of the shaft, was a mining hoist on tracks. This was to be used to send tools or anything that was needed down the shaft when the men were working there. Right now it was an ideal place to keep our foodstuff. A motor operated the hoist up or down "The Hole," as we called this particular pit [the Money Pit], and we found that our food stayed nice and cool down at the thirty-foot level.

With July came the tourists. They came from all over both Canada and the U.S.A. The Bounty was being built in Lunenburg about 15 miles further down the coast. This attracted many tourists and of course a lot of them journeyed on to see Oak Island.

The boatmen who brought the tourists to the island also acted as their guides. They would bring them up to see the pits, tell them the history of the place, show them around, and then take them back to the mainland. Some of the tales these guides told their customers were out of this world. One man in particular told of the hair-raising, narrow escapes he had experienced while working with the treasure hunters … cave-ins, water rushing in, timbers cracking. It was enough to scare anybody to death. I know it did me, there inside the shack listening, even though I knew he had only been employed to ferry supplies to the island.

All our laundry had to be done by hand. I didn't have a washing machine and the nearest laundry was several miles away. It was too much trouble to cart things over in the boat and then on by car, and anyway, the men couldn't spare the time for a special trip to take me ashore. So nearly every day I stood outside scrubbing the clothes in a big tin tub. At first I used to feel rather silly if any of the visitors caught me doing my washing, for they seemed to delight in snapping my picture at such times.

Often the visitors would chat with me. The men were like kids at a picnic … looking around with shining eyes as they eagerly asked questions, listened intently to the answers. Some then would stand silently, looking far off. Perhaps they were seeing themselves at the head of a gallant crew who bravely went down into the pits, and against all odds finally emerged, triumphantly bringing up the treasure.

The wives were a little more practical. They were interested in knowing what it was like to live on an island. These were split into two groups, "For" and "Against." With both, the dialogue was somewhat the same; only the tone inflection was different.

"All alone on the island?"

"No electricity?"

"No telephone?"

"No TV?"

And with each confirming nod or shake, the faces of the 'For's" beamed brighter and brighter. Talking, looking around at the beautiful scenery, then eyeing me in my shorts, bare feet, looking something like Al Capp's Dogpatchers, it was plain to see that they were utterly fascinated by the whole idea. Inhaling deeply of the sweet scented air, they would turn to go, saying, "My, how I envy you."

Those "Against" would run through the same routine but by the time they reached the "No TV?" bit, often their voices had sunk to an incredulous whisper. Then, looking at me pityingly, they would say, "My dear, you have so much courage." That was my cue to straighten up and put on my bravest, martyr-like air. But frankly, I could not have cared less.

The weather was ideal. Even in summer the nights were always cool enough to need warm covering, and lying in bed, snuggled under the blankets, once in awhile, when atmospheric conditions were just right, you could faintly hear the mainland noises coming in through the open window. A soft hum of sounds blended together — traffic, voices calling to one another, a dog's bark, and occasionally the deep rumble of a transport truck. Nearer, the call of the night birds, a gentle rustling of the leaves in the trees. It was like a lullaby. I had no trouble getting to sleep now. It was wonderful to wake up every morning refreshed after a good night's sleep and feel eager to face the new day. For the days were long and sunny, with fresh westerly winds that prevented the awful sticky heat that is so usual in cities during the summer months.

It was almost, but not quite, perfect. True, the nights were sweet, and the days heavenly ... but evenings were hell.

Every evening, not long after the sun had set, the mosquitoes arrived. They came in swarms from out of the woods and from off the swamp. Heaven help anyone who was foolish enough to be out then. It seemed useless to put on repellant for they still found some place to bite, and could they bite, even through thick clothing. I had never encountered such monsters before, or so many of them.

Sometimes, sitting in the cabin waiting for the lantern to be lit, I could hear angry buzzing outside the screened windows, like a swarm of bees. Once the door was shut tight and the light on, we never ventured outside. Even then we were not entirely free, for they would fold up their wings and crawl in at the crack by the door. There was always at least one zooming around, followed by four pairs of eyes, until someone managed to swat it. I tried stuffing the crack with tissues, but still they got in. I soaked the tissues with rubbing alcohol; even that didn't stop some of them, but these were a lot easier to get, probably because they were half gassed from the alcohol fumes. Then around 10:30 with the chill of the night settling in, their ranks would thin, and suddenly they were gone. Then, and only then, did the boys take off down the hill to their cabin.

Just before I left home, arrangements had been made to ship a gas refrigerator to the island. The "Hole" was fine to keep water, fruit, or juices, but a lot of food spoiled when kept down in that damp shaft. What excitement when the refrigerator came! It was quickly unloaded off the boat and placed on a dolly to be brought up the hill. It was towed behind the car, slowly, up, over the rough, uneven path, but then, with only another 300 feet or so to go, the ropes slipped. Before anyone could do anything, the fridge leaned over and gently rested against a tree.

The men straightened it up and were pleased to see that there was scarcely a mark on it. But inside a tube had been broken. We all stood around silently and sadly, watching the ammonia slowly drip out.

We tried to get it repaired but found out that it would have to go back to Ontario to be charged with gas … Well, back to the hole … the largest cooler in the land.

"Aren't you ever lonely?" the tourists sometimes asked. Not much chance of that. During the week we had the tourists who came, saw, and left with their guides or were brought to the Island and left for a time, perhaps to picnic, and were picked up later by their boatman. And the weekends brought the "natives." They came anywhere from Halifax to Lunenburg in their own boats to visit Oak Island. All types of sea craft lay anchored in the coves on either side of the island. Schooners, sloops, cabin cruisers, some quite modern, and a few leaky old tubs.

Although we had put up a corral-type fence in the pit area, this didn't mean a thing to some of these people. They climbed over or crawled under to march up to the shack, peer in through the window, thump on the door, and demand to know what we were doing. Down at the beach kids were shoveling sand, trying to fill in the excavations that the men had spent all week digging out. Grownups were dropping big stones down the pits and climbing all over the equipment, both at the beach and on the hill. It was bedlam. They milled and stampeded around like a herd of elephants. There hadn't been so much activity on Oak Island for over twenty years.

We found ourselves very busy those weekends, running back and forth between the beach and the top of the hill, trying to keep an eye on things. Often we were waylaid by groups who would want to know all about the history of the place. One Sunday, crossing the clearing on my way to prepare a meal, I was stopped by a group who asked me a series of questions about the place. I gave them all the information I could; they thanked me and left. Before I had chance to move on, another group stepped up with more questions. I answered them also, and what I didn't know, I made up. They left and more people stepped forward. I looked around while talking to this group and then it dawned on me that people were "lined up" to the right in large and small groups … All waiting to ask questions, as if I were a tourist guide from some information bureau.

We had left an area around the pits open so that people could come up close to look. Sitting inside the shack, we often had no alternative but to hear their comments.

Some said that the treasure was at the other end of the island. A few swore that the treasure was gone, because it had been brought up over fifty years ago by a poor family on the mainland who had suddenly become wealthy. And some were positive that we were searching on the wrong island.

I was tidying up the boys' cabin early one Saturday morning, when I heard a boat come in to the dock. Presently three men came and stood under the apple tree outside the cabin. I heard them discussing the story of Oak Island, and particularly the number of shafts that had been dug in an attempt to locate the treasure.

"Now I ask you," said one, "what stupid *—* would dig a hole 100 feet deep to bury his treasure?"

Thoughtful pause, then, "Yeah, but what about these other stupid *—*s that keep digging to find it?"

Another pause, then, "Well, come on, let's go and look at them."

I wasn't quite sure whether they were referring to the pits or to us.

To "get away from it all" and to spend some time with people his own age, Bob Jr. went ashore every Friday and Saturday night. Because of the shoals and huge boulders around the island, and the late hour he would be coming home, he didn't use the motorboat. Instead, he walked the length of the island to where we kept a skiff, then rowed across the narrow gap to the mainland. This gap is about 300 feet across at low tide. After dragging the skiff up above the high tide line, he had close to a half-mile walk to where we kept the car. Coming home was the same procedure in reverse. It took him about forty minutes to make the trip either way. When coming home during the summer, if the weather was calm and clear, he often rowed around the island, bringing the skiff to our cove. Ricky then had the use of it until the next weekend.

Bob taught Ricky how to handle the skiff and it was the boy's pride and joy to be able to take the skiff out and row it around in the cove. Sometimes he took one of us along to show off his seamanship.

Opposite Smith's Cove, roughly half a mile away, is an island known as Frog Island. Ricky and I sometimes rowed over to pick the wild raspberries that grew in profusion on this island. On the way we stopped every now and then to look down into the clear water. It seemed that there was always something fascinating to see. Different kinds of fish of all different sizes swam below. Once we saw dozens of jellyfish, from the size of golf balls to dinner plates. Delicate looking things in all the varying shades of pink or mauve. With their long tentacles hanging down like streamers, they looked like so many tiny, gaily coloured umbrellas. We watched them pump themselves along, shooting in all directions.

One late afternoon, when all was peaceful and quiet around the island, Rick and his Dad decided to row over to Frog Island. They took turns at the oars, pausing occasionally to look down into the water. About halfway across and during a resting spell, they saw a dark brown shape surface not much more than a hundred feet off. It looked right at them, then, without a ripple, slid from view. It was a seal.

We often saw porpoise sporting on the surface of the water, either on their way in from or out to the Atlantic. It wasn't unusual to see cranes resting on our shore, standing still and stiff on one leg, looking more like a piece of stone sculpture than a live bird. We saw them in flight, their long necks doubled back close to the body, legs out straight, and their huge wings slowly beating up and down.

This living close to nature was a never-ending source of fascination for Ricky and me. The song birds along the Atlantic coast are many and varied. We were able to study them with the aid of the coloured picture cards given away with the tea we used. Wild fowl, too, made their home on Oak Island, grouse, pheasant, partridge, and on the nearby swamp, black ducks nested.

A pair of beaver had built a lodge at the edge of the swamp, and often in the early evening we would see them cruising around, swimming up and down the waterways among the reeds. Near the bank where we stood to watch was quite an expanse of deep water, possibly eight hundred feet long and ranging, in a sawtooth pattern, from twenty-five to one hundred feet in width. Beyond this, the reeds and rushes grew thickly. The beaver house was at one end of the open water and back, near the reeds.

We saw them diving and swimming, towing newly cut branches to add to their house, and watched as they clambered up the banks to nibble at the new shoots of the bushes that grew at the water's edge. We were always very quiet and still as we stood there, and as the days went by, the beaver seemed to pay less and less attention to us, often coming quite close to the bank where we were.

It became a pastime for us to pay a visit to the Beaver Pond, as we now called the marsh. One evening we watched as one of the beaver went into the lodge, to our surprise we heard a faint whimpering noise, it sounded like the whining of newly born pups, then almost at once it stopped. We kept close watch after that, and sure enough, a couple of weeks later we saw two baby beaver out in the pond with the big ones.

They were learning to swim. One was a natural. It would swim along for ten or twelve feet, paddle around in a tight circle to face the way it had come, dive down, surface, and repeat the whole procedure six or seven times; then home. The other one, however, didn't want to swim. It went through the same routine except that it only swam a couple of feet, bobbed, instead of diving, did this two or three times, and then went in.

The mother must have noticed this, for one evening she followed the lazy one in and hauled it out again. We heard a soft whimper, a loud splash, then up popped Jr. swimming like mad with Mama right behind. For the next few nights Mama went along with her reluctant swimmer. She would allow it to climb upon her back, swim with it a few feet, then slowly sink down, rolling over at the same time, leaving Jr. frantically paddling around looking for Mama, who would surface a few feet away. The little one would head in her direction to start the whole business all over again. In no time at all, he was swimming the way a young beaver should.

We noticed that all the time the young ones were out, the other adult slowly patrolled back and forth between the swimmers and the bank. Sometimes he would wind things up by giving the water a resounding slap with his huge tail. In a flash, they would all be gone.

My household duties were practically negligible. Not having the proper cooking facilities, meals were very simple and easy to prepare. I kept dishwashing down to a minimum to save water. Not that water was scarce, but hauling it was hard work, and having to launder every day gave me more exercise than I cared for. I also had to have plenty of boiled water on hand for the boys to make lemonade and such. The water for dishes and laundry was kept outside in a large milk can. The drinking water was carefully strained (in case there were any wigglers) then boiled and lowered down the hole to cool. Having small living quarters gave me very little housework to do and although house-keeping was awkward, I must admit I'd never had it so easy.

I had one little problem, though, and that was garbage disposal. Everything burnable was burnt, but the tin cans, bottles, and jars were not so easily disposed of. I finally solved the problem with cans by washing and flattening them, then every few days I took them into the woods, dug a little hole, and buried them, carefully covering them over with the dirt I had dug up.

Someone went ashore a couple of times a week for mail and supplies. Not having a fridge this meant that we only had fresh meat twice each week. Cooked meats and bacon were bought vacuum packed, being the only kind we could rely on to keep. If anything was forgotten we had to manage without until the next trip. No running down to the corner store here.

Early in the spring, four young steer had been brought to the island, to grow and fatten up for the market. They were quite a nuisance. Apparently Mr. Chappell often allowed locals to use the other end of the Island for logging, hunting, or grazing. Of course, animals know no boundaries. They wandered all over the Island, but mostly they were where we were. They meandered in and around the workings and, much to the disgust of my sons, left a messy trail wherever they went. They were particularly determined to share our water pond, and we were just as determined that they would not. We put up fences, they knocked them down. Whenever Ricky and I saw them we chased them away. By fall they were chasing us.

Once, Rick and I were going for a swim. We were almost halfway down the hill, when the cows came lumbering around the corner at the bottom, and charged towards us. We went into our yelling and hooting routine to frighten them off, but on they came. Rick and I turned and scooted up the hill. Behind us came the thundering herd. We shot across the clearing, hollering at the top of our voices for help. We made a grand dash for the shack with me in the lead. I've never run so fast in my life. We locked the door, then peeked out the window.

Nothing. Absolutely nothing ... except some tourists by the pits, looking this way and that and then at one another in bewilderment.

The summer wore on, hot and dry. Wells were drying up all along the shore, but our supply of water seemed inexhaustible. The mosquitoes were thinning out and before the end of August were nearly gone. We spent evenings on the beach by a big fire, toasting marshmallows, or just talking. This was when we liked the island best, when we had it all to ourselves.

Our friend, the teller-of-tall-tales guide, sometimes came out to the island of an evening just to pay a social call. We would listen as he spun yarn after yarn about the different legends of Lunenburg County, and there were many ... among them, he swore that he had seen the lights of the *Teazer*.

The *Teazer* was an American privateer ship that made daring raids along the coast of Nova Scotia in the early 1800s. One day the *Teazer* was trapped by the British at the mouth of Mahone Bay, and while the officers aboard her were arguing whether to fight or surrender, a young lieutenant, a British deserter, threw a burning coal into the powder magazine, and suddenly the ship exploded. All but eight men died.

To this day people tell that on certain nights you can see a bright light moving across Mahone Bay. As the light comes nearer, you can see a sailing ship and hear the creak of oars. Suddenly it vanishes in a great burst of light at the exact spot where the *Teazer* blew up.

Our friend told us of another island where no one dared to spend the night, for it was haunted, and shook and shuddered the whole night through. Invariably our storyteller managed to bring in something about Oak Island. He told of the strange fires that were seen on the island on foggy nights. How people who rowed out to investigate were never seen again. He related the sounds of fighting, gunfire, cutlasses clashing, heard by fishermen passing near the Island on their way home; and the ghost of Captain Kidd walking the island, that had been seen several times in the past few years. As for himself, he wouldn't spend a night on Oak Island, no sir. Looking around fearfully in the gathering gloom he would start up his outboard motor and yell a last parting shot, "I wouldn't like to be youse guys sleeping on this here island," as he took off. We were always amused at this display of concern.

There was a black horse on the island, put out for summer pasture. It joined the ranks of the cows. The five of them roamed the island together. The horse was quite adept at nosing up the bar of the gate and letting the cows into our enclosure where, I suppose, the grass was greener.

At the back of the shack, behind the hillocks, a steep bank leads down to a meadow which in turn slopes gently to the beach. This was the way the animals came to get to our clearing, taking their time, munching grass on the way. As soon as we spotted them in the meadow, Ricky and I would hoot and holler, at the same time banging stones together or tossing small stones at them. This was very effective; the animals would stay away for days after that. Eventually they stopped coming — during the day that is. Instead, they came at night.

Several times they had roused me from a sound sleep, clumping around and chomping at the grass nearby, so I always kept a supply of stones at the door ready for use. One could always see at night, even if there wasn't a moon. There seemed to be a grayness to the sky that reflected its own light. Objects like trees, machinery and animals too, were black smudges that could be identi-

fied. Lying in bed you could look through the window
and see the tops of the spruce trees, their edges feathered
with silver, standing solid and clear against a lighter sky.

One night I woke up and could hear the horse nudg-
ing at the bar on the gate, which kept slipping back into
the slots, making quite a racket. I knew it wouldn't be
long before they would all be inside the fence. I got up,
fumbled my way to the door, opened it, picked up a couple of stones, clattered them together, peered out
through half open eyes, and saw the animals amble away.
I closed the door and managed to make it back into bed
without actually becoming fully awake.

I don't know how long I slept, but suddenly I woke
up with a start to the most awful din. The shack trembled and shook, and the front of the building creaked
and groaned. It was as if the whole place were about to
collapse. I clung to Bob, terrified, wild thoughts running through my head. There must have been a cave-in
down the pits, and we, along with the building, were
sliding in. Then there was silence. Suddenly it started
again … clump, clatter, thud, thud, at the front of the
shack. Then, before our startled eyes, a huge pair of
horns sailed by the window. At once we knew what the
ruckus was. The cows were walking across the 24" wide
platform that ran in front of the shack, spanning the
deep ditch. And as they lumbered across the narrow
walk, their wide bodies, swaying from side to side,
thumped repeatedly against the front of the cabin with
a force that threatened to break it down.

With indignation taking the place of fear, I sat up
in bed. "You know," I said to the room, "this is ridiculous," then stopped, for the noise was starting again.
"Here comes another one," I warned Bob, expecting
him to do something, but he just lay there laughing.
That was the final straw.

Jumping out of bed, I ran out of the shack, stopping
only long enough to grab some stones at the door, then
I took off after them. I chased them around the shack
and down the hill, throwing stones for all I was worth.
By the time I got to the bottom, they were disappearing

into the bushes along the side of the meadow. I stood there panting and hopping mad. They won't be back in a hurry, I told myself, and turned to retrace my steps.

Carefully, I picked my way up the stony bank, for I hadn't stopped to put on shoes and now I could feel the sharp stones under my bare feet. Behind me, a low hanging moon showed the way. It also showed me my own shadow, queerly misshapen, bobbing ahead. Quick glances here and there revealed other strange-looking shadows from the bushes, the rocks and nearby trees. For instance, those two boulders halfway up the hill, one a little larger than the other and side by side ... In this indistinct light their edges softened and they blended together looking almost like ... Something was crouched there. Abruptly I switched my eyes elsewhere. I mustn't think of such things. I fastened my eyes on a little shrub on top of the hill, no harm in that. I knew what a scrawny, scraggily thing it was, and that it was only waist high. But from down here it looked thick and bushy, and man high. Maybe thick enough and high enough for someone or something to hide behind. Again, I pushed these ideas away. But no matter how I tried, frightening thoughts kept sliding into my mind. I thought of calling Bob but how could I call out when every time I tried to swallow, my throat stuck together. Walking carefully and trying to think nice thoughts, I studied the apple tree over to my left. How lovely it must have looked this spring when in full blossom. Now, its foliage was thick and it hung heavy with growing fruit. But it was an old tree in spite of its abundant growth; it was stunted and gnarled and the fruit was wormy. And rising straight up from the middle were stark bare limbs ... grotesque arms, menacing me. My heart began to pound. Suddenly I felt a sharp, icy breath on the back of my neck and my hair lifted. A soft moan went through the trees and across the island, then dead silence. I knew it was only a predawn breeze, but it left me trembling and wishing I'd had enough sense to stay in bed. By the time I reached the top of the hill I wouldn't have been at all surprised to find Captain Kidd himself, waiting there.

I walked along to the shack as nonchalantly as I could, but with the feeling that something was behind me. I was too scared to look back, knowing that if anything was there I'd be frozen with fear, unable to escape.

Finally I reached the door, and grabbed the handle. I pushed, but the door wouldn't open. I leaned against it and pushed harder, still it wouldn't open. By now the spiders really were crawling up and down the back of my neck. I pushed again, "Oh, God, why won't the door open?" Then I remembered. The door opened outward.

Once inside I let out a big sobbing sigh, then crept into bed, shaking and trembling, damning cows, treasure hunting, deserted island, but most all, damning that fool boatman.

Working in Eden

CHAPTER 6

Nature study had never been a big part of Mom's life before the move to Nova Scotia, but with plenty of time for exploration and observation, she and Ricky found themselves captivated by the ever-changing sea and the animal and bird life that flourished on Oak Island.

On the other hand, Dad and Bobby had little time to enjoy the pleasures of nature, though they often felt the brunt of it. For them, life on Oak Island was hard physical labour, but they revelled in it. There were never enough daylight hours.

Due to numerous searches on the island, the original Money Pit had become so eroded and damaged that a new shaft was put down in 1931 by Mel's father, William Chappell, where the original Money Pit had been. Later, Gilbert D. Heddon built another shaft right beside Chappell's. Neither of them was exactly over the original Money Pit, but together they had it covered. Chappell's shaft was now breaking down, but Heddon's shaft was still in good condition; Dad planned to use that for his descent into the Money Pit.

It was a struggle to get the pump in place. Dad and Bobby were glad they had taken the time to build the A-frame bridge over the Money Pit. They used it to lower the pump down the shaft to 145 feet and to keep the weight of the massive pump off the cribbing of Heddon's shaft. Dad was surprised and pleased to find that the fish oil grease generously lathered all over the pump parts had kept the pump in perfect condition all those years, even though it had been used to pump salt water.

> July 25th, 1960
> Dear Fred,
>
> Got the wire rope Friday, July 22nd, thanks very much.
>
> Got the pump completed and the cooling problem licked about 14th. Pumped out 30 ft. water July 15th approx and on July 17th pumped out 50 of water in 6 1/2 hrs.
>
> We now have everything ready at last and this next four to five weeks should bring it up. It's a nerve-shattering job. So many unforeseen things come up, it seems just to plague you. This thing is a pressure job.
>
> The long drain across the island is full of sand and when you pump it down 10 ft. it comes in slowly. When you pump it down further it comes in at a rate just in proportion to the pressure difference ... Now we definitely know that at the level we are interested in (118 ft. from the hilltop) we have to remove 140 or 130 ft. [of water]. Measuring from the hilltop, this is from 98 to 108 ft. of water or 49 to 54 lbs. pressure and at this depth the inflow is 450 gallons of water a minute.
>
> This is well within the capacity of the pump but even though the motor is mechanically like new, you can break pump shafts. They have done it before and with motors you can have trouble. If we have to shut down, the water comes in so fast you have to pump 3 days (6 barrels of gas) to get the water out again.
>
> We have this drain problem pretty well untangled. It's crazy how things go but we couldn't check the drains with Fluorescent Quinine as planned because nature has made this bay full of this stuff. Dye is no use because it spreads so and gets so much weaker with mixing, and the sand in the tunnel filters out half the salt from the water and takes out anything like clay. So all our attempts of this kind only gave us a lot of knowledge of what didn't, wouldn't or couldn't work.

No wonder this thing has been unsolved 165 years. When all these things failed to trace the tunnel, we went back to digging and sure worked at it. We now have got the solution the hard way. I am enclosing a few pictures.

We are all ready to wind up this job and bring up that loot. As I wrote you before, I need the rest of the money as this stage of the job has to be carried right through. We have finally found exactly how the pirates intended to shut the water off, and we are going to do it their way except that we will use cement.

Regards to all. It won't be long now.

Sincerely

Bob

The pictures are of the A-frame over the Money Pit, both under construction and completed. There is also a picture of a heavy flow of water coming out of the pump discharge pipe. A note on the back in Dad's handwriting says, "The first time water has been pumped out since 1942." Bobby's journal reports that the water was salty: sea water, no doubt coming from Smith's Cove.

Dad's comment about knowing "exactly how the pirates intended to shut the water off" pertained to his belief that the original design would have included a place to intercept the inlet tunnel. Perhaps they planned to remove some stones and earth, put a sail from their ship into it, and pack it with clay. That would have served as sufficient obstruction to the sea water. No sails and clay for Dad, however; he would use cement.

The men went back to trying to locate the inlet tunnel in Smith's Cove to stop the flood of sea water. In light of the cost of running the pump, this was the most economical solution and would allow a leisurely search in the Money Pit area. It was also the safest way to retrieve the treasure.

Always one to put safety first, Dad believed that working down the Money Pit with pumps running should be a last resort. This was no freshly excavated mine in hard rock or clay. The Money Pit and the surrounding plateau were now honeycombed with shafts and tunnels left by those who did the original work and all of the searchers who followed. The connections and near connections created an underground labyrinth. Once, when Dad pumped water from the Money Pit, a hole melted in the ice covering the large pond (dug in 1951 by Mel Chappell) that was two hundred feet northwest of the Money Pit. Another time, when Dad pumped water from the Money Pit, air bubbles came up in the Cave-in Pit, approximately four hundred feet east. In addition, all those shafts and tunnels were cribbed with timbers that had been lying under water for years. Who could predict how those timbers would react once the tunnels were emptied and relieved of pressure, especially with water rushing in at 450 gallons per minute, scouring passages with sand and clay? Dad and Bobby continued to doggedly search for that sea water inlet tunnel down at the beach of Smith's Cove.

As the men laboured on, my mother and Rick enjoyed the pleasures of Oak Island.

End of Summer, 1960
by Mildred Restall

Skin-divers from far and near came to the bay. The water, nearly always calm and clear in the summer, is a wonderful place for underwater exploration. We had two skin-diving enthusiasts come all the way from New Jersey to try our waters. They arrived at the island early one Saturday morning intending to leave around 3:00 p.m. Long before then Ricky had become friendly with them. He kept an eye on their gear while they were in the water, and in return one of the divers lent him a mask and snorkel and gave some instruction on the correct use of these. By 3:00 p.m. they had decided to stay until 6:00 p.m.; it was such a beautiful day they wanted to enjoy every minute of it. They speared some flounder later in the afternoon, enough for all of us. I cooked it, and we all squeezed inside the shack to drink tea and eat freshly caught flounder. What a treat! What a different flavour fish has, when it comes right out of the water and straight into the pan. After we all had our fill, Bob took our new friends on a tour of the Island. It was dark by the time they left the Island, and this meant they would have to drive all night, as they had to be back at work in New Jersey by Monday morning. Just before leaving, one of them gave Ricky a mask and snorkel as a gift ... This opened a whole new world to my young son.

For the balance of the swimming season Ricky spent hours cruising along by the beach, studying the fascinating sea animal life to be found among the rocks

and seaweed. He collected jars and jars of strange looking creatures, and in spite of the fact that I loathe all
crawly things, I found myself intensely interested at
these oddities.

After the Labour Day weekend our visitors dropped
off noticeably. Children have to go back to school and this
included Ricky. I had applied for, and received, a correspondence course from the Nova Scotia Government to
take care of Ricky's education. Books, paper, and stamped
envelopes were supplied free. The lessons came in blocks
of six, being six weeks' work in each block. Along with the
work, an instruction book is sent for the teacher; me, in
this case. Each day's assignment for the different subjects
is clearly explained. The first few weeks we breezed
through the work during the mornings. Afternoons were
recreation time, for the weather was so good. Evenings,
now getting longer, were for study and reading.

The summer was over. "The best summer we've
had in years," said the natives. For me it was the best
summer I had ever had, anywhere, anytime; so I was
quite happy to stay on Oak Island.

Although the weather remained unbelievably warm,
signs of fall were evident everywhere. The leaves were
changing colour and thinning on the trees; we were able
to see our small, red, squirrel friends much better instead
of just hearing them. They were busy gathering cones
and berries, dashing around, chasing one another
through tree branches and all over the bridge at the pits.
Now that the grass was limp and brown, the smaller
furry animals were also more noticeable. Our brightly
coloured song birds were gone, only the blue jays were
left. The bees flitted from flower to flower in frantic haste
and the ants scurried back and forth madly. All life was
caught up in a tempo that seemed to say, "Hurry, Hurry,
winter will soon be here."

Ricky began to turn his interests inland. He collected frogs, toads, lizards, and even baby lemmings. He
kept his zoo in cardboard cartons that we got from the
food stores when we carried home our groceries. It got
so that I was almost afraid to pick up a box, for I never

knew what I might find inside. Needing a box one day, I looked them over carefully, and seeing one with only a handful of grass inside, I reached in and grabbed … To my horror I found myself holding a fistful of baby snakes along with the grass. "You've got to do something," I shouted at my husband. "Get him a dog, anything, but do something." So, a dog it was.

It was toward the end of October when we bought the dog. Bob Jr. was all set for a big, savage German Shepherd. Something that would keep people at a distance. I thought so too. We went to Halifax, taking Ricky, so that among other business, we could look for a dog.

By the time Bob had done all the things he had to do, there wasn't much time left if we were to get back home before dark. We visited a couple of places, but no German Shepherds.

We wound up at one place where a man had a Belgian Sheepdog, but only six weeks old. I explained that we wanted a grown dog to be a watchdog and to be company for Ricky. The man said this would grow into a big dog and would be a good watchdog. He advised me to get a pup as it would be easier to train, told me what to feed it, said it wouldn't cost much in food, so we bought it.

Later we realized we had the friendliest dog in all creation, with not a watchdog bone in her body; and eat … my God how that dog could eat … three times a day with the portions getting bigger each day.

But that day we hurried back to Western Shore with Ricky sitting happily on the back seat of the car with his pup. By the time we reached the place where we were to be picked up by Bobby, it was raining and getting dark. During our absence a storm had come up and the seas were really rolling. I felt sick at the thought of going in our small boat in such rough weather. We put on raincoats, put the pup into a cardboard carton, and took off. As we drew away from shore, the boat began to heave and roll. It bucked and reared like a wild horse. The waves sloshed over the deck, up over the windshield, right into my face. I had the dog on my lap in her carton, so couldn't crouch down like the others. I sat bolt upright, getting thoroughly drenched every time we hit a wave. I daren't put the box down for fear that the dog would be injured, for after each wave, the hull of the boat smacked back onto the water with a wallop that shook it from end to end. I was so occupied with trying to see (nearly impossible), and with the rain and the waves and concern for the dog that I forgot to be afraid. I had never been out in such rough weather. Since that night, I have been out in far worse weather, but somehow I am not afraid anymore.

We called the dog Carney, taking the name from Carnation milk. She didn't see a person other than our family members until she was about six months old. When she did, she was so frightened that she whined and shook until I thought she was going into convulsions. Around that time she also saw her first dog. Someone came over to the Island hunting, and had a beagle at his side. Carney looked at this other dog and was smitten. She trailed after the dog (at a safe distance) and was oblivious to our calls to her as she followed, star struck, down to the end of the island. Bobby had to go after her; he came back about an hour later with the dog in his arms. She had refused to come back with him, so he had to carry her the length of the island. She weighed around forty pounds by then.

As for Ricky, he was delighted with his companion. The dog attached herself to him and they had a great time. He took her tobogganing, skating, and rambling through the woods, where they tracked the different animals. Boy and dog were inseparable.

In the meantime, Dad and Bobby were busy digging on the beach at Smith's Cove. They rigged an A-frame, hoist, and bucket to carry excavated earth out into the water of the cove. They had to contend with huge stones as well as various qualities of soil, ranging from oozy, previously dug earth to hard clay.

The central part of the beach work put down by those who buried the treasure was thought to be a large reservoir that held water ready to flow into the Money Pit when needed. Later, Dad and Bobby would disagree with this interpretation of the reservoir. But for now, they believed it to be accurate.

More than once, their work was completely destroyed by storms during high tide. Occasionally they were lucky, and after the tide returned to normal and the sea water was pumped out, their beach shaft was intact. Again and again, as they worked, they encountered clues that indicated they were on the right track, as Bobby recorded in his journals.

Wednesday, September 28, 1960
Dad cleared off beach and found drilled rock [hand-drilled rock, first found by Hedden in 1937] at low tide line about 4 ft. from dock. I cut cribbing. Dad welded up engine mount and water runoff for small sump pump.

Thursday, September 29, 1960
Scooped area down below north big rock near dock to start down tomorrow if possible. Went to Chester for coupling for smaller sump pump and braces to fix boat windshield. Coupled up Clinton mill to pump and tested.

Friday, September 30, 1960
Found north edge of reservoir just about 3 ft. north of big rock near wharf. Rained rest of day.

Saturday, October 1, 1960
Worked in same hole again and possibly found NW corner of reservoir exactly 7 ft. true east of half-buried rock near wharf.

Sunday, October 2, 1960
Worked on south end of beach in general area of SW corner of reservoir. Cleared an area off down to stones, but found only clay below. We have to go closer to the water, according to measurements [of earlier treasure hunters].

Monday, October 3, 1960
Rigged up sump pump so coupling won't slip. Worked in hole at S end of cofferdam. Cleared off two areas for excavating. [The cofferdam consisted of

the remains of a crescent-shaped stone wall built by
earlier searchers to hold back the sea and permit
them to examine the reservoir.]

Tuesday, October 4, 1960

Worked on beach but results were uncertain. Picked out
centre of 242 ft. ends of old cofferdam and found sand in
layers according to coarseness. Apparently water passing
through sand in volume caused this.

Wednesday, Oct. 5, 1960

Worked on the beach. Found an area just inland of
sandy area that has rocks like reservoir but mixed with
clay and a layer of clay on top.

Thursday, Oct. 6, 1960

Made adaptor for heater. Fixed windshield of boat.
Worked on beach and put in one long trench and two
small holes towards wharf and one to the south.
Apparently found reservoir about 10 ft. down from
high tide.

Friday, Oct. 7, 1960

Locate approximate position [of reservoir] shown in
old photo in booklet "Pirate Gold" by Freda. [They
compared what they could see of the reservoir with
a very old publication.] Worked on beach. Set up log
dam with rocks and started to level off the area for
a hole.

Saturday, Oct. 15, 1960

Chappell and Johnson, a treasure hunter negotiating for
rights to work on another part of the Island, came to the
Island. Work was shut down while they hashed things
over and finalized an agreement. [This was one of the
several occasions when Chappell granted rights to someone else to work on parts of the island while my dad's
contract was in force. Dad was to receive a percentage of
any Johnson recovery.]

Tuesday, October 25, 1960

Storm last night was probably the worst since we came here. Completely filled 18' shaft [on the beach], tore out the log dam in front of it. Ripped out stone dam and drove log dam back, and completely filled the hole we were working on. Went to Chester for machine work, etc. Pulled stakes, cleared debris and started digging again.

Work continued on the beach. On November 6 they found something significant. My brother Rick recorded his recollection of that discovery.

The 1704 Stone
by Richard Restall

It was a beautiful day, and my mother and I went for a walk on the beach, near where my father and brother were digging a great many small holes in an effort to solve the mystery of the flooding Money Pit. The material from these excavations was loaded on a dumper suspended on a cable between two poles, which allowed dumping below the tidemark. The tide would wash away the lighter debris, leaving the stones. These stones ranged in size from that of an ostrich egg to that of a football, though they all tended to have at least one flat side.

It was early in our time on the Island, a happier time than what was to come, and both my mother and I were still enjoying this change from suburban Hamilton, Ontario. As an immature boy, I was mostly interested in the sea life that teemed in the tidal pools along the Smith's Cove shore, and my mother was of course interested in seeing I didn't pocket any aquatic life forms that would make her job, laundry, any more difficult than it already was in a wild overgrown place that hosted innumerable muddy holes old and new.

Something in a pile of freshly washed stones caught her eye, and she carefully pulled out a slate rock and tilted it under the afternoon sun.

"Oh, look at this. I wonder …"

Bob Lee (Restall).

Mildred Lee (Restall).

Speedy Bob Lee (right) with his U.S. motorcycle racing team members.

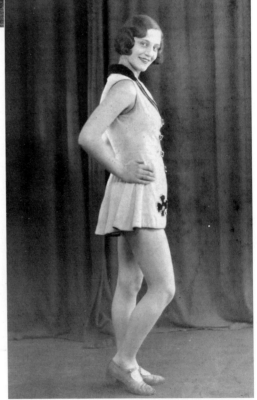

Mildred Shelley, the dancer.

Bob Lee trick riding in the drome.

Mildred Lee riding the drome, or Wall of Death.

Bob and Mildred Lee (second and third from right) in Hamburg, Germany.

Living the high life in Germany.

Advertising for the Globe of Death, Munich, Germany, 1934.

Publicity shot, Canada, 1938 or '39.

Bob, Mildred, and Lee Restall return from Hawaii.

Canadian National Exhibition, Toronto, 1937.

Ricky, Mildred, and Bobby test one of Bob Restall's adult carnival ride cars while suspended from guy wires.

The Ski Lift in action. Another Bob Restall creation.

It took a lot of squinting to see that the stone bore some chiseled characters. I wasn't sure what it meant, but my mother thought "the men" should be informed.

I ran down the beach at her request, to tell my father that something of interest was at hand. It took so long for the two men to stop work that my mother had left the spot and was coming to them. A discussion ensued as to precisely where the stone had been, and a subsequent search revealed that this was the only number-bearing stone. My father and brother, at first annoyed that their work had been interrupted, both voiced the idea that this was some local's idea of a joke. But as the days passed, the men began to think less that it was a practical joke, and more that the stone had some connection to the Island's mystery.

What joker would leave the stone's discovery to pure chance, buried in among countless other stones, under a deep layer of beach sand? The darkness of the carving indicated it had been buried for some time, and immersed as well, for as the stone dried out, the carving became lighter, so that in a few months it was easy to read in any light, "1704."

N.B.: Beneath the beach sand there was a layer of coconut fiber over a layer of what was thought to be eel grass, though most of this was decomposing dark matter resembling black jelly. Under these was the layer of stones that fit together to form a paving layer.

The carving on the stone was later examined for authenticity. It was verified that both the seven and the four were carved in a style that was common in England in the year 1704. The stone itself was not sent for carbon dating or any other scientific testing because my parents had already learned that everything that left the island to be analyzed or authenticated never returned. They were determined that the stone would not meet the same fate. The 1704 stone is still in the family's possession.

Here is another little piece Mom wrote that fall.

Culinary Delights
by Mildred Restall

Fall was well underway. Although the days were fairly warm, the nights were getting quite cool. Too, the evenings were getting longer. I was beginning to find out how awkward this camp life was. Rick was no longer breezing through this school work, he was past the review stage and now really had to work at his lessons. I had to read ahead and make sure I was ready for each lesson. I thought we deserved a reward.

By this time, our daily fare was monotonous, so I decided the time had come for a change. Having to spend more time indoors with Ricky I thought to put it to good use by preparing more elaborate meals. Up to now we had only had stove-top meals. But now I wanted to start using the oven for foods like casseroles or cookies.

Along with the fridge, a huge monstrosity of a stove had been sent. It took up nearly the whole side of the room. It was an old relic but it had an oven. One day I decided to make some hot biscuits to accompany our stew, so I lit the oven. It had a thermometer, but no oven control dial, and the oven wasn't insulated. As the temperature of the oven rose, so did the temperature of that small room. I opened one window, then the other, and finally the door, wide. Now the oven registered the 425 degrees I wanted. I lowered the flame and popped my biscuits in, and turned, as I heard a voice call out, "Why is the door open?" Bobby stood in the doorway. I started to explain, then thought of my biscuits. I saw the thermometer now registered over 500. I took the biscuits out and left the oven door open to cool a little. "What are these things," asked Bobby, poking at the twelve black cinders. "Shut up," I responded. Just then Bob Sr. came in; it was supper time. I popped the rest of the biscuits into the oven and shut the door. I quickly set the table and ladled out the stew and went to take the biscuits from the oven. They had flattened out and looked like little plastic doll plates. We all sat down to eat, silently, faces lobster-red from the heat. So much for my first attempt at baking.

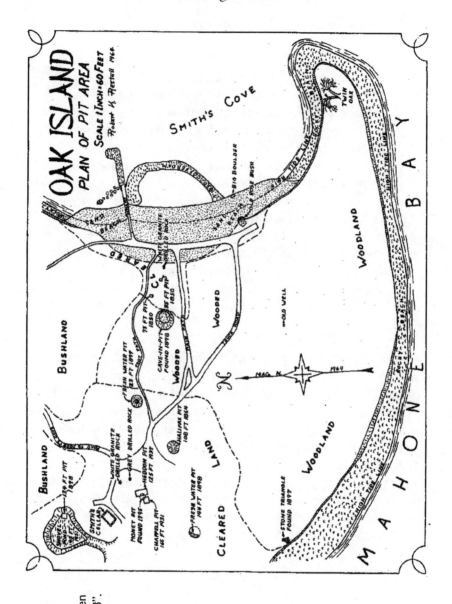

Figure 2: Bobby Restall's map. Original size between borders: 16 5/8" x 12 5/8".

On November 22, 1960, Dad wrote to Fred Sparham. He started with small talk and then indicated the direction that future work would take.

> Our position regarding the place is this. He [Chappell] has promised us the place next year. It's not in writing. We intend getting next year. Our plans for this next six weeks are to get after the treasure in the 118 ft. shaft and we are slow principally because, in our state (financial) we cannot take the chance of pumping day and night while we work down the shaft. ...
>
> I don't know if I told you before but apparently Prof. Hamilton put a well-cribbed tunnel within three or four feet of where we feel sure the 118 ft. treasure is. I will close now. Will keep you posted. I'll bet I am more impatient than you are, it's just the most annoying thing in the world. If you get time, drop me a line.
>
> Yours truly,
> Bob

When Dad said that he would go after the treasure in the 118-foot shaft, he was referring to a shaft that was put down by the Truro Company in 1849 about twenty feet south of the Money Pit, as shown on Bobby's map (see Figure 2). At a depth of 118 feet searchers tunneled towards the Money Pit. The water that usually floods the Money Pit broke through the earth between the Money Pit and the new tunnel. It flooded the tunnel and the new shaft, bringing with it the end of a yellow keg and other debris believed to be from the treasure. Dad and Bobby now believed that the treasure would have come to rest in that Truro Company shaft at the 118-foot level. That is where they planned to concentrate their search.

Winter in Paradise

CHAPTER 7

Winter presented special problems on the island. Groundwater continuously seeped into the Money Pit and froze, coating the sides of the pit and the ladder rungs with ice, making descent and ascent treacherous. On the beach, digging frozen earth was difficult and slow. Equipment parts and tools became fragile in the frigid air. The need to shovel snow was constant. Simply surviving the weather took a mighty effort.

The winter of 1960–1961 was the second winter for Dad and Bobby, but it was the first for Mom and Ricky.

Winter '60–'61
by Mildred Restall

Winter really came to stay shortly after the New Year, 1961. The thermometer dropped down to zero at nights, often lower. During the day, it never once climbed above thirteen degrees for over six weeks. The bay froze solid. Ice began along the shore, and daily crept out further and further. Every morning after breakfast, I hurried down to the beach to see how close the ice was coming to our end of the island. Overnight it advanced fifty, a hundred feet. Finally we were completely icebound. The calm weather and zero temperatures had brought the severest winter in nearly forty years.

It was bitterly cold. We found birds frozen to death, one a great hawk. You could walk through the woods and hear tree branches snap like a pistol shot.

People on the shore skated over to the island and we could skate to the mainland. For the first time in living memory for some of the residents, there was ice-boating. Even cars could be driven over to Oak Island. Some of the younger set took to having car races on the ice. At night it was a sight to see … huge bonfires lit along the shore for skating parties. As far as you could see there were acres and acres of ice. It made one think of dog teams, huskies and sledges, fur-lined parkas and snow shoes. It was cold, bitterly cold.

The cold penetrated the thin walls of the shack. We had the heater on full blast, but even so I wore my snow boots all day while working around in the cabin. At night we sat on the bed with our feet curled under us; it was too cold near the floor. You froze from the knees down. From the knees up to the shoulders was fine, but the rest of you was too hot for comfort. Now it was too cold to do any laundry outside, so every day I rinsed out a few odds and ends indoors. With daily dishwashing, cooking, and laundry, the shack was very humid. This warm, moist air floated up to the ceiling, and as the sun moved off the roof it froze. Next day, when the sun hit squarely on the shack, this ice would melt. Starting at around 11:00 a.m. it would drip all over the place … on the bed, floor, even on Ricky's school work. It began to collect around the bottom of the walls and freeze. By the end of February we had ice an inch or more thick all around the bottom of the walls and up to a height of two feet in some places.

It was so cold that whenever the door was opened, the outside frigid air swept in and collided with the warm, moist air at the open door and there they struggled, a huge cloud of vapour rolling back and forth in the doorway. So cold that when I threw out a pan of dishwater it bounced on the snow. More than once after throwing out water, I unconsciously reached for the metal door handle with my bare moist hand, and promptly snatched it away as I felt my fingers adhere to the metal.

How we stuck it out I'll never know. I worried about Ricky, who was susceptible to ear trouble. But in spite of all the miseries of cold, and lack of conveniences, we were as healthy as horses. Not one of us got even the sniffles.

I went to the mainland only once during this cold spell. It was the day after St. Valentine's Day. Fine powdery snow had fallen the day before, and everything looked beautiful and clean. It was bitterly cold, and the sun shone on the field of snow out over the bay, making it glisten and shine so that it hurt the eyes. Bob suggested that we walk across to the mainland and visit some friends. I quickly agreed that it would be nice to go visiting for a change.

We set out right after lunch, cutting through the woods in the deep snow that brought us to the large cove facing Western Shore, where we were headed. The days of snow, followed by bright sunny days, had caused a crust to form on the snow that covered the frozen bay between the Island and the mainland. As we stepped onto the ice, we broke through the icy crust and found ourselves walking in about six inches of snow.

Every step we took, we broke the crust. It was hard going. I soon tired and decided to follow in Bob's footsteps; it was much easier. Besides, there was a brisk breeze blowing from off shore and my face was getting quite stiff. Bob thought it was a good idea, he would walk ahead and break trail for me to follow.

It was all right at first, but I found it hard to match his footsteps, so every now and then I took a couple of mincing steps that brought me up to his. The glare of the sun on the snow made my eyes ache; my feet felt like lead. As we walked on I could hear a mumbling ahead. Bob was talking to me but I didn't bother to answer, for by this time he was a good twenty feet in front of me. I plodded on, my head bent low against the wind, just following his prints. I nearly ran smack bang into him, for he had stopped. When he got no reply to something, he had looked around and discovered that I was far behind.

It was so warm, I could feel myself beginning to get sticky under my parka. We rested two or three times, as we didn't want to perspire and then get a chill.

Eventually we reached our friends' place. It must have been a good two-mile hike. I was exhausted. I took off my snow boots and felt my feet spread out and out, and I wondered if I would ever get my boots back on.

By the time we got through the return trip I was dead beat and stumbled around for the rest of the day in a state bordering on unconsciousness. "This is what the men go through every time they go for supplies," I thought. "On top of that, they have to drag the groceries home on a toboggan. No wonder they sit around exhausted for the rest of the day."

That winter it seemed to take all our effort just to survive. Not only did we have to think about bringing in food, there was also oil and propane to get over to the island. This, too, had to be brought across the bay and up the length of the Island on a toboggan.

I had one thing to be thankful for during this hard winter. I no longer had to haul water. This job was given to Bob Jr. The pond was frozen over and each day it was necessary to chop a hole in the ice with an axe. My husband didn't trust me with an axe, probably thinking I might chop a leg off. This was fine by me. I was tired of carrying pails of water; I was beginning to develop a pair of shoulders that would do credit to a boxer.

Of course, we had our lighter moments. Skating on the marsh, tobogganing down the hill. It was a great winter for sports. Our pond was well sheltered from any and all winds, and sometimes on weekends some of Bobby's friends would come over for a game of hockey. I went out more than I ever did at home. I had to. I couldn't stand being cooped up in that tiny little shack day in and day out. I walked for miles through the woods. Rick and I had been collecting animal cards that were being given away with the tea we used. And through them we learned how to distinguish the tracks of different animals. We saw the tracks of the fox, with the small, neat round holes it made, one in front of the other. The cottontail and jack rabbit, whose long leaps could be plainly seen in the snow, and made us wonder just how big was this creature. Egg-shaped depressions, revealing where three large birds had lain in the sun. The mink with two tiny little paw marks spread such a long way apart. It was fascinating, all of it, even the signs of struggle where a few feathers and red stains showed that some bird had met a violent end.

On January 5, Dad wrote to Fred. The letter begins with descriptions of the storms they are enduring. Then it turns to details of what they have uncovered in the reservoir area. Dad included a photo of the 1704 stone and commented:

This brings us to the fact that Kidd was hung three years before this beach work was done. [Kidd was hanged in 1701. As far as Dad was concerned, the treasure of Oak Island could not be Kidd's.] It also brings into a time when the big pirates had to lay low or get out of the business. This all fits in with the Theory that this is tremendous [treasure], that it was leisurely buried and that it was dug up from somewhere considered not safe and buried with this drain system so it would be safe against everything. This is the way it appears to be. If Prof. Hamilton's tunnel is as close to the 118 ft. shaft as we believe, it sure was a close one. ...

We can be sure that there are millions involved but we don't want to be cutting it up anymore. What can you do? I know things have been very bad for lots of business around the country, I believe.

Now that we have got this drainage system unscrambled we have to keep right on that end and cement it up. One thing is that because the drain is full of sand, it is no use pumping cement with Quick Set into it as it would flow up and down the drain but not be able to displace the sand across the whole diameter of the drain.

It's a wonderful lot of Treasure here, we intend to get it up as quick as we can consistent with not taking any chances that would risk the success of the job. We have got a lot of work done for the money spent here up to now. While it's not going to take any fortune, we will have to find another two thousand. This will surely complete the Job. I will phone you about the 10th.

Yours truly,

Bob

Dad needed more investment money, but he was concerned about giving away too great a percentage. Fred had already been assigned 25 percent. You can't give away too many quarters before you have nothing left.

Maintaining their existence occupied a lot of their time in those winter months. They made windbreaks and used layers of evergreen branches on the roofs of the shacks for extra insulation. They plowed and shovelled. In his journal, Bobby mentions temperature of -3 degrees Fahrenheit with winds up to 35 miles per hour. But even in that weather, they dug another hole on the beach.

On February 11 they ran the big pump at the Money Pit for four and a half hours and lowered the water in the Money Pit to about seventy feet. They pumped out their latest hole at the beach but could hear nothing: they were hoping to hear sea water as it flooded back through the inlet tunnel into the Money Pit. Was the tunnel to the side? Was it lower? They needed to find it to plug it.

On February 14, Bobby wrote in his journal, "Went to Chester for food, etc. On the way home we had 46 cents to our name."

The letter from Dad to Fred on March 6 hinted at the toll this expedition was taking on the family.

March 6th 1961

Dear Fred:

I received your Telegraphed Money Order Wednesday, and we were right flat. It was a great help. Not hearing from you, I didn't know what you were planning to do. Thought you would either be sending another $50 later by wire or that you were writing. I didn't phone, as it's not sensible to keep phoning collect. I sure can't phone and pay for it on this end.

I have written to the shopkeeper friend who put $500.00 in at first (before you did) he put in another $500.00 in Dec or was it November. I know he can't do much (if anything) but any help right now will allow time to raise some more money. I do know he will help if he possibly can …

How have you been making out, I would like to know. If you appear to get people interested what seems to be the point where they cool? I hope you haven't lost any confidence in this venture yourself …

I am enclosing a sketch of the pirates' work on Smith's Cove as proved out by a year's hard work and 65 test holes into their work [See Figure 3]. First you must understand the records of 165 years of work here are incomplete. Not mentioning all the work done from 1850 to 1860 or from 1868 to 1893 (this includes a dozen shafts back of Smith's Cove) and another dozen in the area of the money pit (but 25' or more away). But all this time Smith was living 50 ft from the money pit and no one got near the treasure. Another great trouble have been the errors in the records. Making two ways

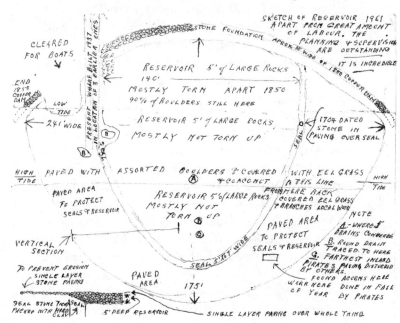

Figure 3: Enclosed with letter of March 6, 1961.

that everything at every step has to be checked. Is this true or false. Was this done by the searchers, etc.

I want to give you a report on absolute fact.

The Reservoir at Smith's Cove with its Paving to prevent erosion, its seals to keep mud and sand out of the reservoir, is absolutely incredible. We are the only people who examined this work from one end to another. When the 1850 outfit found the water running out of the beach in 1850 they uncovered the beach and found coconut at low tide. When they decided a Coffer Dam had to be built to examine this work, they uncovered [a strip of] this Coconut till they came to both ends [of the beach] (Incidentally, they removed the coconut from this whole strip) under it they found a layer of stones like Cobble stone paving.

Obviously this was man's work. They [the 1850 group] built a Coffer Dam in a crescent to span this work exactly 241 feet. When this Dam was built and the sea shut out they started in the Middle and removed a few hundred tons of rock finding the rock work 5' deep and 140 feet wide and from their Coffer Dam inland about 50'. On the bottom of this rock work they found 5 drains (box drains) these they followed inland (Hop scotch) reaching a place where they converged joining a round larger drain. When they attempted to follow the round drain they succeeded only for a short distance. The ground and gravel letting in so much water (they had no pumps) they had to give up. At this point a storm along with Spring Tides overflowed the Dam and when the Tide went out the whole thing went to pieces. The sea brought sand in and reformed the beach in the open work.

Now because the Main Drain across the Island to the money pit is 110 ft. deep (30 ft. hill) the drain is approx. 80 ft. below sea level <u>40 lbs. pressure</u> this is enough to force the water through carrying sand with it. Where the level of the pit is down 10' the pressure is only 5 lbs. It takes a week to fill the Pit back to sea level at this low pressure. But pump it down 40' (120 lbs. pressure) it comes in at the rate of 250 gal. a minute. Pump it down 80 ft. and it comes back from 450 to 550 gal. a minute. When the water is pumped down 15 feet (7 1/2 lbs.) or more it brings a great amount of sand with it. This sand pumps up with the water. This proves the drain across the Island is full of sand and that it constantly gets new sand from the beach with the water.

Note on the sketch that the place is marked where we got the dated stone out of the Pirates' work covered with decayed vegetation. The grease from this is right into the stone, I took this stone out of this work where its location, and condition proved that it had not been disturbed since placed there when this work was done and is therefore undoubtedly authentic.

I may phone you before you get this as there are two people I tried who have the money and who might come in, but you may know them, perhaps I should write them from here. In which case I would have to have their Addresses.

The winter here has been terrible; the ice is breaking up, the pieces floating by are 18" to 20" thick with some over 2' thick. This on Salt Water yet. They are still using cars on what is left. There is a storm on now. Waves are only 3 to 3 1/2 ft but not too close together, this gets the chunks of ice (tons) enough momentum to give things an awful beating.

I am going ashore on foot this afternoon. The other half of the Island is in solid ice yet. So will mail this then. We have to wind this job up fast (it's here, we can get it, and we are going to get it) but we can't stand much more of the way we have been living, its enough to drive anyone out of their mind. Do the best you can and we have got to get enough for eating and stove oil, etc. Best regards to all from all of us.

Yours very truly,
Bob

Dad was providing Fred with a bit of a history lesson here. This information on the Truro Company would have been well known to Oak Island aficionados, but not to Fred. He needed to understand the beach work thoroughly if he was to describe it to potential investors.

Dad had mentioned sand and the problems it raised. The 1850 searchers had uncovered part of the reservoir in Smith's Cove and found it consisted of a layer of coconut fibre and a layer of a jelly-like eel grass. They believed the reservoir acted as a sponge to hold water for the inlet tunnel so it could flood the Money Pit. As Dad and Bobby found, the reservoir certainly held sufficient water to make digging in the beach difficult, but more importantly, it had actually acted as a giant filter, screening sand out of the water so that sea water travelled with force to the Money Pit. But by this time, whenever the Money Pit was pumped down, the water that came in was mixed with plenty of sand, because the 1850 searchers had disturbed the original work during their explorations and had broken the reservoir seal, compromising the reservoir's filter function. A cross-section of the pirates' beach work shows one of the five box drains that lie under the water in Smith's Cove (see Figure 4).

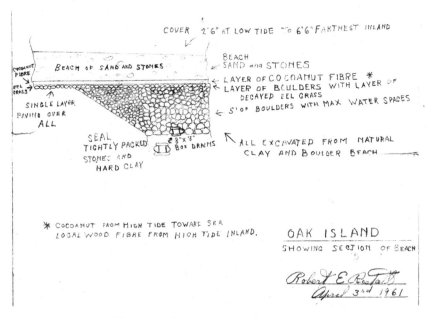

Figure 4: Bob Restall's sketch. Cross-section of seawater inlet system at Smith's Cove.

Late in December, Chappell had dropped Dad a note to extend their existing contract until March 31. Then, on March 23, he sent a letter, long but worth reading.

March 23, 1961
Dear Mr. Restall:

Apparently I have been somewhat lax in replying to your letter which is dated March 6th. As a matter of fact, I believe the letter arrived in Sydney the evening of the day I went to Halifax on practically a whole week of Hospital Meetings, hence I did not get it until I got back from those meetings. [This refers to Chappell's position as a member of the hospital's board.] I believe it was March 16th. And incidentally, this old hip of mine is giving me quite a lot of trouble in moving around. It does not bother me much in sitting down or even lying down, but as soon as I start moving, it begins to kick up quite badly.

I have had several letters during the past number of weeks from parties who have all sorts of ideas about Oak Island. I am enclosing you a copy of one in particular from a party who has been corresponding with me every spring over a number of years, in fact seven or eight years, I believe. He also corresponded with Mr. Blair before he died and that is about eight years ago. Just what this man has behind him, I do not know; but I have written my son in Washington, D.C. asking him to check up and let me know what the resources are behind this company and what this man's record is for carrying out work that he undertakes.

I have a letter from Calgary, Alberta, in fact, two. The first one came from a firm of solicitors and the second one came from a party who was their client; and he seems to be extremely anxious to get going on some sort of a proposition this spring. I have written him asking what his proposition is, so when I hear from him, will let you know if I think it is anything worth considering.

You remember the fellow in Boston who phoned me and said that he could raise practically an unlimited amount of finances. I had another telephone call from him yesterday, and he is anxious to come down the latter part of April and visit Oak Island with me and discuss matters with you. He seemed, according to conversation, quite willing to work in any kind of a proposition. I would gather he is a highly qualified engineer from the conversation I had with him, or if he is not, he has highly qualified engineers at his command to look into any technical angle.

Due to the extremely severe winter weather, we have not been able to get together as early as I had anticipated, so in order to keep things on the level until we can get together I am dropping you a line extending our time from March 31st to May 10th. The reason I say May 10th, is that there is a possibility I may be going in the hospital about that time to see what can be done in regard to my hip condition; so, we must come to some final decision before that date.

Incidentally, regarding the balance of the Island, or at least the portion that was formerly owned by Beamish. I do not know for sure that it covered all of the balance of the Island or not, but I am having a solicitor check the records and make sure. But in any case, the option is being taken up so that we will have possession of the Beamish portion anyway, and if there is any other which he did not own, it must be a very small portion; but I hope to learn within the next few days just what it is. [Chappell had incorrectly thought he owned the entire island, but he had found another piece that was for sale and was going to acquire it.]

You remember the boat that used to lay off there on the south side last summer. Nobody seemed to know just what they were doing, who they were; well I have just learned what was going on. Apparently, a couple of skin divers were operating the boat and looking for the entrance to the tunnel to the money pit; and they claim they discovered it. So far as I can find out, they are both local boys, that is from around Halifax, and they have three or four Halifax men, some of them fairly well off, who are interested with them. I do not know any of the men, in fact, I do not know the names of them, but they have asked me to meet them on Monday, the third of April, so I expect to be in Halifax, Monday morning, and meet them and learn what they have discovered and what their idea is. Of course, I suppose I have no jurisdiction over them doing work out in the water, but so far as coming in beyond the shore line, apparently, they realize that my licence protects me fully. So, it will be interesting to find out what they discovered and what they have in mind; that is if they will tell me.

The discoveries that you have made during the past season are certainly interesting. I am hoping that the weather will clear before too long so that I can get down and look things over and have a chat with you.

Yours truly,

M.R. Chappell

It is obvious that Chappell kept up a running correspondence with many other would-be treasure hunters, as he had with my parents before awarding them the contract. Déja vu. It sounds as if Chappell considered some of these correspondents to be possible replacements for my family, and others, like the man from Boston, to be a possible source of financing to help Dad's operation. The comments about the entrance to the Money Pit refer to previous searchers who had speculated that there was a walk-in tunnel from South Shore Cove. These 1961 skin divers were claiming to have located it. Even if that were true, they needed Chappell's permission to proceed because under the Treasure Trove Act only Chappell had the licence to recover treasure. This is an example of the intrigue that constantly swirls around Oak Island.

But the only thing my parents cared about was their contract. In Chappell's letter to them just before this one, he indicated that he was highly satisfied with their work. This informal extension to only May 10 must have driven my parents mad. They needed a contract so that they could use it as a basis for raising capital. Who would sink large sums of money into a recovery operation that could be out of business in thirty days?

Raising operating funds relied on having a contract. In their less than six years on the island, my parents had twenty-five investors who, altogether, put in $57,883. Some invested large sums, some invested as little as $100. 1961 was a very bad year, as a formal contract for the entire year never materialized. And although investment money came in during every other year on the island, in 1961 not one cent of investment capital was secured.

Money raised by Dad went exclusively for the recovery operation. My parents lived in self-imposed penury, but the big pump in the Money Pit virtually inhaled money. Equipment and services had to be purchased. Workmen had to be hired. It would have been unsafe to run the big pump with Dad and Bobby working down the Money Pit together. One of them had to be on top to deal with emergencies.

For the recovery operation to have a chance, it needed a steady flow of capital. And that could be raised only with a contract of reasonable length. But Chappell was not one to give long contracts. It seemed he needed to wait until the end of one contract to be sure that work was progressing vigorously. Then he would entertain an extension. Even when he did promise a new contract, bad weather or the state of his health could delay the signing for weeks. More than once Dad had an investor, cash in hand, unwilling to part with it until the next contract was signed. Contract renewal was a serious source of concern for my parents, and delays resulted in several periods of time lost from the recovery operation.

Attempting to get contracts signed in a timely fashion was such a challenge that all else seemed trivial. Yet there were other frustrations. Chappell was continually contacted by people who promised to unlock the secret of Oak Island, and he seemed compelled to hear them out. He was bewitched by the idea that someone somewhere might come along with a unique idea that would instantly solve the mystery and yield results. He even expected Dad to play tour guide to these wannabe treasure hunters or to let them camp on the island. Sometimes he wrote asking Dad to provide measurements of certain landmarks so they could make more accurate drawings. Chappell seemed to need to inform Dad of all of his correspondence with these people. It was hard to take.

There were other players. A number of adventurers had theories that involved locations on the island that were not near the Money Pit. For a time Chappell entered into contracts with these people in three-way deals that obligated them to share any findings equally with Chappell and Dad. Later, Chappell divided the island for purposes of contracts. Dad had rights to only the Money Pit end of the island. Dad didn't care about the other parts, but he would have much preferred no other presence on the island while he went about his own work.

It must have been very difficult to work so hard, make so many sacrifices, and then have to listen to Chappell's enthusiasm for someone else to come in and raise the treasure. In the 103 letters from Chappell written between October 1959 and August 1965, Chappell's comments and questions indicated that he was wholeheartedly behind Dad's recovery operation. And yet in sixty-two of those letters he mentioned other people who wanted a chance at the treasure once the Restalls were finished, or while they were still working.

The Grip Tightens

CHAPTER 8

Breakup
by Mildred Restall

It was well into March before the breakup came. I think everybody we knew was glad to see the end of winter. "Worst winter we have had in years," the natives said. It was certainly the worst for me.

As the ice began to break away from the mainland, it floated past our island. Great slabs, some big enough to put a fair-sized house on, went floating by, and many swirled around the end of our wharf to lodge in the cove. They piled up on the beach where the receding tide left them, making miniature cliffs from four to ten feet high.

The western side of the island, on down to the gap, was clear of ice in no time, as was the part of the mainland lying to the west. So by docking at that part of the mainland, we were able to use the boat once again.

Before the men could put the boat into the water, it was necessary to clear away some of the ice that was floating in the cove. To the boys, this was great sport. Taking long poles, they jumped from one ice mass to the next until they were nearly at the outer edge. Then pushing with all their might, they forced the ice out to where the current would take it past the island. Often, when they got back, they would find ice right back in the path they had cleared, and would have to go through the whole business again. Some of the slabs were nearly three feet thick. Hard work.

While living on the island, Bob and I had made it a custom to go for a long walk every Sunday. At present, it was best to walk through the woods, as the whole shore was ice-covered, but this particular Sunday, we decided to go down to the cove to see what effect the rough weather was having on the ice. From the top of the hill we could see the white caps dancing on the water and we knew that this would really make an impression on the ice still left along the mainland coast. Down at the cove waves were flinging themselves over the ice ledge on the beach, and huge cakes were ramming against the dock. The cove was full of floes that dipped and bobbed with the waves.

Ricky and the dog were with us, and we all huddled under the apple tree by the boys' shack, out of the wind. Suddenly I saw a dark brown object moving along the beach. I nudged Bob and we all watched as a little brown animal hurried with an undulating movement over the ice. It stopped by the wharf, right in front of where we were standing, then began to poke among the seaweed. We stood very still and quiet, studying the animal bobbing up and down in search of something edible.

"It looks like a weasel," said Bob softly.

"Can't be," I whispered back. "Its coat would be white at this time of the year, just like the rabbits." Then I saw the little white patch under the animal's throat. This confirmed my suspicions. "It's a wild mink," I said firmly, confident in my new knowledge of wild animals, courtesy Red Rose Tea.

Just then the dog spotted the mink. Off she went, after it. The little animal leapt from the dock and landed on the floating ice. Carney followed, but the mink jumped from one ice platform to the next. Soon it was on the outer rim of floes. The dog gave up the chase as soon as she landed on a piece of ice that rocked up and down with the waves. Meanwhile the mink, without hesitating for an instant, dove head first into the heaving sea and soon we saw a little brown head bobbing up and down as it swam along with the waves. About a hundred feet down the beach it turned toward the Island and began to come into shore. I saw with what force the waves were dashing onto the ice ledge, and wondered if the mink would be injured. But by gauging its distance and waiting for the right wave, the mink rode a crest and landed safely, then quickly disappeared into the woods.

In April, at Fred's suggestion, Dad made a quick trip to Hamilton to give a presentation to a group of prospective investors. Although there was keen interest, and some of those people did invest later, there were no immediate results. So that the trip would not be a total waste of money and effort, Dad brought back a load of the family's belongings from storage.

Comforts of Home
by Mildred Restall

When we first set up housekeeping on the island we had bought all the necessities as cheaply as possible. Our mattress was felt, and was downright uncomfortable until we put an air mattress we had underneath. As time went by it became increasingly difficult to keep the mattress filled with air. It was getting porous and added to that, the bed was used to sit on during the day, so had a lot of wear.

Every night I had to make our bed over, for it would be somewhat rumpled. I found I had to give the air mattress a few puffs also. As the days rolled by, more and more puffs were needed to bring it up nice and tight. First one side and then the other. Night after night, I blew my little heart out while my big lug of a husband sat reading. Finally one night, as I lay back on the bed exhausted and looked at the room spinning and tilting at crazy angles I told my husband, "Something has got to be done, I can't take it anymore." So he said he would take care of it and he blew the darned thing up. He did, that is, for one night. The next day he got hold of a bicycle pump and expected that to be the answer to his problem. It didn't take many nights of pumping like a fiend to find out that this, too, was hard work. He knew he would be going back to Ontario soon and vowed he would bring our own bed back. And that's what he did two weeks later.

It was April when Bob went back home. He had gone to take care of the usual problem … money and to arrange more permanent storage for our furniture in Hamilton. He came back loaded with stuff he thought I might need. Our box spring and mattress, books, clothes, and, of all things, two huge mirrors from the backs of the dressers. "Whatever did you bring those things for?" I asked. "There wasn't any place to put them," he said. "Besides, I thought we could use them." It was useless to argue. It was done and that was that. So we put one in the boys' cabin and one in ours.

We installed our bed in the cabin and stored the felt mattress. Along side of the bed we put the mirror, where every time you went near the bed, like it or not, you could see yourself.

Several times the first day I stopped, momentarily surprised by my own reflection, then remembered. It was only me. About the third time I really looked at myself. Was that really me? True, I had lipstick on, but wasn't it a little cockeyed? And while my hair had some curl, it was kind of long and stringy looking. And this shirt of my son's that I was wearing didn't really do anything for me. Up to now we had only a small hand mirror. I hadn't seen myself full length for nearly a year. And now before me was a bedraggled stranger, not matching at all my memory of myself.

The next time Bob went ashore, I went too. I had my hair cut, bought some face cream, a home permanent, and set about making myself presentable. From then on, I kept a closer watch on myself — shaken by how easily I had slipped off the scale of presentable.

Here is another piece written about events that took place around the same time.

CBC
by Mildred Restall

Sometime toward the end of March, Lloyd McInnis from CBC called in to see if an interview could be arranged for his program "Gazette." It was to be one of those "on the spot" interviews.

It was a rare spring day on the last Saturday of April when the camera crews and staff arrived to do the shooting. They began to bring their equipment over to the island at 9 o'clock in the morning. By 10:30 cameras were set and we had been briefed on what type of questions would be asked. Then they began to shoot.

Mr. Chappell was there, of course. Since he retained all movie rights pertaining to Oak Island, CBC had to get his permission to take the film. He and I stood to one side, well out of the working area. The cameras were rolling and light reflectors were up, and the interview with my husband was taking place. It looked so professional and business-like. I was quite interested, and Mr. Chappell looked very, very pleased. After watching for awhile he nudged me playfully, and said, "Hollywood next."

At this time, no one knew about our connections with show business. We had not wanted our unusual background to eclipse the work we were doing on the Island. We had let it be known that my husband had been in the construction business all his life. Which is true. Bob always worked at least part time at his plumbing and steamfitting trade. But, show business was a line he went into years before I met him as a means to travel and see the world. It also served as a means of earning a good living when jobs were scarce in the building trade. And they often were, during those first few years after he brought me to Canada.

As for me, I was born and brought up in the theatre world, a dancer. Bob and I knew the ins and outs of the theatre business, and we both knew the outdoor show business well. But the art of putting a show on film was new to us. We had been interviewed in a studio, but our experience ended there. Now we were eager students.

Under the expert guidance of Glen Sarty, the show was wrapped up and we had the island to ourselves by 2:00 p.m. Three weeks later Bob received a check for $100 and a letter telling him when the show would be on. We all went to a friend's house to watch, and learned a little more.

That summer, Cyril Robinson and photographer Louis Jacques came to the island to get a story and pictures for the *Weekend Magazine*. Right away Louis Jacques recognized me from a story he had worked on five years before, out West. At that time, he had been with another writer and they had been doing a story of the Western Fairs. He had seen our motorcycle act, and met us all then, while travelling around with the show.

We all squeezed into the shack, had lunch, and a good long talk. It was a happy visit for me. It was like talking with old friends. Louis took his pictures, and Cyril had his story. But it definitely let the cat out of the bag about our show business past.

From that time on, articles on Oak Island referred to us as stuntmen or daredevils.

With no contract and no investment money coming in, Dad and Bobby kept on digging. They located a gravel bed eighteen inches under the roadbed, but it did not look promising. Then they brought the winch up to the clearing from the beach and started to look for the 118-foot shaft sunk by treasure hunters in 1850 near the Chappell and Heddon shafts. Bobby's journals comment on finding "all sorts of odds and ends ... nails, old 3/4" die, wire, etc." They had to pull out old drill rods to continue their digging. They got down past stones to clay and started hitting wood towards the north.

Soon they abandoned this work and returned to the beach. They needed to relocate the drilled rock referred to in all the Oak Island lore so that they could triangulate markers and shafts in the area. Bobby noted this in his journal.

May 19, 1961

> Finished taking brush off main shaft [put in for insulation during winter]. Dad found drilled rock about 6 ft. south of its alleged position [according to measurements provided in early written accounts of markers on Oak Island].

Three large stones have been found on Oak Island. Two are white, fairly large, and bear identical hand-drilled holes. The other is slate, bearing a matching hand-drilled hole. They are thought to be marker stones left by the people who buried the treasure, possibly as a reminder of where things lay under the ground. They have become part of the puzzle for searchers. Lines are measured from the stones, drawings are made, hypotheses are formed. They are thought to be an integral part of the solution to the Oak Island mystery.

Having relocated the drilled rock, Dad and Bobby continued probing at the beach, now working out from the drilled rock, noting the composition of the earth near it and running lines between the drilled rock and other markers or shafts.

June 2, 1961

> Located a vertical hole about 12" in diameter. Found small dome of beach stones and hollow space below. It is about 8 ft. SE of drilled rock.

June 6, 1961

> Found hole to be about 18" across and possibly 5 ft. down. Bar passes through stones at about 8 ft. and enters open space. Ran Big Pump with no effect on water in hole.

The dome of stones that Dad and Bobby found was slightly inland at Smith's Cove. When they pumped out the Money Pit they hoped to see the water rise or fall in this new hole, indicating that it was connected to the sea water inlet tunnel and the Money Pit. When there was no perceptible change, they cribbed the hole with twelve-foot two-by-fours then, using the compressor, forced a half-inch pipe down to about forty-three feet below zero tide level and ran the big pump again. This time, listening through the pipe, they thought they could hear water moving.

They were certain that the hole with its dome of stones was the work of those who had buried the treasure. It had not been discovered by earlier treasure hunters. At last they had uncovered something new and significant. By now they were calling this hole the Vertical Shaft.

With nerve-racking anticipation, Bobby and Dad concentrated all their attention on this shaft for weeks. Then Dad wrote Fred a letter.

July 4th, 1961
Dear Fred:

We got [found] the drilled rock OK and also the old original Shaft. Dug this shaft down to 2' above Zero low tide so that I could examine exactly how it was built. It was 12" to 13" in diameter lined with stones and had a stone dome over it. Half the stone dome and part of the stone lining had gone down, over the 256 years.

I was able to carefully examine about six feet of it. Then we put 2 lengths of 3/4" pipe and with a 125 lb air hose on it got it down to 43' below Z low tide level. It was partly stopped at three levels with stones and clay. However, had no real trouble getting the pipe down. Found the level the drain joined it from the five drains and also the level the drain leaves it to go inland. The shaft was completely clear between these two levels. I then put it down to the lower level and with the Air wide open I blew up about 75 lbs of very small stones scoured by the Water (approx 1/4" dia stuff). There was no way that we could get further information from it. We then got a 2" casing down with a steel point that we removed with a 3/4" pipe key. Then, by holding the point down and raising the casing we had an open 2" casing right where we wanted it. We got everything ready in advance that we possibly could.

Got a mixer over and screened a lot of sand. On Thursday we tried but got rained out.

So put up canvas for Saturday, rain or shine. We got a new shipment of cement just arrived from Cement Co. Got an Air Ram built from 10" pipe with a blank with gauge 1" plug for dip stick, a 3/4" pipe for the float valve, a feed valve for air and an air exhaust valve. Mixed 2 sand 1 cement with water and Quick Set. Got 1st load down and air blew it all away. Float valve did not cut off air when cement had gone down because of bumps in cement. As we had cement down now with Quick Set, had no alternative but to continue.

Took float valve out and put next load (about 3 cu. ft.) down by balanced air pressure. No go. The sand was so sharp it packed in casing. This load the casing was already full and pressure did no good. Spent 3/4 hr. clearing casing with 3/4 pipe and 125 lbs air; got it clear at last (also a cement bath) put balance down no sand. Very tricky with balanced air pressure; however, got it all down, each load taking a little more pressure than the one before, showing by the gauge that it was packing in great. However last load was trouble as by this time pressure needed was greater than the seal around the casing would stand. Our seal was canvas around the casing then spread flat with 5 ft of sand and gravel to hold it down. We actually had it, but it blew up through our seal on the last half of our last load.

Nothing we could do about it. Impossible to know how much pressure the seal would take (blew at 55 lbs). We now could pull the casing, wash it out and try again or because it blew upward the chances seemed good that the bottom 2/3 of the cement would be OK and do the job. Decided to let it set and see. Let it set 48 hrs. Pumped the water down 37 ft and 7 ft came back in 1 hour. That is about 350 gal. a minute and right exactly at that pressure difference. So now we knew the air had penetrated it all and the cement had gone out the drain at low tide with 3 lb of pressure, approximately, to help it along.

Now our casing is full of cement (bottom half and has a lump of cement on the end large enough so we could not budge it with a hydraulic jack. Bobby got a bad whack when the jack slipped. [He chipped a front tooth and split his lip.] Managed to get the top half of the casing by screwing it apart at the coupling.

Our whole effort was shot through such a small trifle. Who would ever think that they have lumps in all their cement down here. When they want some smooth, they sift it.

We can, of course, get another casing down and now we have the levels, and the pressure the seal will take is another story. Instead of a flat rubber to close the float valve I will have a metal needle about 45 degrees on the face that will close every time, lumps or no lumps.

It was discouraging after going to so much trouble to have everything right.

The telephone I was using has been moved from the booth, and everyone in the restaurant can hear what you are talking about.

If you have any of those people show a little interest, try to get them to come in on the thing.

When I found this stuff I just couldn't take the chance of making a single all-or-nothing attempt. I am trying everything that I can from this end.

By, the way, send me down [name withheld]'s proper address, would you. ... Would be glad to get all these addresses as soon as is possible.

It seems to me incredible that after 156 years of searchers working here, it has been possible to get all the real facts so straight, and separate the misleading records that caused such confusion.

Best regards to all from all of us. Never thought it could take so long, but we're getting there.

Yours truly,
Bob

As he had been convinced that the Vertical Shaft was the shut-off point where the pirates planned to stop the sea water to recover the treasure, Dad was palpably disappointed. Despite his best efforts, most of the cement that should have sealed off the intake water tunnel had instead, under pressure, blown out to sea.

Next they brought Professor Hamilton's drill rig over to the island and began to probe into the Vertical Shaft. Work did not go easily. Bobby's journals report more than a month of drilling in the shaft and adjacent ground. Exceptionally hard stones played havoc with the drill bits. Ultimately, the drilling bore no fruit.

Fred was already on the island working with Dad and Bobby on the Vertical Shaft when my husband, Doug, and I and our three children arrived on August 5 for a two-month stay. Dad described the

Vertical Shaft to us. He was clearly disappointed that his attempt at cementing the shaft had spoiled that location. Cement could not be tried there again.

During our time on the island, Doug and the kids and I slept in the tent trailer that Dad had built and took turns — the five of us, then the four of them — eating in Mom and Dad's cabin. Our daughter, Sandy, was four, our son Barry three, and our other son, Brook, just two. The kids and I played on the beach, dug for clams, dove for mussels, and picked buckets of huge blackberries in the overrun gardens of farmers many years departed. This was Shangri-la.

Meanwhile, Doug enjoyed his own version of paradise as he laboured alongside the men on the beach and down the pits.

I expected solitude on the island, but tourists were everywhere, taking pictures and asking questions. A steady stream of locals also came to the island to picnic by the famous rose bush. Some expressed disapproval at all the activity on what they considered to be their private island.

Media-wise, Oak Island had never had so much attention. The CBC crew with Lloyd MacInnis started it all off with their documentary. Cyril Robinson and photographer Louis Jacques kept the excitement alive with their *Weekend Magazine* article. A reporter from the *Chronicle-Herald* came over to take pictures and gather information for an upcoming article. Several others followed, including a reporter and photographer from the *International Harvester Truck News*. That piece contained an excellent photograph of Dad and Mom in front of the A-frame over the Money Pit with Mom holding the 1704 stone.

Dad was delighted with all the publicity. He was confident that sooner or later it would generate interest from someone in a position to invest in his search.

In spring, Dad had written to Fred telling him that he feared that if he were unable to raise adequate financing, Chappell would insist on him taking in a moneyed partner. After this much work Dad did not relish the thought of giving a large, perhaps major, portion of the booty to some latecomer. One side effect of all the publicity was that after years of being besieged by enthusiastic treasure hunters with virtually no money, Chappell now was being courted by very wealthy adventurers.

Dad's fears came true when Chappell connected with a wealthy man from Boston who offered to back Dad's search. But as discussions progressed, the newcomer revealed that he wanted to direct the recovery operation. At that, Chappell balked, telling the man that he wouldn't hear of anyone having any say in how Bob Restall did the job.

Dad was grateful for that vote of confidence, but his reprieve was short-lived. That summer, Chappell introduced yet another prospective treasure hunter. I will refer to him as Mr. Z. He was a multi-millionaire who arrived on the island in his twin-engined Beechcraft airplane, accompanied by his son and his pilot/bodyguard.

This affluent interloper was prepared to finish the job, but not in any partnership; he wanted control of the island to conduct his own search. However, after seeing the island, he said that he would prefer to set up a big dragline and screening plant and open-pit the whole end of the island. Chappell blanched at the thought of his beloved Oak Island being destroyed, and that was the end of that ... for the moment.

Finally, the summer was over and the tourists vanished. The work continued. On September 12, Dad wrote to Fred describing the current work:

> We got nowhere on the hole we were starting when you left. We couldn't get through the mess of boulders. We got cribbing and built a bucket to use with the power winch and put an 8 ft. extension on that shaft on the beach. Made really good progress and got down as deep as the other one. Eleven feet below Zero low tide, 23 ft. below the ground where we drive the Plymouth back and forth to beach the boat. Now we know for sure the drain was not north of our shaft and it appears that we were most likely right when we thought last October that it would be south of the shaft.
>
> Every time you learn something. We sure worked hard on this one. It appears that by the old fashioned process of elimination it has to be to the south. We're going to try 8 ft. south of our shaft and if we don't get the drain we will go right ahead at the Money Pit. [The rest of the letter refers to mechanical problems and proposed solutions.]

The next letter, written on October 19, described the work in the same area. They had put an eight-foot cribbed shaft directly north of the last shaft on the beach. Much to their disappointment, they did not intersect the sea water inlet tunnel; instead, they intersected an underground sand streak with surface water coming in at twelve feet below the surface.

Despite unwieldy boulders they then put in a four-foot by three-foot tunnel that ran from the shaft eight feet to the south. But they ran into hard clay on both sides of their shaft, thereby showing it was not part of the work of those who buried the treasure. Through these attempts they learned that the Vertical Shaft ran to a depth of thirty-two feet and deduced that the sea water tunnel was considerably lower than previously thought. Now they set up Hamilton's drill slightly inland to probe across the line where they believed the inlet tunnel lay (see Figure 5).

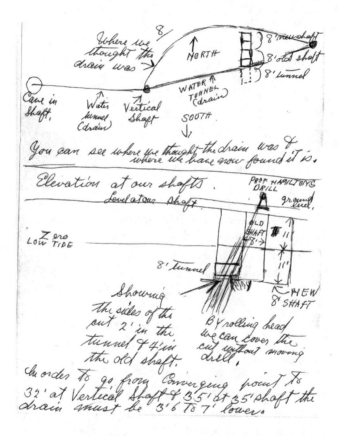

Figure 5: Enclosed with letter of October 19, 1961.

Certain that he was nearing success, Dad wrote to Fred, "I have sent up to Montreal for a couple of revolvers (Just to have them on hand before we start working down the Heddon Shaft)." Further in the letter, Dad described pressure from Chappell for success, and commented that he didn't blame him. Dad then returned to the never-ending topic of money: "Regarding money, we are still OK and can make it till the end of November [Fred was supplying them with cash infusions]. I should think that with the publicity, it might be possible to raise a bit. If you or anyone you know wants to put in $500 that may be all we will need. If you can get someone to put some in don't turn it down. The most we will take into the project is another $1,000 and as far as we know half of that may be enough ..." The rest of the letter dealt with requests for equipment such as a blower to provide fresh air down the Money Pit.

The fact that Dad sent to Montreal for revolvers indicates how certain he was that they were within days of finding the treasure, and that he knew it would be all too easy for a well-organized group to hijack the treasure the instant it surfaced.

A month later he did not sound so confident:

> Nov. 18th 1961
> Dear Fred:
>
> We received everything OK. The Blower is just right. We found the original trench dug by these people 14 ft. to 15 ft. across and 19 ft. down our beach shaft.
>
> We found the drain to be definitely lower than we thought. Figures say (with our new information) 3 1/2 ft. to 7 ft. deeper. So we set up Prof. Hamilton's Diamond Drill to bore 10 holes across this trench 10 to 11 ft. deep. We are No.8 hole now. No's 6, 7 and 8 all struck close-set boulders at 3 ft. and on down. In no. 6 hole we hit a very hard stone that carbeloid won't cut. We will come back to this later if we haven't got the drain. No.8 hole is only 3 ft. deep yet. We are most anxious to finish this one and No's 9 and 10. We will only put in an 11th if this stone work continues and we haven't got the drain.
>
> From what we have done here so far it appears that the cut is wider than necessary and that the drain was built on the North side of it. The floor on the south apparently being used for work space. We hope to finish this in a week. We got some of these holes down in a day and a half. Unfortunately it's all a matter of the type of stone. Some drill very well with carbeloid.
>
> It's a lot of red tape drilling [in] this weather. The suction hose and water pump, etc. have to be drained each night.

In any case, our finances and the owner dictate that we must get down the Money Pit after the loot, starting December 1st. So the hour has finally come.

We got 18 barrels of gas over 10 days ago, took 12 up for the pump and left 4 at the beach shack. Also got over 2 barrels of stove oil. The weather here has been unseasonably warm. Mosquitoes (they don't bite now), flies and moths are really out again …

Don't know where I am going to dig up money this time. Expect this to be the very last. Would like very much to wind this up soon, successfully of course.

Well, I must close now, let me hear from you. I will keep you posted as regards results. Best regards to all from all of us here.

Yours truly,

Bob

Where was the money coming from to buy those drums of gas and oil? Since I know for certain that no outside investment capital came in, Fred must have come through. Several of Dad's letters to Fred that year mention small amounts of money received in Fred's letters, and in one letter Dad refers to having received a cheque for $440. In another, Dad mentions that he hopes Fred got the $1,500 job he was bidding on; possibly part of that had been earmarked for Oak Island. Throughout the years of Dad's search, Fred worked assiduously at his plumbing and steamfitting business, and his son, Eddie, told me that many times his father's attitude was, "Twenty dollars for us, twenty dollars for the Restalls. We can't have them starving to death out there."

In December, my husband flew down from Ontario to bring a diamond drill to the island, then stayed for a few weeks drilling with Dad and Bobby.

Dec. 12, 1961

Dear Lee:

Just a note to let you know what is going on.

On Sunday a fellow named Tobias came down from Montreal by plane to talk to your dad and see the operation. He had written some weeks before mentioning his interest. He wants to invest in the operation, but we don't know what terms exactly he has in mind. Your dad is to fly to Montreal tomorrow (Wednesday) at Tobias' expense to discuss it and arrive at some sort of contract terms. He is in the packaging business somehow. The *Financial Post* had an article on him awhile back. He took a bankrupt business over and ran it up into a million a year ($ that is) operation. A week or so should make a difference here, any longer and it will be too late, can't afford to bicker back and forth a month or more.

Monday morning we started the pump on the main shaft [the Money Pit], ran the water down about 50 or 60 feet, took 9 hours. We put in four sets of ladders and four platforms so now we have everything finished over half way to the bottom of the shaft, including an extension on the hoist track. We worked till 9 o'clock Monday night. Were we beat. We have come to the conclusion that shutting the drain off is one hell of a lot better than trying to make it with the pump running.

We did not have much luck with the diamond drill (don't say a word about any of this to anyone). We could not tell whether we were going through the drain or not at the beach. The water we pumped down the drill just disappeared, then it would come up, then it wouldn't. So we could not tell a thing for sure. We have now decided to move the drill to a spot just behind the vertical shaft in solid ground where there is no sand for the water to disappear into. If we hit the stone drain there, as we should, we will know because the water we pump down will stay down.

If your dad makes a deal with Tobias it will make a big difference all round (I hope). I hope he plans to go at it hard this winter. I would like to have you all down here ...

On December 20 Doug flew back to us. It was time to concentrate on his business in Hamilton.

In the meantime, Tobias indicated that he was prepared to make a considerable investment for the final push. Nothing could stop them now.

1962: High Hopes

CHAPTER 9

In 1961, the year in which there was no Restall/Chappell contract, Dad was unable to raise any outside financing. Then, in October 1961, David Tobias wrote, introducing himself and expressing interest in financing the recovery operation. By the end of December, several letters had exchanged hands, Tobias had visited the island, and Dad had visited Tobias at his office in Montreal. Hopes were high.

In order to accommodate the need for further capital, on January 11 Fred agreed to reduce his interest from 25 percent to 19 percent. With Tobias scheduled to come on board, it looked as if funding for the operation was under control at last.

To secure Tobias's financial involvement in the recovery operation, Dad needed a contract with Chappell — a sure thing with adequate financing for the recovery now arranged. However, Chappell was not quick to renew the contract. He promised Dad that during his trip to visit his sister in Montreal he would arrange to meet Tobias, but then did not make contact. Instead, he had a financial investigation of Tobias carried out, which, of course, did not go unnoticed. Dad feared that Tobias might take offence, but if he did, he kept it to himself. Then another obstacle arose. Before Tobias would put money into the venture, he wanted a copy of Chappell's Treasure Trove License and a copy of the deed to the land. Chappell balked. Now Dad began to doubt Chappell's dedication to his search.

Dad's worst fears were realized when he met with Chappell and his lawyer in Halifax on January 22. Chappell made it clear that he had no intention of entering into another contract with Dad. He would let Dad continue working without a contract but only until contract details could be finalized with another treasure hunter. Mr. Z, the wealthy businessman from Oklahoma who had flown to the island with his son and bodyguard during the summer of 1961, would now dragline the entire south end of the island.

In the lawyer's office that Monday afternoon, Dad made an impassioned plea to Chappell to spare the island. Once the treasure was up, the historical significance of the island would be monumental, and the island would be a source of wonder for generations to come.

He struck a chord. Chappell did not want to be the one who sanctioned the destruction of the island. So, as tempted as he was by his millionaire's deep pockets and as driven as he was by his own impatience, that day Chappell agreed to give Dad another year's extension. Chappell's only stipulation was that he retain the rights to dig for treasure on the rest of the island. That left him free to enter into a contract with Johnson, another treasure hunter, to work in an area north of the Money Pit. Dad's new contract covered the south end of the island up to one hundred feet north of the Money Pit to the Cave-in Pit line.

On February 8 Tobias and Dad signed a contract, and payments for the recovery operation began. Ironically, during those first weeks of 1962, several other backers, after perhaps a year of hesitation, jumped in with investments of between $200 and $500.

With a new Chappell contract in hand and investor participation, especially the substantial infusion of cash from Tobias, Dad was now in a position to tackle the recovery operation aggressively.

In the meantime, Mom was still at work on her memoir. Here is a small piece from this time:

Winter, '61–'62
by Mildred Restall

Our second winter was well underway. Actually it was the third for the men, but for Rick and me it was our second. While it wasn't nearly so cold or severe, nevertheless, the evenings were just as long and draggy as last year. The bad weather didn't start until February, then it was blizzard after blizzard. It was impossible for the men to work at anything, in fact all they seemed to do was shovel snow, and more snow. Sometimes when they had to go ashore, it took nearly a whole day just to shovel their way down to the beach, walk over to the mainland, and shovel their way up to the highway.

The evenings found us all huddled inside, where it was cozy and warm. Not like last year. Even so, it was too much togetherness for me. Ricky underfoot all day, the men in and out and all together at night; it was too much male companionship. I got awfully tired of the male point of view. No matter what the subject under discussion, they all agreed with one another. They stuck together like glue. All for one and one for all. Just like the Three Musketeers.

March was a perfect month for weather. It was so warm that there were times when I considered putting on shorts instead of my jeans. But come April, it turned very cold. It snowed and hailed, then poured with rain throughout the whole month. May was bleak and miserable. It never really warmed up all year. The summer went by and didn't bother to stop. It was our wettest, coldest year on the Island.

Mom's complaints about the male point of view are not surprising. Due to their isolated situation, very little of what was going on in the world reached the family. Dad, who prided himself on his knowledge of world events and scientific advances, was cut off from the flow of new information. Oak Island filled the gap. Soon no topic of conversation other than Oak Island and its treasure survived more than a few moments, then it was back to how many feet to this, what happened in what year, how this had been misinterpreted, how that would be key. Night after night, Dad and Bobby debated interminable hypotheses. Even Rick tried to distance himself from these tiresome arguments by immersing himself in reading.

Bobby's journals support Mom's comments about the weather. He and Dad drilled constantly from mid-October 1961 to February 3, 1962, but then, due to weather, they were forced to turn to maintenance chores and preparatory work.

As soon as they were able, Dad and Bobby continued their under-ground explorations. First they tested the holes they had drilled across an original trench they had found in their latest beach shaft. Then they focused on the work of earlier treasure hunters. They cleared and explored the thirty-five-foot pit and the seventy-five-foot pit (see Figure 2).

Sunday, April 1, 1962

Tested drill hole and drain connection. Ran Big Pump about 6 hrs. Pumped water down drill holes. No reaction. [In other words, they found no physical evidence that there was a connection between the Money Pit and the holes they had drilled on the beach.]

Monday, April 2, 1962

Pumped out Money Pit and explored 35 ft. Pit. Ran pump from about 10:30 a.m. to 6:05 p.m. No reaction around drill holes [ie. water movement]. Ran it down to 57 ft. level in 75 ft. pit. In four hours it came back to 43 ft. Water in 35' Pit dropped to 36'6" level. Rigged ladders and went down. Found tunnel from 36 ft. level with roof at 32 ft. Apparently were of 3 x 8 planks every 8–10 inches with dirt face and floor. Water had eaten in about 6" and clay was stony and hard otherwise on walls. Six inches below water there is another tunnel in SW corner facing S. Noticed water pouring into the 75' Pit at around 35 ft. level and it stopped at the same time as the 35' Pit level stopped receding [proving an under-ground connection between the Money Pit, the thirty-five-foot pit, and the seventy-five-foot pit]. Found several drill holes on S and N walls starting at 30 ft. in the 35' Pit at 14" levels. 10 ft. of water was left trapped in bottom of the 35' Pit. End of tunnel was uncribbed and part of end has caved in and it is half-filled with ooze in the last 10 ft. Shaft cribbing and ladders are very good below water line.

Saturday, April 7, 1962

White Granite drilled rock near Pit. Ran drill down to about 10 ft. Added casing. ... Located a drilled granite rock about 21 ft. from slate drilled rock. ... Drilled rock is apparently the original, although it makes the 25 rods distance wrong, but the holes match with the beach one. Early in April, Doug and I received a letter from Dad.

April 8, 1962
Dear Lee and Doug:
 We have had good working weather lately and have got six holes down across the trench the drain is in [the sea water inlet tunnel]. Two of these came out of the stone work and into the hard clay of the island at 38' 6". All six holes went through soft clay (soft as cereal) from approximately 20 ft down to approximately 32 ft down. We reluctantly are forced to the idea that owing to this, there is no use of grouting here. Freezing or a cribbed shaft then filled with cement would work here (but not on our budget).
 Did I mention Mr. Hay [owner of a company that specialized in synthetic expandable grouting] was down here? He had a good look around. He appears to be a very nice chap.
 After putting these holes down we pumped the pits [the Money Pit] down over 50 ft. and as soon as we got the salt water coming through good, you could see the clay in the water. Before drilling here we pumped the pit down much farther several times and never pulled the clay through like this. This confirms that the water is passing through where we put our six holes.
 We have got to accept the fact that this place is a sea of soft clay. That brings us to the fact this spot is useless to us (as we can't consider either freezing or a cement wall at this time). What we can do is this: 1st, drill near where they claimed to hit the drain in 1897 (we know from our experience in the shaft you helped us with that the fill here was mostly sand and rocks and gravel). We got the first hole here down 23 ft. and it's apparently a trench. It appears that we came out of the bottom of the cut at about 20 ft. Our next hole is going to be 4 ft. north, where we hope to come out of the cut at a lower depth. If its not so then we will have to go south instead. I am enclosing a sketch, so you can see what we are about. [See Figure 6.]

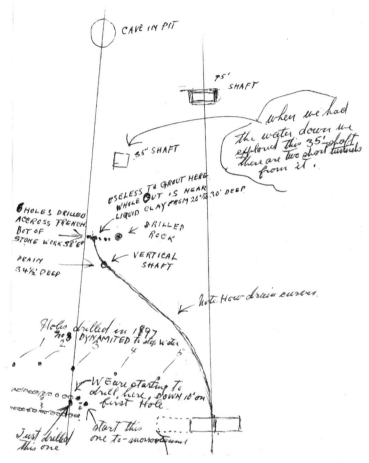

Figure 6: Enclosed with letter of April 8, 1962.

There are only three things left that we can do before using the pump steady, and we intend to do them. 1st, try to find if there is a by-pass as the 1897 story claims. 2nd, try to get down the remaining four or five feet in the shaft you helped us with and make sure the drain here is inactive. The 3rd thing left is to put a hole down about 20 ft. back of the Cave-in-shaft and try to get into the drain where it is 30" x 30" and filled with stones. Actually where the drain or drains cross the back of the beach is best, as we know that the fill here is something we can work with. The whole area around the Vertical Shaft is like a sea of soup down below.

We have been having motor trouble. The Wisconsin had a warped head and two inlet valves out of some other motor (cut down) so naturally the one used as an ex-valve warped. We have been using the Lawson to charge one battery at a time, but with the weather getting warmer there aren't enough fins to keep it cool in steady running. We are going to have to find a small car motor, water-cooled, and mount it properly with an extra transmission on the hoist so that we can also charge two or three batteries at a time. I was wondering how the Anglia you have there is. If you could look it over and turn it over, perhaps you could see if it's still all there and if it appears to have compression. I would like to know. There wouldn't be much use getting it down here if parts were missing or if it needed a lot of work on it.

By the way, our Mr. [name withheld] came in on the treasure hunt for $500.

I have had the second diamond concave bit for quite a time now. Our diamond cutters are just about done. Have to get a new set of them to complete the job. Just got notice from Joy Manufacturing Co they were sending the allowance on the returned concave diamond bit. Haven't got it yet, but at least it's coming.

The wind tore up the canvas on the folding camping trailer. Have had it repaired and had extra reinforcements and wind bands sewn into it. We had a lot of starting trouble with the Johnson, but a new set of plugs put it right quick.

Our Mr. Johnson [other treasure hunter] is coming down with another theory (from Vancouver) about 18th. Bill [Sawler, tour boat owner] was over the other day. He came by little outboard. Will be putting his boat in the water in a week. The ice went out so we can use Western Shore Dock again (went out ten days ago).

Hope everything is coming on O.K. up your way. Sorry to hear you have such a lot of grief [a run of mechanical failures with Doug's excavating equipment] and hope the children are well now.

Best regards to you all from all of us.

Yours, Dad

On May 20, 1962, Dad wrote to Fred. The letter started with a brief reference to television crews currently working on a documentary, then described what was going on with Johnson's crew, who were working on the other part of the island. His account of yet another treasure hunter is amusing:

> ... Chappell brought a woman over who had a secret sort of metal finder. She has been back twice since. Mildred calls her Witch Hazel, and it's more fun than a barrel of Monkeys. She runs around dangling a piece of plastic hose (clear) with a piece of metal in it that looks like a steel and brass plum bob. She has the whole lot hanging from a chain. She also has a gadget she takes out of a bag that looks like a pair of horns. Then she puts these horns against her forehead and goes around like a Moose. You just can't believe it at all. Bob and I are much too busy to waste any time on this stuff. But Ricky and Mildred are getting all the dope. Ricky has been made Mildred's Official Spy No.1 and there isn't anything going on that they don't get to know about.
>
> Regarding our own work we are pressing on with it to our best ability.
>
> I am doing considerable work up by the pit [Money Pit]. Have got an Austin set up to run the hoist in such a manner that it can charge 3 batteries at once as well and also drive the grinder. As soon as I can find a 12 V generator it will be able to do 4 batteries at once. All our lights below [in the Money Pit] will be 1 seal beam from 1 battery with always 2 where we are working and one by the hoist and ladders. We have not got the duct for the fan all built yet. Are using off-standard-size plywood at $3.50 a sheet to make 12" x 12" wood duct with 2" x 2" corners and mounting them 4" apart with old inner tube joints. This is both reasonable and practical. [Dad went on to say he wanted to bore out to locate the treasure before tunneling, and an Oster power vice would be the right equipment for the job. He provided specifications, asking Fred to try to locate one for him.]
>
> As to our progress on the beach, it is now definite that the drain goes under our beach shaft (though it

appears to be inactive) at 27' depth, curves around to the Vertical Shaft (34 1/2 ft deep) then curves slightly in the opposite curve toward the Cave-in Shaft. The whole area inland from the Vertical Shaft and around the Vertical Shaft is soft clay (like cereal). The water in this part goes in at from 4 to 14 feet above the drain. The drain level is 34'6" at the Vertical Shaft and 38'6" only 8' further inland.

We moved the drill back to the beach on the line where they claimed to have drilled and dynamited the drain in 1897. Our first hole proved the clay had been removed and the trench filled with rocks and gravel. We came into the clay of the island about 20 ft. We moved 4' north and put in the 2nd hole. Came into the hard clay of the island approx. 22'. Put in 3rd hole 1' south of second hole and 3' north of first hole, same results as 2nd hole.

This stuff here is in good shape and the trench is filled entirely without clay. It's very hard on diamonds and also wears all the rest of the stuff away very fast. We have a full week's work up on top. During that time I am going to decide whether to drill anymore here, now that we have the picture. [The rest of the letter dealt with the pros and cons of drilling.]

Apparently Fred was able to get the power vice, for in Dad's next letter he thanked Fred and put in his next order for parts.

Early in this summer, Mom wrote a few small pieces, some just fragments.

Bored?
by Mildred Restall

"Don't you ever get bored?" some people asked. Who could be bored with so much to see and do. Walks in the woods where squirrels scold us as we go by. Finding birds' nests and daily marking the progress of the newly hatched chicks. The mother grouse with her brood following in single file who, at our approach, sends her young off to cover while she draws our attention by scurrying along the ground, one wing drooping, uttering plaintive cries. The baby black ducks on the swamp out for an evening swim, with one parent in the lead and the other bringing up the rear, maneuvering about, this way and that, like ships at sea. Then at a signal, performing a quick about face to head back to the reeds. No, I wasn't bored. I just hated to see each day end.

Others
by Mildred Restall

Just wish they would leave us alone, Dammit. This is serious business, treasure hunting. But these people act as if it is a joke.

Fresh Competition
by Mildred Restall

One day Bob came into the shack with a broad grin on his face. It was a Sunday afternoon and there were a lot of visitors about. He told me that while taking a walk in the woods nearby, he had come across a couple of fellows with a metal detector. "And," he continued, "they seemed very excited, from the sound of their voices. When they saw me they tried to appear nonchalant, but they looked as guilty as hell."

I asked Bob where the men were and he told me. "Oh," I said, putting down my book, "I think I had better tell them that …"

"No, no," interrupted Bob. "Leave them alone, let them enjoy themselves."

I thought of those treasure hunters several times that evening, and wondered if they would be back when all was dark and quiet. Later, in bed, I listened, my imagination running riot. I was sure I could hear the faint clunk of a shovel hitting a stone every now and then. I laughed to myself, visualizing the expression on their faces, as they uncovered deposit after deposit of my old flattened tin cans.

Phosphorus
by Mildred Restall

Many times my husband and son had tried to describe the phosphorous they had seen on the water of the bay. I couldn't quite grasp what they were talking about, but finally I had the opportunity of seeing this minute sea animal for myself.

The boys had gone down to the cabin for the night, when a few minutes later Bobby came back to tell us that there was phosphorus in the cove. Bob and I hurried down to the beach and found Ricky gently throwing stones into the water.

I have never seen anything like it before. I tossed in a handful of small beach stones; instantly a myriad of sparkling lights appeared, then quickly vanished. Then I threw in a larger stone and the water sprayed out like a molten silver fountain. Bobby dipped an oar into the midst of the phosphorous and it came out glistening as if it were silver-plated with silver spangled droplets that made even more twinkling bright flashes as they returned to the water. Walking along on the seaweed momentarily revealed ghostly silver footprints.

What a rare sight. I could have stayed and played all night.

In May, Karl Graeser, a Long Island marina operator, had written a brief note referring to a visit to the island the year before and expressing his intent to visit again. On July 8 he arrived at the island and introduced himself. The next day he and his wife took my parents to the Sword and Anchor for dinner. On the following day, he came back to sign an investment contract.

From that moment on, Graeser was a keen participant in work on the island. He visited often. Many visits were spur-of-the-moment to see whatever had just been uncovered or to work alongside Dad and Bobby. He invested sums again and again to keep the work going. He located information, sometimes at Dad's behest, sometimes to follow leads of his own. He attempted to interest other investors in Dad's operation. And over time, he became a deep personal friend of Dad, Mom, and the boys.

Back in Ontario, after years of boom, the housing industry had gone bust. My husband had prospered as an excavating contractor in the good years but was unable to compete with the hoards fighting over scraps in these lean times. Doug and I decided to take ourselves and our three children down to Oak Island to devote ourselves to Dad's venture. In almost every one of his letters Dad pronounced, "It's within our grasp … We're only weeks away … We're into a final push." He truly believed that and welcomed us. He certainly wanted trusted family members at hand when the treasure came up.

It wasn't long after we arrived that we realized this was no repeat of the idyllic summer of '61. The sun was scarcely seen. Dad insisted on building another shack, saying the tent wouldn't serve. We argued. But he was so right. A cold wind whipped up that hill each night, under the tent-trailer, chilling us to the bone. The new shack couldn't be ready fast enough.

Soon Mom and Dad moved into the new shack (painted silver in contrast to the old black one) and my little family settled into their original shack. It was perfect. By then it had grown from its original tool shed size of eight feet by twelve feet to include a three-foot-by-six-foot extension on the front, a two-foot-by-four-foot extension on the side, and a decent stove. We had eating and sleeping space for all five of us. It was quite cozy. Dad gave us a small allowance for food. Lack of refrigeration was still a problem, so meals were kept simple.

A few weeks after we arrived, the men were pulling the boat up on the beach, using the power winch, when suddenly the eye that screwed into the bow of the boat let loose, and with all the force of the winch behind it, the eye, bolt-end first, flew like a gunshot up the beach and embedded itself in Doug's leg. It knocked him off his feet. The wound didn't bleed much, but you could see right into the bone. Because it was already dark, we waited until the next day to take him over to the hospital. The doctor ordered an x-ray, cleaned out the wound, bandaged it, prescribed an antibiotic, and sent Doug home. After a few days, he was propping himself up down in the hole, working alongside Dad and Bobby again.

But soon a huge sore erupted on Doug's leg next to the wound. Then another. He returned to the hospital, where they prescribed a different antibiotic, informed him that he had a staph infection, and said that since it was highly contagious they preferred that he not return, unless, of course in dire (unspecified) emergency.

Soon, one by one, huge, angry, red, puss-filled sores rose up on his legs and then on his back, his chest, and under his arms. No sooner did one disappear than two took its place. They were hideous and deeply painful. Antibiotics did nothing. We didn't know what to do. Dad looked at the mess gravely, then said, "You know Bernard McFadden would attribute this all to diet." I moaned softly. Not *that* old lecture. But we were desperate. We would try anything. Dad searched his memory for the appropriate homeopathic remedy, then told us that Doug should eat nothing but bland food: oatmeal porridge, Cream of Wheat, mashed potatoes — no meat and absolutely nothing acidic. He suggested we make an oatmeal poultice for each of the boils. Within a week, almost every one disappeared. We were relieved and grateful, though somewhat chagrined. Once again, Dad knew all.

Working together, the three men had accomplished a lot, but now somehow Doug's enthusiasm for the project had abandoned him. A guy with boundless energy, who loved to work, now went about his tasks like an automaton — grim, silent, stone-faced.

Christmas on the island was wonderful. A simple meal, of course, but all day long we nibbled on nuts and fruits and chocolate. The week before, we had chopped our own little tree and the kids and I spent hour after hour making an assortment of ornaments since there would be no electric lights to jazz it up. We had a calm and totally natural Christmas, truly beautiful and unforgettable.

But the moment Christmas was behind us, Doug and I made plans to leave. We no longer believed that all that was needed was just one final push. It seemed to us that this treasure recovery operation would go on forever. We kept our pessimism to ourselves, but we had lost faith. The search for treasure on Oak Island was my parents' dream. Now it was time for Doug and I to return to Ontario and get on with our own destiny. On January 8, 1963, we piled into our old station wagon and headed for home.

Dad was sorry to see us go, but he understood that we could not put our own lives on hold forever. He was grateful for the substantial progress the three of them had been able to make throughout those five months.

The men had completed a cribbed shaft twenty-five feet deep in the beach, then carefully prepared the Money Pit and the Hamilton tunnel for major underground work.

They cleared the pit and tunnel of mud and debris, made a duct system to pump fresh air in, set up a horn signal to alert everyone whenever the pump stopped, welded up track for the power vice to ride on, and generated electricity. Then they made a window in the wall of the Hamilton tunnel and systematically drilled a series of probes out into the surrounding earth, in search of the 118-foot shaft and the treasure that had come to rest in it.

Bobby's journals provide details. Here are a few excerpts.

Saturday, Dec. 29, 1962

Cut another window in tunnel and it's similar to last one. Used wood auger and drilled hole in roof around bend in tunnel just past dam. Drilled six more working toward S entrance every 2 feet. Holes #1 and 2 in hard dry yellow clay. #3 soft damp blue clay. #4 soft damp blue and yellow mixed. #5 & 6 soft damp blue and #7, hard yellow. These holes cover area of two windows. Noticed yesterday lots of sand in S end of Pits and tunnel. Found cribbing came apart where water enters in tunnel running to Cherry tree. Put prop in to hold it. Worked in evening.

Sunday, Dec. 30, 1962

Bored holes in clay through windows but it was all yellow. Bored two new holes in roof away from Pit and on in middle. All had yellow clay. In holes 3 to 6 we got up about 7 ft. with wood auger. All were soft and we found bits of wood in nos. 4 and 6. No. 3 was wet clay and in no.5 we hit stone. Put window in Pit side of tunnel and dug it out. Put auger up on angle and hit blue clay just above tunnel roof level. No wood, but dry, fairly solid blue clay with some red in it also.

Monday, Dec. 31, 1962

Put window in N side of tunnel near 1st hole with blue clay in it. Ran drill out into solid yellow on approximately 70 degree angle up. Drilled two holes in S roof of tunnel opposite holes no.4 and 5. Hit soft blue clay and bore through a plank over 5 ft. up. Bored a couple of holes through earlier holes on angles but learned nothing new. Almost certain to be under an old shaft. Storm took end off wharf yesterday.

Tuesday, Jan. 1, 1963

Took careful measurement to cross beam near floor of Pit and it is just over 124 ft. Plan to drill N. Checked out power vise drill rig. Cut cables clear on air ducts to be drawn out. Pump wasn't keeping water out so we stopped to switch plugs we salvaged after I couldn't get any ashore. One broke off so we got shell out and pulled head to clean insides. Lots of hard tan coloured deposits. Put it together and it pumps much faster with different plugs.

Wednesday, Jan. 2, 1963

Got power vice ready. Put drill in bed in place and set up equipment and started hole. Got in about 16 ft. with pipe auger and casing. In yellow clay. Last few inches seemed soft. No stones.

Thursday, Jan. 3, 1963

Worked in tunnel. Found tunnel floor is roughly 118 ft. from approximate old ground level. Started drilling sideways towards Pits for 118 ft. shaft. Got food and letter from Mr. Chappell to the effect, "No recovery, no extension." Sent one back to the effect "No extension, no recovery." Horizontal drilling hard due to bit dragging.

Friday, Jan. 4, 1963

Drove pipe auger to over 20 ft. towards N. Pulled rods and casing. Set rig and started hole in below. Got in about 11 ft. Casing jammed damaged threads. Jacked it all out. Very hard yellow clay and brown clay that comes out in chunks sometimes in last hole.

Saturday, Jan. 5, 1963

Water wasn't out of Pit. Engine isn't up to revs. Went ashore for flashbulbs and to phone Tobias re telegram. He and Chappell were in contact and a deal may be underway for a time extension, etc. Sent telegram to Chappell saying will see both of them in Halifax on 15th. Water was out of Pit. Set drill bed in new position but after dinner water came back in so we took photos and shut pump down.

1963: The Year of Troubles

CHAPTER 10

The pages at the end of Mom's notebook held a few fragments of sentences, phrases without explanation or elaboration. One of them read, "1963 — The year of troubles."

Dad wrote twenty-four letters to Fred Sparham in 1963. Almost every one of those letters described mechanical failures, breakages, or needs.

Somewhat prophetically, the year started with a crisis. Communications with Chappell had deteriorated to near disintegration. In a registered letter Chappell wrote:

> January 2, 1963
> Dear Mr. Restall:
>   Today is the 2nd day of January, and I have had a call from [Mr. Z] asking how soon he can make final arrangements to get his equipment on the Island this summer. Since I have not heard from you recently, I am assuming you have not uncovered anything of value.
>   I would ask you to refer to our agreement made one year ago. It was with the definite understanding and plainly stated that unless you made a recovery

to the value of at least ten thousand dollars that the agreement would expire December 31st, 1962.

I am registering this letter, and in case my last letter did not reach, I am enclosing a copy of it. Please let me hear from you without delay.

Yours very truly,

M.R. Chappell

David Tobias stepped in to try to smooth the waters. He arranged for a meeting between Chappell, himself, and Dad, hoping to persuade Chappell to give the Restall search a little more time.

In a letter to Fred dated January 9, Dad mentioned the meeting that was scheduled with Chappell the following week. In it he made his only allusion to what he believed the treasure to be.

> I am to meet Chappell in Halifax next week re contract (we have our fingers crossed and how). After all we have been through we sure hope we can arrange it. Actually we have progressed so far with our knowledge as to feel 85% sure whose treasure it is. If we are right and I feel confident we are, then it would be insane to put a dragline shovel into this treasure. From what we can find out, this stuff should contain a lot of priceless stuff worth far more than metal value. We hope this will tip the balance in our favour.

In this letter Dad outlined some of the obstacles that had slowed progress. Due to the very rainy October, they had found it necessary to timber off the south four compartments of Hedden's shaft above tide level to preserve the shaft and work in safety. That task had consumed considerable time. The coldest fall in fifteen years (down to 2 degrees Fahrenheit) made the oil so thick they couldn't lubricate, so they had to shut down the big pump. This was followed by the worst storm in ten years. Dad continued:

> We found a tunnel crossing Prof. Hamilton's tunnel. Drilled 17 holes into it. Proved it to be a shaft with some old wood in it, got a lot of pieces of old wood, made a complete check up. It's not the shaft we want [the 118-foot shaft] but one that was put down right adjacent to

it (and two Prof. Hamilton found). We now know the proper level in the old days as compared with today. That is a wonderful piece of information to have. We find the bottom hard yellow clay and lower brown marl. All the tales about it being a soft mixed up mess are just fairy tales. It's just as hard and firm as can be.

Dad's enthusiasm for his recent discoveries and his determination that a dragline not be used on the treasure must have served him well in his meeting with Chappell, because on January 19 he was able to notify Fred that he had a contract until June 30. To keep Chappell on board, he had promised to get a diesel engine to run the pump and to concentrate his search on drilling from the Money Pit.

Shortly after, Dad left for Hamilton to try to locate a suitable diesel engine to drive the big pump in the Money Pit area. He and Fred located one that had been in a destroyer.

On February 27, Dad wrote:

Dear Fred:

The Diesel Generator arrived today, Wednesday, Feb. 27th. We got it off the transport into a 3 ton truck we bought cheap. The only way to get it on the barge and off and up the hill was by putting it on a truck. We got a 3 ton Dodge V-8 with dual axle ratio, pretty cheap and it has lots of power. We had to throw on a spruce plank platform. We got the unit from the transport to the truck by jacking it up and putting 2" pipe rollers under it while we pushed it on with bars (down hill) and held it back with a chain fall I borrowed from Hawboldts. Got the other stuff over to the Island already.

Bought 20 ft. x 10 ft. of 4-thousandths plastic and covered the outfit. We will build a plywood shack on the truck with hinged sides, also will bolt the unit to the truck before we move it from Gerald Stevens (Middle River).

The Back Harbour is no good at all for a transport. They can't turn around and it's too steep and slippery except in summer. I was able to phone St. Johns to switch delivery to Middle River in lots of time. The driver said in one 16 hour stretch he only made 35 miles. From Rivière de Loup to Amherst was very bad.

The bay has frozen over again, also the hill here is all sheer ice. It will be at least two weeks till we can bring it over to the Island.

Have any of your prospects shaped up? Looks to me that we are going to spend a total of $1,500 to get the outfit here and running. The reason being that after going over Prof. Hamilton's Motor (it has been standing 20 years) I wouldn't attempt to run it without having it re-wound. Before considering that, get hold of Stan and see if he knows where to find a 440-volt 1200-rpm 60-cycle 3-phase motor and starter. A lot of stuff like this was used in mills around Ontario. I am going to advertise down here for a few days, as well. Stan is pretty good at finding stuff. See if he can dig up anything.

Sorry this is all so much trouble. Got the contract signed. Will get the one for you up to you within a week.

Yours sincerely

Bob

Give my regards to everyone. We sure have our work cut out down here now.

P.S. You can see dampness has ruined the motor insulation (armature).

In mid-February two more investors came in, one for $3,000 and one for $500. (Almost all investors received 1 percent of Dad's share of the treasure for each $1,000 invested.) Back in August 1962, a contract for 2 percent had been drawn up in the name of Fred's son, Eddie Sparham, to give credit for all Fred's advances of cash, equipment, and parts. Now, in order to make room for more investment money, Fred agreed that his own share, which had originally been 25 percent and was then reduced to 19 percent, be reduced to 12.5 percent.

In a March 4 letter to Fred, Dad described the job he and Bobby were doing, constructing a plywood body on the truck with sides that hinged up so that there was both ventilation and complete weather protection for the diesel. Ice was in the gap again, but they were still hoping that the barge would be able to bring the diesel engine over in two weeks. He had placed an ad for a motor but received no response, and he now wondered if Fred or another friend, Stan, had had any luck locating one.

In Dad's March 7 letter he reiterated the specifications for the motor. He hoped Fred had been able to get the brushes for the diesel, and commented that they would probably cost plenty. He mentioned that two more potential investors had shown interest in providing financing.

Bobby's March 20 journal entry indicated that Karl Graeser visited the island again. The visit was followed by a cheque for $500. Another investor came in for $1,000 at that time as well.

On March 28, Dad wrote to Fred that he had purchased the 75-horsepower English Electric motor with the rewound old-style starter that Fred had found for him. Now Dad was mounting truck wheels on the generator so that it would ride lower on the barge and was planning to bring the Dodge truck, motor, and starter over first but would need to hire an outfit with a tractor to push the load on. Dad faced other problems as well. There were eleven leads from the electric panel for the diesel generator, all marked; however, only half of them corresponded with terminals, and the manufacturer could supply no manual. Dad hoped the electrical engineers would be able to figure it out. Snow and ice still covered the island, making it impossible to use the car.

A new problem was cited in Dad's letter of March 30. He'd wanted to start the diesel with air but found the eighty-five pounds the compressor put out was not enough; now they needed a thirty-six-volt generator. Dad mentioned that some aircraft and boats used thirty-six volts. He expected the barge to be in the water that week. Then he could get the diesel to the island.

Tobias wrote to Dad on April 15, referring to the next ten weeks of drilling, upon which "the whole gamble is based." He urged Dad to keep Chappell up to date on the operation and suggested that Dad invite Chappell down during the drilling so that he "sees what you are doing and why you are doing it and knows you mean business." Dad acted on Tobias's suggestion and invited them both down once drilling was set to start. But more frustrating delays would intercede before that day arrived.

On April 16 Dad wrote to Fred, thanking him for the starter and motor. Most of the equipment was at the government wharf ready to load and bring over to the island, but a twenty-mile-per-hour south wind was forecast, and the new owners of the boats would not launch until the storm had passed. The potential investor from Boston was there for a visit and needed to investigate tax implications before proceeding. Dad had arranged for the diesel people and the generator engineers to come as soon as the equipment was set up on the island.

On April 28 Dad wrote to say that the Dodge truck with motor and starter were brought over on Friday morning, and the diesel generator on Saturday morning. It got rough both days before they were finished, but they landed without incident. He still needed to get the generator up the hill.

The electrical engineers spent May 13 and 14 working on the panel wiring for the diesel, but the problem was not resolved. Dad's letter of May 17 was a continuation of a telephone conversation and telegraph message about a broken starting motor gear reduction shaft. The electrical engineers for the panel wiring couldn't come again until the next week, so Chappell delayed his visit to the island. Dad mentioned that Chappell had never been on the island when the Heddon shaft was pumped out and was very keen to see the diesel running.

Dad's May 18 letter was brief. He thanked Fred for the switch and related that the diesel man came and started the diesel up, but the electrical engineer for the starter couldn't come until Monday; he explained, "All this delay is hard to take."

On May 21 Dad wrote that the electrical engineers had just left, having gotten the outfit to pump just before noon. The roads were in such bad shape that Dad and Bobby hadn't been able to get oil up the hill, so they planned to spend the balance of the day getting oil so they could run the pump steadily. There was still a problem with the voltmeter, but it was not urgent. The switch Fred had sent for the power vice was larger than the last, so Dad had to weld up a larger box. He also asked Fred to send the name and address of the place where the family's belongings were stored so that he could send some rent money.

The letter of June 1 was a short one. Dad had received the six-inch Ell and had it on. He had the test valve on No.1 cylinder re-ground and it was okay, but they had a lot of trouble with the cylinder safety valves popping. He asked Fred to get three safety valve springs for the diesel engine.

On June 3 Dad wrote that he'd made a temporary fix but urgently needed the three safety valve springs. He had just discovered that the water getting into the crank case was from a leak in both the outer and inner cylinder head seals on No.2 cylinder and would have to be repaired by the diesel expert. With all these troubles Dad was feeling low and wondered if the diesels were lemons, but he was assured by the repairman that these things could happen any time. He closed with, "Needless to say all this extra delay and extra expense is destroying our finances. The weather has suddenly turned very hot and the mosquitoes and black flies are terrible. Sorry I haven't any cheerful news at the moment. That will come later, we hope. Best regards."

The letter of June 4 came in a large brown envelope. It contained a gasket.

> We finally got to the bottom of our troubles (or we sure hope so). Look at the enclosed exhaust gasket. Note that it has been put on backward, cutting about 60% of the flow. How could anybody pull a boner like that. This what has been causing all our troubles from local hot spots. There can be no doubt that steam pockets formed in the liner and head. This is from No.2 cylinder. We have just had No.2 head and sleeve pressure-tested and the cylinder is cracked at the ports. As I have had water in the air box and water in the crank case sump right from the start, there is no doubt at all that this must have been done right after this gasket was put in. Now remembering that time is vital, the diesel people are putting in a new sleeve and gasket set … You can be sure we are taking the Ex manifold off to see if No.1 and No.3 gaskets are in backward. I think we are lucky the head wasn't gone as well. We sure hope that this is the end of our diesel troubles.

According to Bobby's journals, they started the diesel and started pumping on June 5. Work continued despite frequent breakdowns. After talking with Professor Hamilton and the members of his crew, then Charlie Hatt and Harry Adams, Dad and Bobby were able to cut more windows in his tunnel and locate another tunnel that crossed it at a different height. But they finally decided to give up the search for the 118-foot shaft due to the uncertainty of its location.

Dad's next letter is worth reading in its entirety.

> June 20th, 1963
> Dear Fred:
>   We got the controls Tuesday and thanks very much. Got them on right away. They are not quite the same; the new ones have a final adjustment that saves time putting them on and makes it possible to get a very fine adjustment without taking anything apart. It was get-

ting pretty hard running the boat from the back when it's rough weather. I still haven't sent you the little piece for the lawn mower. We have had so much happen recently that I will try to bring everything up to date.

As our fuel would only last till last Sunday and the Montreal investor was flying down and bringing Chappell on Wednesday (yesterday June 19th) I got him to charge 14 barrels of fuel and 10 gal lub to his account. On Sunday (we got the fuel Sat and got it over after a big day's work underground and got it on the 3 Ton dodge 7:30 p.m.) We were so tuckered out that we left it at the beach and we had a heavy rain. Sunday morning I got it up OK but while we were putting 3 barrels into the tank and covering the others with plastic, one of the empty ones went off the side of the truck and knocked me with it. The truck slopes sideways here and the oil and water on the platform was very slick. Our barb wire fence is 6" higher than the platform. Knowing it would trip me, I managed to jump over as I went. I landed very hard with my left arm out and it feels as if it tore the arm out of the socket. Meanwhile the drum came down corner-ways and landed square on my right leg between the ankle and the knee. Fortunately my leg was flat on the ground and I have strong bones. It didn't break but it is the most bruised leg and foot I have ever seen, right from my knee to my toes and right across the bottom of my foot. It is improving rapidly and another week should see the last of the bruises (I hope). I can use my left arm OK as long as I don't reach above my shoulder or let a wrench slip or try to move it too fast. If it's not a lot better in another week I will get x-rays taken just to be sure.

Tobias had a lousy trip down on Tues. night. The plane couldn't land, took him back to Moncton. He came by bus from there. He could have done better taking a sleeper on the C.N. Railway. He brought a lot of food with him and we had a meal in the cabin. They [Tobias and Chappell] left at 2:20 p.m. to get 4 p.m. plane. Everything went fine. They both took a lot of pictures and the set-up here impressed them both. We have until

December 31st 1963 to bring up some loot and whatever time needed after that. Tobias has agreed to have all the fuel oil and lub. charged to his account. Approximately $600 a month for the full 6 months if necessary.

Our other expenses (bare expenses) are $35.00 a week to cover $24 getting oil over $11.00 a week boat car and any small hardware. Plus $65.00 a week for living expenses, etc. This is $400 a month. That we must dig up somehow. On top of that there is the Con. Equip bill, the Westinghouse bill, Fraser's bill and Featherstone. A couple of thousand dollars would wipe these four right off and the $400 a month shouldn't be too tough.

We were drilling nicely this afternoon when our first pump shaft broke. So now we have to pull part of the pump apart and put a new shaft in. We have several spares but there is a little machine job. Prof. Hamilton broke shafts every summer but this is our first and we hope we don't have more.

We found old broken up cribbing and big timbers apparently in the No.6 shaft. We probed all over the bottom and sides. No loot yet. We are pretty sure the clay here is moving toward Chappell's shaft a few inches each year. As we are now sure this decoy treasure is between Prof. Hamilton's tunnel and the Chappell Shaft. We had made up our minds last fall that should this prove to be so, we would get after the big treasure and get it out before going into this section.

So Mon. we pulled everything out of the area and Tues we started a hole at 127' depth magnetic N.W. We drilled 3 holes north (true) last winter and had hard yellow clay in two and brown marl in the lower one. We set up with clay tools and got nowhere, 3' only and we were into coarse sand and fine gravel brought up from the beach. You can imagine the excitement. Wed. was public relations [visit from Chappell and Tobias]. Today we took the diamond and everything needed down. We got all set up and in the same hole and only a few inches of progress when the shaft snapped. Mildred heard the change of racket at once and nearly had a fit. We got everything out of the way and loaded in the [hoist] car in time. Could have done it faster but you know how these sudden emergencies are, both of us tried to do what the other fellow had been doing. We soon saw that was no good so we just went back to loading the [hoist] car as if we were through for the day and let the hoist car bring up the electric cable.

I got $300 from the bank Tuesday for 2 months. This will handle ordinary expenses. We will sure have to start writing out in all directions for more funds. Well anyway Fred, in spite of everything. We now have the time. We have the fuel expense. What remains may look big but it's the small end and we will get it one way or another.

We have an oil leak into the cooling water. We are going to take the oil cooler off now. I think we will find a split from water frozen here (in the Lub oil) from some time in the past from the cracked cylinder liner. It will be interesting if this is so. I will let you know. This will be easy to test and we hope not too hard to fix. The diesel runs very well, good oil pressure, etc. The only other bother was the tach cable broke, it was bent too sharply where it came out of the case. We shortened the outer and inner 2" and had it running in 30 minutes.

Well, we're getting right close in now and we just can't wait to get going again, perhaps the broken shaft is only 40 ft. down or so. Should be in the top half (the break). Best regards to all,

Yours sincerely
Bob

Dad and Bobby began repairing and replacing the shaft and trying to solve the persistent cooling problems. Graeser came to help out.

July 10, 1963
Dear Fred:

I want to thank you very much with the speedy help getting the Oil Cooler down to me. The fellow from Long Island [Graeser] was up for 8 days and helped us a lot. We found the cooler was going to be locked in an express car from Friday night till Tuesday morning. So we drove to Halifax to meet the two trains. It wasn't on the first one and the second one was 3 1/2 hrs. late. So we made out an order to have it sent to Chester Basin instead, as they are open on some Saturdays and were open on this one. Karl (from L.I.) Picked it up 10:30 Sat. morning.

Thank the fellows at Red D Arc for me, and Eddie as well.

We broke our first shaft and got it fixed OK, luckily it was near the top. We put the cooler in and pumped the shaft out and the three of us were only 3 1/2 hrs. working when the fresh water cooler clogged up. The oil in the water system amalgamated with rust particles and put the combination into circulation. This stopped the small slots in the fresh water cooler. The cold seawater ensured that the stuff chilled and thickened the only place there are narrow slots. This ran the temperature up and gave us no end of trouble. Finally after cleaning the cooler (fresh water) four times we realized we needed some safety gadgets.

I would have put a filter or strainer in the system but couldn't get anything here. I put on two thermostats and ran a separate line into our shack and down the pit. Down the pit we have a yellow bug light. If it goes out we know the temperature is going up. Over in our shack we have a 60 watt lamp that lights all the time the diesel is going and a solenoid that holds up a contact. If the light goes out the solenoid drops the contact and a house electric bell 6 v wakes us up (hooked to a 6 v battery). This gives us good protection on temperature rise. I put 2 flaps in the run off pipe with copper contacts so that if a shaft breaks or the pump stops, these contact blow a 12 volt horn in Bobbie's shack.

I also checked the low oil pressure cut off. It's OK. We are going to make a flap felt covered that swings up and cuts the air to the blower and stops the motor. This is so that in the event of an oil line breaking, etc. the motor will be stopped before any damage is done. I am putting a pressure switch on the fuel oil pressure line and in the fresh water system so if the fuel pressure drops or the fresh water pressure drops the same flap will stop the diesel at once.

These things are all made for this diesel. A full kit to do is about $250 without installation. I am sure our outfit will be just as good and cost less than $50.

We have sure been going like mad. So much so that we have had no time to cut grass or anything like that.

We lost the bottom jaw of my rigid 14" wrench and the teeth on the top one are worn out. Could you get me an upper and a lower jaw for a rigid 14" wrench and the piece for the lawn mower. We just have to move the jungle back now. It's been cloudy and fog patches for over two weeks now and the mosquitoes are multiplying like mad.

The Long Island fellow has come in for an additional $400 a month. So we have $600 a month guaranteed in fuel bills and $400 a month for all other expenses. We can just manage on it as $100 a month goes to Stevens for bringing four loads of fuel oil over each month. The other $300 will only just cover machine work, lumber, gasoline, oil (car and boat) food and the drug store. This covers everything except the accounts. Diesel repairs, lumber since May 1st, Fraser, Westinghouse and Red D Arc.

If someone would come along with a couple of thousand it would clear every one of these things away. We have a prospect or two, but nothing definite yet. Also, with our present set up, to properly service everything keeps us running. What we need is four men, two to work with Bobby and two to work with me. Then we could work two shifts drilling and actually drill about three times as much as at present.

We have drilled into the ramps that spiral down clockwise. The Chappells came into this in 1931 in the S.W. corner of their shaft. These ramps were about a 12" pitch per lap and appeared to them to be between a 30 ft. and 40 ft. in dia circle (judging from the curve of the small part they saw). Well, we drilled into the very same thing. The diameter is about 32 ft. and the centre was the Original Money Pit. These ramps are full of beach sand and gravel but there is over 6 ft. of hard brown marl under the floor of each ramp. We also drilled out into the top ramp on the north and found it about 11 ft. wide here. Perhaps we were where the walk-in tunnel joins the ramp. At this point you could put a drill in such a distance in the sand and gravel now filling the old excavation. These things were not cribbed.

We held the water level pretty high, approximately 31 ft. and when we broke the shaft and had the cooler trouble, oil first then fresh water clogging up, we were shut down long enough to pressurize bubbles up the walk in tunnel to our pond [Mel Chappell's excavation two hundred feet away] and up the water tunnel to the Cave-in Pit. So we go on learning something every day.

We now must assume there is a walk-in tunnel to magnetic north about 14 rods; that it was to be used to get to the spiral ramps; that these ramps at the south are (floor) 118 ft. 130 ft. 142 ft. We must assume the big treasure was either put in the bottom end of the spiral (most unlikely) or that the treasure was put just outside of the spiral at the bottom of the ramp.

We have just completed our fifth hole and must work out a way to get more holes drilled faster. It still looks as if the 30 degrees to 40 degrees covering Magnetic N to True N with a bit extra W of Magnetic North is the right section.

I have had some more 2 ft. rods and couplings made. Only 2 ft. rods and casings work well in such limited space. [His letter concludes with a request for lawnmower parts so they can control the mosquitoes.]

Dad's letter of August 11 started with thanks for the information that Red D Arc never had the panel and voltmeter hooked up. Dad then requested a transformer to replace one that had burnt out, as well as fifty hexagon bolts. The rest of his letter casts more light on the ramps referred to in the previous letter:

We are doing our best with the drilling but it is slow hard work. It's almost unbelievable the way this thing is built, am enclosing a sketch showing what we are into now. We know the treasure is at the bottom of the ramp but we do not know for sure where the ramp ends.

Apparently the treasure was put outside the ramp but we haven't any way to be sure. The big treasure is below 142 ft. because Chappells found the ramp on the south side at 118 ft., 130 ft., 142 ft. Now if the ramp ends opposite on the north side, we have got the ramp here at 124 ft., 136 ft., but we have not got into the lower level. It could very well be that the ramp curves down to either 148' ft. or else to 145 ft. and we may have to drill a lot of holes yet. In the two sketches A & B, I have tried to show you the two ways that seem most likely to us [see Figure 7]. However, we will not know for sure until we drill into the stuff.

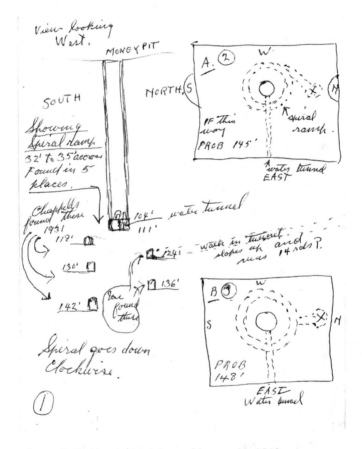

Figure 7: Enclosed with letter of August 11, 1963.

Give my regards to all and we will keep you informed.

I used to get bolts very reasonably from Wilkenson and Kompass. If you can't, surely you know someone in steel fabricating or something who can.

Yours sincerely
Bob

Dad and Bobby became convinced that there were two treasures on Oak Island. They believed that in 1897 the drill went through the smaller of the two treasures. They call that the decoy treasure. Theoretically, it would have satisfied the gold lust of any treasure hunters who had managed to deal with the water that flooded the Money Pit. That would leave the big treasure undisturbed. Dad and Bobby now concluded that a walk-in tunnel spiraled down from the Money Pit to a more important treasure ("priceless stuff worth far more than metal value," as Dad wrote). Among the papers left by them is a sketch of how they envisioned this spiral tunnel (see Figure 8).

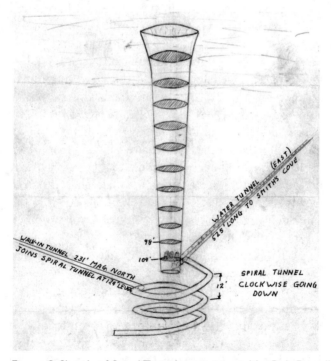

Figure 8: Sketch of Spiral Tunnel as envisioned by Bob Restall. Based on measurements obtained through drilling.

On September 17, Dad wrote to Fred referring to a telephone conversation that they had just finished about power vice parts and tachometer and tachometer cable. But now the pump shaft had broken again, this time very low down. They were in the process of pulling the whole pump out and repairing the bearing. Now Dad needed mechanical tubing urgently as well as the tachometer, cable, and power vice parts. He concluded by saying, "Sorry that our troubles seem to run in bunches. Seems incredible that we have got up three of the pieces from below the treasure and three from above it. That's almost as close as finding the chest itself."

A letter written on September 20 elaborated on the reference to the three pieces.

> September 20th, 1963
> Dear Fred:
>
> We have got all the pump up except the impellers, etc. The casing and inner casing is very bad in places. We were only using 140 ft. of the 200 ft. down the pit. So we can at least weed out the poorest 60 ft. of each. [He went on to provide detail regarding how he would improve the inner casing of the pump.]
>
> I don't like to think of the machine work bill, but have to get right on with it and then find the money somewhere. The Bearings are in the machine shop. As soon as the tubing arrives we will have it cut into 7-7/8" pieces and welded on the shafts. Then when the pieces are shimmed to fit the bearings we will have that rot set and get on with the impeller piece that has a long shaft and five bearings. I sure hope the main shaft is usable again. We have decided to put the pump down to the same depth. If we put it lower we may have too much sand in the sump.
>
> What is more important is this. We now know that we have the pieces from the platform that was under and over the decoy treasure. So with a couple of fellows to help us we are going to get after the decoy treasure as soon as possible. We now know that we can follow the spiral tunnel to the big treasure later. Since we now know that to get this we must work down to 150 ft., we don't need to drill. By getting after the decoy first it

would give us working capital and we could cement the drain for good.

With all our work to date and the new knowledge re the decoy treasure and the spiral ramps, we should get the money we need with ease … The *Star Weekly* are sending a photographer down with the writer who did the Imperial Oil News story. They come Sunday. This may help us but don't know yet what date it will appear. … [Here the letter included several paragraphs of details of parts received and new needs.]

P.S. Thanks for the fast action and sorry to keep bothering you but it just can't be helped.

On September 26 Dad thanked Fred for the tubing. His six-page letter contained mostly details on the work to get the pump going again, a plan of action for the next work, and some discussion of bill payments and finances.

His letter of October 7 continued discussing work on the pump. It concluded with, "We are just about biting all of our finger nails to get back after the treasure, now that we have so much of what points to the exact position and level."

Dad's letter of November 12 was the last of the year. It announced yet more bad luck: Hurricane Ginny had struck.

November 12th, 1963
Dear Fred:

Thought you would like to know that we are still alive. Actually we weathered the Hurricane down here OK. We put plywood over the two most exposed plastic windows, so they were OK. Two others went, but this a small matter. Several trees went down (big ones) and our wharf was torn to pieces. It's only a stone pile now. 64 ft. on the outside end stayed together, but landed a hundred yards down the beach. We are going to manage without a wharf until March or April.

I have worked out a system to bolt a chain around the oil drums and throw them overboard. We will have 165 ft. of steel cable hooked to the 3 Ton truck and pull them up the sandy beach by the rose bush. Steven's boat will have to use two anchors and 165 ft. of handline to pull the chain and cable back each time. I expect it to work O.K. Then we will roll the drums up planks on to the truck platform and take the 14 up the hill as we now do.

Several weeks ago the lower (underwater) end of the Johnson [boat motor] went again. It cost us $187.00 fifteen months ago. It's just as bad again. It's been in the shop since and they have everything except the two aluminum cases. We had an awful time for two weeks with only the skiff. Then we got a rental motor (a little 10 hp). Our boat needs about 35 hp but it sure was great to be under power again.

We got all the pump together, ran it many times up to 1 1/2 hrs. so as to give it every chance. We started it up steady and after 3 1/2 hrs. the bottom end seized up. You should have seen the bridge sway when it seized. The diesel poured more fuel in and it really struggled while I was running the 100 feet to the main switch to cut it off. We put a 24" wrench on the impeller shaft and it twisted up like a spring. It's 1-1/4" steel rod but 150 ft. of it sure is springy. We had to take it all apart again and the motor torsion, when it seized, sure screwed the rods together. It took all we could do with 6 ft. of pipe on the wrenches to break the joints. We got it up in 15 1/2 hrs. just the two of us and it rained steadily all the time. There are five bronze bearings in the bottom. Two were completely seized up and other three were free with absolutely no clearance. This time we are giving it ten thousandths per inch of shaft diameter. This is the way they do the boat propeller shafts. So the four on 1-1/2" shaft will have 15 thou and the 2" bearing 20 thou. It took us a day to get the bottom apart (on account of it being seized up so bad).

We are hoping to have it all back in by the weekend. The year's coming to an end and we want to come up with some treasure before the 31st. We are still pretty short of cash. The fellow in Texas put in a thousand (his second). We would squeeze by nicer if the bank didn't want me to pay their $500 back on the 25th. I am going to try to get them to settle for half this month and half next.

All our Garlock gaskets are done. They compress too much. The narrow 3/16" steel flanges concentrate entirely too much pressure. I am going to try lead rings this time. That is what Prof. Hamilton used for years.

When we get our outboard back it will be in good shape and should do over a year without trouble. We hit a reef and cracked the case. This wasn't where you could see it. The grease got out and the salt got in. This ruined all the bearings, gears, shafts, seals and etc. About the only thing any good was the rod that shifts the gears. No damage was done to the engine, but we are having a new head put on as one of the spark plug threads has been very bad for two years.

Well Fred I will close now, hope everything is going well up your way. Sure hope that we will have some real good news soon. I will cut strips from 8 lb sheet lead which is easy to get down here. Give my regards to everyone and hope your wife is OK. [Fred Sparham's wife had suffered a severe stroke a few months after her 1961 trip to Oak Island.]

Sincerely yours

Bob

P.S. <u>Note</u>: don't have to write for anything this time. This doesn't happen very often.

Gulls
by Mildred Restall

Storm warning, just a light breeze nearly all morning; suddenly it starts to blow hard. The gulls come screaming in from the Atlantic, and with wings outstretched, some pause over the cove on the southwest of the Island. Wings motionless they hover and soar, dipping and diving, swooping low to soar to fantastic heights, then side-slipping in a wide circle, just riding the wind.

Finally, as the wind grows more intense, they sail over the tree tops and away to the mainland for shelter. The hurricane is upon us.

Hurricane Ginny
by Mildred Restall

> In-rolling tide. The heavy seas played around the dock
> then lifted all 130 feet of it off the rocks and rocked it
> around as if undecided what to do with it, finally tired,
> dumped it 100 ft. further down the beach … sixty feet
> of it in one piece, and the rest smashed and scattered all
> down the shoreline of the island.

The process of locating parts, repairing the pump, and laboriously reassembling it began one more time. By November 27 the pump was running and the men were able to go down the Pit and assess conditions. Bobby recorded the events in his journal.

November 28, 1963

> Pit was dry by 12:00 noon. Went down pit and pulled
> rods and casing and looked around. Lots of muck.
> Cooling pump to diesel lost prime two times. Shut down
> to get boards, etc. Readied and enclosed diesel, etc. This
> evening noticed pit by cherry tree caved in and left 20 ft.
> dia. 15 ft. deep hole. Likely occurred yesterday when we
> felt shock like dynamite at about 2:00 p.m. Also accounts
> for dirty discharge water and muddy shaft.

To the end of the year the diesel was plagued by electrical problems, underground work progressed at a crawl, and the campaign to secure more time continued. Dad went to see Chappell in Sydney and found him determined to bring in Mr. Z unless treasure were found immediately. Small amounts of money continued to come in from investors. Graeser sent a letter telling of the expansion of his marina and regretting that he could not come in person to work. He enclosed $300 to, "hopefully, hire men to work in the Money Pit."

1964: Persevering

CHAPTER 11

Down the Pit
by Mildred Restall

Winter was on us and it was too cold to leave the diesel shut off for five hours and expect it to start up without a lot of trouble, so we had to enclose it.

The men built a room around the diesel and put a small space-heater inside to be lit when the diesel was shut off. As the diesel was set up on the sloping ground by the pit, one side of the enclosure was higher than the other. This put the door sills about ten inches up from the ground. If you were in a hurry to get in or out you hopped back and forth. Up to open the door, back to let the door swing open, then up again to enter.

It was the middle of December [1963] by the time we were ready to roll once again. Bob arranged to pick the men up at Grandall's Point on the mainland, and to bring them over to the job in our boat. They were to start December 19th.

We woke up that morning to find a howling blizzard raging outside. Swirling snow so thick we could hardly see across the clearing. Occasionally we caught a glimpse of a dark sea, tossing and raging back and forth with the same steady roar that we have heard so often. We couldn't even think of trying to put the boat in the water. So, to get something accomplished on this inclement day, Bob decided that he and Bobby would bring the barrels of fuel oil up from Smith's Cove where they had been left by the boatman.

They had been gone only about an hour when they both came back, chilled to the bone and blue with cold. The truck had broken down halfway up the hill. I made coffee, and while they sat sipping it, we listened to the news. The weather report told us that the temperature was 7 degrees above zero with winds of 50 mph and gusts to 70.

This was one of the worst blizzards to hit the area in years. The snow blew in the crack at the door and froze solid. If you were in, you couldn't get out, and if you were out, you couldn't get in. The ice kept on building up and soon the door started to curve. We ended up with a permanent warp that let the cold air seep in, until we put in extra hooks to hold the door in tighter … weeks later, of course.

It was several days before the weather eased up enough for the boat to be put in the water. Then began the task of getting the workmen over to the Island.

What a job. Every morning my husband and son went to the mainland to get the men, and every morning the men weren't there. The first day, Bob and Bobby left at about 7:30 and the last I saw was the two of them in the boat disappearing into the mist. It was very foggy. They weren't back by 10 o'clock and I began to worry. Finally they got back; it was just before noon and just before I had a case of hysterics.

After reaching the mainland and finding none of the men waiting, they had walked up to the highway to where we keep our car and where the men were to meet every morning. One fellow was sitting in his car waiting for the others. They all piled into our car and went to round up the rest of the crew.

One fellow was home sipping tea, waiting for his

friend to pick him up. They had to drag the other one out of bed. But then his car wouldn't start, so he decided to stay home and work on his car.

The next day, the other fellow's car wouldn't start. It stayed cold day after day, sometimes barely getting above zero, and seldom as high as ten degrees above. Every day either Bob or Bobby had to drive in for one of the men. Sometimes our car wouldn't start either.

Actually, the men thought we were out of our minds wanting to work in such bad weather. And with typical Nova Scotian philosophy, they didn't worry. In this kind of weather the best thing is to sit in front of the fire and wait for things to warm up a bit.

They didn't put themselves out at all, and seemed quite content to let my family do all the running around. We could never get more than two men in to work. It was like trying to round up a bunch of kids who didn't want to go to school.

For us, it was rush, rush, rush. Get up before seven, gobble breakfast, chase all over for the crew, bring them over, work overtime to make up the hours lost in the morning. Everything was on the double and without realizing it I found myself running everywhere. Running to the boys' cabin, make beds, tidy up. Running down the hill to check how far the ice had advanced. Running to set the table, to get water … man comes to the door, "Missus, yourhusbandwantsthefiftyfoottape." For a minute I thought he was speaking in a foreign language. Bob and Bobby were on the run too, take the men home, eat a quick supper, check the diesel, start it for the night, all get washed … and so to bed. It was always way past midnight before we got to bed, and after more than a week of this we were all dead beat. Then we heard on the radio that a storm was forecast for the next day. Thinking he wouldn't be able to go for the men, Bob left the pump off that night.

We were still asleep the next morning at 9 o'clock when a pounding came on the door. It was Bobby to tell us that the men were here. They had walked across the ice bridge between the mainland and the island.

From then on they got to work themselves, and they never missed a day regardless of the weather. Now there was no holding them back, though the weather was dreadful. It was the stormiest winter we ever put in and one of the worst on record.

While the others were working down the pit, it was Bobby's job to do the running around. Check this, check that. Keep an eye on the diesel. Take the empty barrels to Chester by boat. Order supplies, bring back supplies. And if anything was needed down the pit, he loaded it on the hoist and sent it down. Signals were arranged so that he knew what was wanted.

It was New Year's Day; Bobby and Ricky had just got back from Chester and before they had time to haul the boat in, the horn sounded for Bobby to get to the pit head. He hurried up the hill, leaving Ricky hanging on to the painter. But there was a little breeze and before Rick could do anything, the boat swung around and beached itself. The spring tides fall fast, and in a couple of minutes the boat was above the water line. Bobby came down in a few minutes and tried to move the boat, but it was stuck on a rock with a hole punched in its bottom. Fine way to begin the New Year.

Soon the boat was patched up and things went along fine for awhile. Now that the ice was good and solid at the end of the island, the men could get to work without any trouble. But getting oil and supplies from Chester was another matter. Everything depended upon the weather. It was the deciding factor in getting the barrels to Chester to be filled with oil, and for the boatman being able to bring them back to the island.

It wasn't possible to carry full barrels in our small boat, so Bob arranged for a friend who had a 30 foot fishing boat to transport all oil and gas from Chester to the Island. In order to carry as many barrels as possible, Gerald, our boatman, had put a deck on his boat and 12 to 14 barrels were loaded on top.

When we got to the island, a line was thrown to our shore and the barrels were tied on, then thrown overboard to be pulled in by our men. This was the only way we could get the fuel landed now that we no longer had a dock. The unloading was done in a matter of minutes. Several times the weather delayed delivery, and we needed a boat load at least every six days. We kept 500 gallons in reserve just in case, and there were times when we dipped well into this reserve because of bad weather preventing delivery.

By now we had plenty of snow around from many snowstorms. Before coming here, snow was just snow to me. But now I was noticing things more. I saw the kind of snow that covers everything up in no time. Big fat flakes that settled on everything, hiding the rough, jagged shapes, leaving soft contours, just like a huge white blanket. Snow that glistened and slithered about, resembling something like mica. Another kind that looked for all the world as if detergent were spilled all over the place. And now, it was superfine, the consistency of cornstarch. When it was walked upon, it didn't crunch or shush, it squeaked.

The men had been working down the pit for about ten days when we had our first spot of real trouble. It was after lunch and everyone was getting into rubber suits ready to go below. Bob made the rounds as usual, checking the diesel and everything, including the motor room where the big generator was connected to the pump. As he opened the door, a cloud of smoke poured out and a grinding racket could be heard all over the clearing. A bearing had seized up. That meant the pump had to be stopped and taken apart. Unfortunately, all the tools were down the pit, and on top of that, the tunnel they were working on had to be boarded up. It was a new tunnel, and was across the pit from the hoist. To board up the end of the tunnel would take quite some time, but it had to be done, otherwise the whole end would collapse as soon as the pit filled up and the water started to wash soil in.

None of the men fancied going down without the pump operating, and water pouring in at 450 gallons a minute. But they went. The trouble was lights. If the diesel wasn't running there wouldn't be any lights so it was up to Bobby to keep it going as long as possible without letting it overheat.

The cooling system for the diesel depended upon the water from the pit being pumped around the cooler. No pump, no water. Without the cold inflow, the diesel got warmer and warmer. Bobby had cut down the revs as much as he dared but still it was getting too warm. He started to shovel snow into the cooling barrel. Then he called for his brother to help. They were barely holding their own, for Bobby had to keep running into the engine room to check the gauges. They used all the snow nearby and were having to go farther afield. Next, I was outside, shoveling like mad, heaping the snow inside the fence where it was in easy reach of the boys.

Finally, the long-awaited signal came. Up came the hoist, up came the men ... looking very pleased with themselves. It had taken forty minutes to block the end of the tunnel and load the tools. By that time the water was washing over the cat-walk they were standing on.

While repairs were being made to the pump, the men cleaned drilling rods, sharpened tools, cut timber, and made logs ready to be used down below. For me, this was something of a relief from the hustle and bustle, and I could give more thought to my household duties and teaching Ricky.

But the hiatus didn't last long. One day Bobby came rushing into the cabin, one hand tightly gripped by the other. Blood oozed from between his fingers and dripped onto the floor.

"Oh," he moaned, "I've cut my hand to the bone."

"What happened?" I asked, startled.

"I was sharpening the chisel on the emery wheel when it slipped and my hand banged against the wheel."

He sat down, white and shaking, while I got water, antiseptic, bandages, and anything else I might need. I wiped the dirt off from around the wound and took a look. It wasn't bleeding so much now. There was quite a hole all right. And it would take a couple of weeks to fill in. But a little bandage took care of it. Looking rather surprised and a little self-conscious, Bobby went back to work, while I made myself a cup of coffee to steady my nerves.

The following day one of the men cut his hand and had to have it attended to, nothing serious though. Then less than an hour later Bobby came staggering into the cabin with both hands pressed to his head. "Quick!" he groaned, "I've split my head to the skull. I'll have to go to the doctor and get some stitches put in." My stomach flipped. Trying to appear calm and composed as I gathered my first-aid equipment, I asked him what had happened. He told me that he had been chopping the bark off some logs with an axe, when he had swung his arm back too hard and conked himself on the bean with the axe.

I managed to pry his hands loose to take a good look. I had to look really hard. There was a cut on his forehead, maybe half an inch long, from which a drop of blood was struggling hard to surface. I cleansed his wound, slapped a band-aid on it, and sent him back into battle.

By this time I was feeling more jittery about work above ground than below, and was glad when the men started to work down the pit again.

Several times during this busy period visitors came to the site. They never said anything, just looked around very carefully, then left. It is unusual to have visitors at mid-winter, and I wondered what made them walk all that distance just to stand outside a barbed-wire fence. We found out later that a couple of our men, real comedians, spent much of their weekends at the local pub and, of course, kept their friends enthralled with stories of the job ... even to throwing out strong hints that we had located the treasure.

We were getting low on fuel once again, hadn't had a load for over a week and were now on our reserve. There was enough oil to run the diesel until 7:00 or 8:00 that night. So we thought.

About 4:30 Bobby lit the lanterns ready for when the men would be finished and the diesel shut off. He brought one to me, and just as he got to the diesel room with the other lamp, the motor slowed down, then stopped altogether.

The sudden silence was startling. I grabbed my lantern and ran out to the diesel room where I found Bobby hopping in one door, out again, into the other, back and forth like a jack-in-the-box.

"What are you doing?" I asked.

"Trying to get the damn thing going again," he said as he hopped back over the doorsill.

"How can you? Aren't you out of fuel?" I asked, hopping after him.

"There's a few inches in the other tank." he said, hopping outside. I hopped after him.

"That's no good. By the time you prime it and everything, it will take fifteen minutes to get it going again. What about lights?"

"I know," he screamed, hopping back into the diesel room. "What the hell do you think I am trying to start it for?"

"Stop hopping about," I hollered, "and do some thinking. Have they any lights at all?"

"They have safety lamps … I think," he said, hurrying over to the pit.

I knelt beside him as he pulled back the trap door. We both looked down. I was shocked. I had never seen such blackness before. It was like looking into nothing. We couldn't see a thing, not even a pinpoint of light. Except for the steady sound of running water, and now and then the loud plops as seepage from high up fell 100 feet to the water below, there was absolute silence.

Thoughts of my husband and crew drowning like rats in that black hole had my hair standing on end. Just then a voice far below came rolling and echoing up the shaft and burst out loud and clear, "Lights! … Lights!"

"You've got to get a light down there," I told Bob. "They can't even find the ladders."

"I can't carry a lantern down there. You need both hands free to hang on. Everything is wet and slippery." Even as he was talking, Bobby reached out, grabbed my lantern and his own in one hand, swung himself over the trap door, and started down. All the while protesting, "It can't be done I tell you, it can't be done."

The Money Pit
(foreground) in
October 1959.

Bobby reaching
layers of stone
and vegetation.
Oak leaves and
acorns found.

Dump system for earth and stones removed from beach holes. Ridge of stones in water is the cofferdam.

The car arrives on Oak Island.

On left, tool shed that became their first home. On right, A-frame under construction to keep weight of pump off deteriorating Money Pit.

Discharge from Money Pit pump: 450 gallons of sea water per minute drawn into the Money Pit from Smith's Cove.

Mel Chappell (right), owner of Oak Island, visits the island with a *National Geographic* photographer, 1960.

CBC television crew with Lloyd McInnis preparing to film for the "Gazette" in spring 1961.

Bob and Mildred in front of the Money Pit A-frame. Mildred is holding the 1704 stone found three feet under the beach at Smith's Cove.

International Harvester photograph. Nov–Dec Issue, 1961, International Truck News. Courtesy International Truck and Engine Corporation.

The Vertical Shaft is discovered. Spade and pick stand over hole with stone dome. Hand-drilled stone discovered by Hedden is in foreground.

Fred Sparham,
Bobby Restall,
and Doug
Helland drill
into the Vertical
Shaft.

Storms and high tides wash away progress, time and again.

Tourists "walking the plank" to Bill Sawler's boat. The wharf was repeatedly destroyed by storms, rebuilt, and destroyed again.

Bobby Restall running gasoline generator for drilling-down the Money Pit, December 1962.

Air bubbles cause ice on Chappell's pond to melt when Money Pit is pumped, proving an underground connection.

New diesel generator in housing arrives at the Money Pit.

New 250-gallon fuel tank and drums of fuel are delivered to the island.

Money Pit pump breaks down.

Photo by John Max.

The "Year of Troubles" takes its toll.

Photo by John Max.

Winter at the
Money Pit.

Laundry day.

Karl Graeser and Bob Restall tour the Halifax Tunnel.

Crew members remove earth and stones from the entrance of the Halifax Tunnel where it joins the Hedden Pit.

Jim Kaizer emerges from working down the Money Pit.

Hewn timbers found underground behind Professor Hamilton's tunnel.

Trench at Smith's Cove where broken china was found.

China pieces glued together. They were likely buried by those who created the Money Pit and the sea water inlet system.

Carney, Rick, and Mildred exploring.

Bob Restall Sr. and Bob Restall Jr.

Photo by John Max.

Carney at the death pit.

Courtesy Weekend Magazine, Nov. 6, 1965. Frank Prazak, photographer.

I don't know how he did it, but he got down all right. There were shouts of relief when the men saw the lights coming down. With a flashlight, I shone a light onto the hoist from where I was at the top of the pit. I could hear some plain and fancy language as they all busied themselves loading the equipment on to the hoist, but I knew that everything was all right.

The men came up, all smiles. There had been some anxious moments there for awhile. They had safety lights all right, but as quitting time drew near some "got-a-date-tonight" chap started loading things not being used onto the hoist. The 12 volt battery that operated the two tractor beam emergency lights was the first thing to be loaded. For all the good they were, they might as well have been in Timbuctoo. But by now, it was all a great adventure. "Never a dull moment," they said, and hurried off for the mainland. Probably, to tell their pals in the pub all about their latest thrilling experience.

It was getting to the end of January and we were lucky to keep operating, for the weather was getting worse. Coming from Chester with a load of fuel one day, our boatman lost the whole load overboard.

It was fairly calm when Gerald and his mate set out to deliver oil to the island. As they neared Frog Island, a huge swell keeled the boat way over, then back, throwing fourteen barrels overboard. Luckily the barrels weren't tied down or the boat would have gone over too. Gerald hurried to the Island for help. Bobby, with one of the men, took off in our boat to help round up the barrels, which, by his time, were spread out all over the surface of the water. Some on their way out to sea.

It was quite a job scooting among the islands, rounding up the barrels. They managed to herd them all into a cove in the lee side of Frog Island, intending to haul them onto Gerald's boat.

By now the waves were big enough to send the spray flying, and in no time everyone was soaked and chilled through. Trying to tie a rope around a barrel with icy-stiff fingers was practically impossible. Sometimes the waves pushed the barrel under, and it would bob up too far away to grab. Or the thing would bob up right under the little boat, nearly upsetting it.

Finally they gave up trying to get the barrels aboard, and looped a long rope from one barrel to the next, then towed them to the Island, all strung out like sausages. It was nearly dark by the time they were through, and the cutter scurried off to Chester as the seas began to heave and the wind howled through the trees.

This was quite a storm. It broke up the ice bridge between the mainland and Island. Now the crew had to row over. They didn't care for this and were glad when it started to freeze over again. Even so, they couldn't wait for the ice to get good and solid, but tried to walk on it too soon. One man broke through and had to go home to change. Of course, the others went with him and that made them all late. In fact, they were hardly ever on time, now that they were rowing over.

What with the difficulty of getting supplies, and the men having trouble getting to work, Bob decided to shut down for the winter.

I, for one, was glad of the rest from the nagging worry of perhaps something going wrong. For the next few days we all relaxed and caught up on our sleep.

During February the storms continued. We had snowstorm after snowstorm. Now my husband and son had to walk the length of the Island, across the ice bridge, and on the mainland, to the highway to get supplies. Sometimes the drifts were too deep to get through, and a couple of times we ran very low on food. But somehow we made it through.

Early in January Dad learned that Mr. Z, the millionaire who wished to replace him, was insolvent. Chappell was told about this but still would not commit himself to extending Dad's contract. Instead, he began to talk of selling the island.

When Tobias had agreed to pay fuel costs in the summer of 1963, it was believed that the treasure would be found in weeks, or at worst in months. But by January of 1964 no end was in sight. In February 1964, Dad received a letter from Tobias indicating that as he had far surpassed the amount of money he had intended to invest in this treasure hunt, he would not be responsible for future fuel bills.

It was a loss, but not a surprise. Tobias had generously supported the recovery operation for a long and critical time. No one expected his deep pockets to be bottomless. The relationship between Tobias and Dad remained cordial, and Tobias retained his keen interest in the work on Oak Island.

In 1897, members of the reorganized Oak Island Treasure Company had been working from the Money Pit when at 153 feet they drilled through 7 inches of soft stone, 5 inches of oak, and then some sort of "soft metal." Of course they believed the soft metal to be gold in oak caskets. Attempts to retrace the path of the drill were unsuccessful because the drill was thin and had been used without a casing. On its journey to the "gold," it could have been deflected by a stone and wandered in any direction to any location that its length allowed. The exact location of where the drill began its journey and its length are recorded in the Oak Island archives.

Interestingly, it was William Chappell who had been operating that drill. Later he would say that he had found traces of gold on his drill bit, but had wiped the bit clean and said nothing. No doubt his little secret motivated him, and later his son, to mount his own search on Oak Island.

In 1963, Dad and Bobby had set up a drill in the Money Pit where the 1897 drill had purportedly entered the ground. Then they systematically drilled holes to cover every possible location for the gold that fell within the arc that could have been made by Chappell's drill, no matter what the point of deflection. Their careful calculations and painstaking work yielded nothing tangible. That work, as well as the rest of the 1963 work down the Money Pit, was probably on Dad's mind as he wrote to Fred in March 1964. The envelope contained a letter with one sketch showing the beach and illustrating the connection between the two drilled white granite rocks and the 1704 stone (see Figure 9) and, stapled together separately, another sketch with a long notation written under it (see Figure 10).

March 16, 1964
Dear Fred:
Some of this information will not be new but from January 1st we worked underground except two days lost on account of two storms and also a short break-

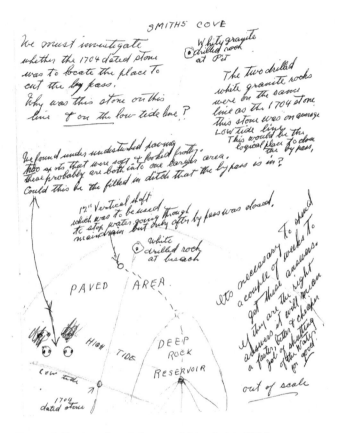

SMITHS COVE

We must investigate whether the 1704 dated stone was to locate the place to cut the by pass.

Why was this stone on this line & on the low tide line?

White granite drilled rock at Pit

The two drilled white granite rocks were on the same line as the 1704 stone. This stone was on average Low tide line. This would be the logical place to close the by pass.

We found under undisturbed paving two spots that were soft & looked frothy. These probably are both into one larger area. Could this be the filled in ditch that the by pass is in?

12" vertical shaft which was to be used to stop water going through & maintain but only after by pass was closed.

white drilled rock at beach

PAVED AREA.

HIGH TIDE

DEEP ROCK RESERVOIR

Low tide

1704 dated stone

Its necessary to spend a couple of weeks to get these answers. If they are the right answers it will mean a faster, better & cheaper pot of shutting off the water for good.

out of scale

Figure 9: Enclosed with letter of March 16, 1964.

down when the bearings on the countershaft went. Then on Feb. 28th one of the fellows fell through the ice on the way to work and by the time they got him home and dry clothes it was past noon. We got the half day.

When we started the pump that night the countershaft got so noisy in an hour and the bearings heated up so we shut down knowing it wouldn't last till morning. When the fellows came over we spent the day putting everything ship shape. Good thing we did because for the next two weeks the ice was thick enough to prevent using the boats and too thin for walking on, and tight-packed floes held in by the wind prevented any crossing.

Since then we have had nothing but snow storms and blizzards. The sun is getting very warm and it won't

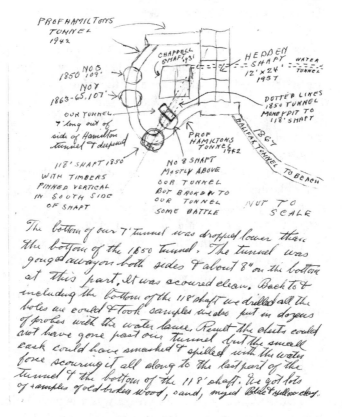

Figure 10: First page of three-page note accompanying letter of March 16, 1964.

be long now. We have had a real job digging out of storms one after another and getting supplies.

We investigated the 1850 tunnel and the 118 ft. shaft very thoroughly. Enclosed sketch, etc. With the shape the Chappell shaft is in we can go no further with this now without jeopardizing the works.

I have been in touch with Mr. Chappell and was up to see him in Halifax … Apparently he won't think of doing business with [Mr. Z] except by selling him the island. He has agreed to give me first chance to find someone to buy the island if [Mr. Z] or anyone else is serious about buying. Why he would even consider selling now is quite beyond me. People 80 years old do some queer things. I am to phone him again on the

25th of March and hope we get our contract without further messing.

Our finances are very short now. A man who visited two years ago has put in $500.00. This was a godsend but by the time I squared some of the most pressing things and sent Red D Arc $100.00 [against purchase of the diesel generator] there was some hole in it. We sure hope that we get the thing set and get seriously down to the job again.

We expected to be able to look into some things that look important re the bypass [drain], but 4' of ice on that shore prevented it. It has now melted down to 1 ft. so we will soon be able to investigate this.

Hope things are picking up for you now. We expect that things will be soon straightened away down here. We have got to do it this year and by October. That will make five years and besides we will then be without further percent to sell. So you can see it has to be done this summer. Best regards to all.

Yours truly,

Bob

By now Dad and Bobby were sure there was a bypass drain. That was why, when the main drain was plugged with clay in 1868, water still found its way into the Money Pit. The following note was attached with staples to the second sketch:

The bottom of our 7 ft. tunnel was dropped lower than the bottom of the 1850 tunnel. The tunnel was gouged away on both sides and about 8" on the bottom at this part. It was scoured clean. Back to and including the bottom of the 118' shaft we drilled all the holes we could and took samples. We also put in dozens of probes with the water lance. Result the chests could not have gone past our tunnel but the small cask could have smashed and spilled with the water force scouring it all along to the last part of the tunnel and the bottom of the 118 ft. shaft. We got lots of samples of old broken wood, sand, mixed blue and yellow clay but no loot. Of course the biggest trouble

was that we went as far as we dared without undermining the Hamilton Tunnel.

In the part from our tunnel to the Chappell Shaft
we drilled and got samples every where we could and
used the lance in dozens of other places. There are no
chests along the 1850 tunnel.

Where are they?

Only one place remains, as they were not found in
the Chappell Shaft. They must have been in the first 4 ft.
or so of the 1850 tunnel immediately south of Chappell's
shaft. Now, if they were there in 1931, the underground
pressure would have pushed them North (toward the
shaft) that being the only way the pressure was relieved.
Now, if they pressed against Chappell's shaft they would
move down with the clay and stones that moved down
over the last 32 years. Prof. Hamilton put a few feet of
fill between the two shafts each spring (on the surface)
to replace the stuff that got away through the cracks in
the cribbing.

This does not mean that this is lost. No one can tell
whether these chests sunk 2 ft. or 50 ft. The important
point is that to tear into this would bring the whole thing
down unless a very expensive job were done. The money
this would cost could very well bring up the big treasure.
So it would be folly to try further for the decoy treasure
at this time. We must set this aside until we have the big
one and we must work at the big one with all we've got.

With no contract, and with virtually no money coming in, the men
returned to digging at the beach in search of the elusive sea water tunnel, rebuilding the wharf, and maintaining the pumps and vehicles.
Fortunately, on April 30, one investor brought $1,000 to the search and
another invested $300.

On May 7, Dad wrote that he had arrived safely back from Ontario.
This was already the second trip of 1964, but no money had been raised.
Dad informed Fred that he now had the contract for 1964. He men-
tioned possible investors and asked Fred for their addresses.

In the following letter to Fred, Dad described an unexpected find
and announced that at last they'd gotten to the bottom of the problems
that had plagued them with the generator for almost a year.

July 25th, 1964

Dear Fred:

Our weather has been almost all fog and drizzle this season with only a few sunny days, these had 100% humidity and after them the fog and drizzle were welcome.

We sure dug the beach up plenty, even finding a couple of plank dams underground and a wooden trough through one of them that was made of 2" x 14" on top and bottom and had 2" x 4" for the side. This left a 4" x 10" waterway. This had a shut off gate of wood. It was surprising to find this. This strenuous workout didn't do us any good. Neither did the 27 ft. trench we put in further south and further back than we had located the paving before. Here the vegetation on the south end was 5 ft. deep and had a lot of broken dishes among it (very old). All the pieces were above the stones of the paving which was on the hard clay at 6 ft. depth.

Enclosed is a photo of two pitchers and a plate that I was able to glue together. There were also a dozen pieces of an old cup that we could not glue together. The plate has raised pattern around the rim. Roses and Thistles together and Shamrock separate.

These are repeated many times all around the rim. So this is old British. There was a man and his wife visiting who claimed to know about old dishes. They claim the plate was old, probably 50 years old when it was buried and that the cup and one pitcher is 17th century English.

It's very interesting, but does not get us the loot. As far as I am concerned, the people who put the treasure here in 1704 threw their broken dishes in on the paving to get them out of sight, while the paving job was underway.

We altered the Apt Sump pump so as to be able to dig down to the main drain. [The letter goes on to discuss difficulties they encountered and technicalities of the next planned beach shaft.]

The lumber is to be delivered Monday morning. We are most anxious to know for sure whether this drain is active or not. Whether the 1704 dated stone is to locate the by pass or whether it is just a red herring. We hope to complete this before the month runs out and will try real hard to get a picture of it.

Time sure runs away and money is short. I got another hundred and a half from the fellow in Long Island which will keep us eating.

I finally got the real expert down re our generator outfit.

Here is the situation.

There was one wire too few from the exciter to the panel. The 550 volts for a year did in one of the four resistances (rheostats). The high voltage into the panel has done in the Cycles gauge and resistors, transformers, etc. that allow it to operate. The Excitor motor was reverse-polarized, causing the current to aggravate instead of smoothing out so the voltage drop when load was applied took far too long to recover and this may be why the [manufacturer's engineer] had turned it up to 550 volts, otherwise the big switch would kick out. It's running OK now. We can plug an old electric clock (which we have here) into the circuit (110 v) and check cycles that way.

We haven't paid anything yet. If you can get anything going, finance-wise, it will sure help. I will let you know how we make out re the main drain. There have been almost no visitors. Was hoping perhaps to find some help that way. We are all keeping well. Give my regards to all.

Yours sincerely,
Bob

Work resumed on the beach. The diesel generator control panel was, at last, correctly fixed, but without adequate financing working down the Money Pit was out of the question. They confined their efforts to digging or drilling on the beach and maintaining equipment.

Graeser continued his lively participation in the operation, visiting the island, contributing money, and working out his own theories regarding the treasure.

Suddenly Chappell announced that he was definitely selling the island. His October 5 letter to Dad stated that he wanted $100,000 for the island and his licence rights (which was considered to be an exorbitant price at the time) plus a yet-to-be-determined percentage of the treasure when it was raised. Shortly after this, Dad learned that Chappell's business was struggling financially.

In a November 2 letter, Chappell advised Dad that several groups were interested in purchasing the island. One was a Danish group; another was someone who had visited the island a month earlier. Chappell had by now decided he wanted $100,000 plus 10 percent of anything recovered. With the price finally set, Dad needed money to keep his recovery operation going and money to buy the island.

On his own initiative, Graeser placed an ad in the *New York Times* that generated a response from some very wealthy investors who wished to participate in the recovery operation. It fell to Dad to break the news to those would-be backers that the arrangement proposed in the ad was not feasible; it would change the Canadian tax situation so that the government could take the lion's share of any treasure, as opposed to the 5 percent it was entitled to now.

At least one of these *New York Times* sources expressed interest in buying the island. He was an agent responsible for presenting investment opportunities to moneyed clients in England. However, Chappell refused to provide the paperwork committing himself to sell, so those negotiations did not come to fruition.

At the beginning of October another investment of $500 was made in the recovery operation, and one for the same amount came through on December 30. A contract for investment by Karl Graeser was issued in December 1964, but that covered sums provided through 1963 and 1964, not an infusion of new cash. New money had all but dried up.

Early in December, Dad drove to Hamilton again in a desperate attempt to raise money. Mom, Bobby, and Rick faced Christmas on the island without him. One of Mom's fragments was written at this time:

Money
by Mildred Restall

Sometimes the financial situation was so bad I felt like digging a hole and hibernating until the famine was over.

1965: The Power of the Press

CHAPTER 12

W hen Dad travelled to Ontario at the end of 1964, he urgently needed money to keep the search afloat and to buy the island before someone else did. If an outsider were to buy, that would be the end of the Restall search for treasure.

But Ontario was still experiencing an economic downturn. Money was tight. As well, the season was wrong. People were preoccupied with Christmas festivities and not eager to turn their thoughts to treasure hunting.

Dad used our home in Oakville as his home base, but this was not a happy visit. I remember our conversation coming in fits and starts during the interminably slow drive to visit Doug at Princess Margaret Hospital, Toronto's cancer hospital. A year earlier, after months of mysterious illness, my husband had undergone an exploratory operation that revealed cancer of the bowel. The primitive chemotherapy of the time, although leaving him weak and nauseated, was ineffective. The cancer advanced. Now, a new diagnosis — cancer of the liver. He had less than a year to live. Doug was stoic, but already frail. I shuffled about in a zombie-like state, trying to comprehend what was happening to my life. Dad was deeply saddened by our plight. We didn't talk much. What was there to say?

It was well after Christmas before Dad could arrange his meetings with potential investors. In all, he raised only $500. A week of January was gone before he arrived back in Nova Scotia in his beat-up, barely road-worthy car. While he was in Ontario, Mom had written to him:

> December 29, 1964
> Dear Bob:
>   All hell has broken loose here. Someone sent an article from Hamilton about you trying to buy Oak Island. I am enclosing the clipping from the *Chronicle Herald* (front page yet), it was in Monday's issue. We heard it on the radio and it was on TV, so we hear. When Chappell was finally located for an interview he said that he hadn't heard from you lately about purchasing the island, and that he hadn't heard about you only being thirty feet from the treasure. Didn't you tell him last winter that you thought it was a matter of feet? I thought you wrote that in a letter to him.
>   Can you make an offer? Even if it's way below what he wants it will put you in the clear. This way it looks as if you are trying to push him out, when God knows, the man has been impossible to do business with. I wouldn't accept his offer of another year, you do need two. And I would want a change in the percentage. We need more percent to finance the job. As things stand, it isn't worthwhile to carry on. Providing you *can* get any financing. It looks pretty bad. Do you think you will have to stay in Ontario this winter and work for a few months?
>   We have had nearly twenty letters from all over the States about the *Reader's Digest* bit. If any more come I am going to pack up and leave. All in the same vein, wanting to tell you how to do the job in exchange for a percent.
>   It was a very lonely Christmas, I am glad it is over. Maybe you had better get a job for a while and try to save up enough money to get the stuff out of here in the spring. I am fed up with it all. It isn't worth fighting about, and it certainly isn't worth the sacrifices. How about it?

So long for now. Take care of yourself.
Love from the boys and myself.
Mildred
P.S. Chappell also said that our contract terminated Thursday, December 31st. If you can make an offer, do it in writing, no more phone calls. You have no proof he offered to extend your contract.

During the summer of 1964, a reporter from *Reader's Digest* had come to the island and interviewed my parents for an upcoming article. It appeared in the January 1965 issue of *Reader's Digest*, which reached some homes just before Christmas 1964. The history of Oak Island was accompanied by a sketch of the Money Pit with its oak planking every ten feet as it might have existed before any of the many treasure hunters wreaked their havoc. The article described the work of various treasure hunters and included a brief report on the Restall search.

During the years the family was on the island there had been countless newspaper and magazine articles about Oak Island and the Restall search. It is hard to imagine what it was about this one particular article that so galvanized readers throughout United States, Canada, Britain, Germany, France, Belgium, Netherlands, Portugal, Africa, and more, but excite them it did. Hundreds wrote. They offered solutions of every imaginable kind; some wanted to be paid for their services, others just wanted to be helpful. Here are some examples:

Hamburg, Germany
July 8, 1965
Dear Sir Restall!
From an article in *Reader's Digest* I learned about the various unsuccessful efforts to find access to the hiding place. I have been thinking about this problem for some time and may have found a simple and convincing solution which, according to the above mentioned article has not yet been tried.
Providing you are interested in my ideas I would suggest the following. The process I have in mind could be managed with a financial minimum. I have some of the equipment on hand and can make the other parts available — unless you prefer to purchase them yourself.

I would need to know some geographical details i.e. does the ground consists of rocks or sand, etc?

I would also need, of course, a detailed map or drawing of the island so that I can explain to you how my plan works.

I presume that you are legally authorized to handle the project, and will understand that, providing you use this plan, I would want a 30% interest in case I do the job.

If you should decide to do it alone, I would claim 10% of the finding.

If you are interested in discussing my view with respect to your project, please let me know.

Sincerely ...

More than one person sent telegrams, like this one:

MERRITT ISLAND FLORIDA.

NO OTHER WAY TO GET TO TREASURE WILL ACCEPT TEN PERCENT OF FINDING IF MY SYSTEM USED. CONTACT ME ...

From Pittsburgh, Pennsylvania:

Sir:

I have read of Oak Island's "Mysterious Money Pit". If you, and all parties concerned would like to see the solution, and bring up all that there is down there, Let me know, When after I view the area, and If the percentage is right. I will solve the problem.

Until I hear from you I remain ...

Not everyone expected to benefit from the treasure; many merely want to share their theories, and others wrote because they were intrigued by the story.

Doetinchem Holland
Feb. 25, '65
Mr. and Mrs. Restall

Perhaps you might think a letter from Holland, what will that be?

Well, a couple of days ago I read in *Reader's Digest* about you and of course about the mysterious hole in which you and so many others before you have been looking for the big treasure that has to be found in it.

I'm an eighteen-year-old scholar and I am very interested in archaeology and other things that have something to do with antiquity. This is not really archaeology, but I think it's very interesting and I should be very glad if you would tell me something more about the Island and the treasure.

I'm very curious to know who made the hole with all these wooden floors, but in the article I read that nobody knows who did it. Is that true? It must have been very ingenious men. I think I'd better stop now, for I have still some home work to do. I could have done it first but I thought this so interesting that I had to write first.

Mr. and Mrs. Restall, I wish you good luck and I hope to hear something from you soon.

March 26, 1965
Pacoima, California
Dear Mr. Restall,

You have very likely received numerous letters since the *Reader's Digest* article about your island, but I, in another *Reader's Digest*, read about a Paris sewer installation that had to be stopped because water seeped in faster than it could be pumped out. They used liquid nitrogen poured into pipes driven into nearby soil. The soil froze rock hard and stopped the seepage and the work was completed. This article is entitled "Nitrogen — the stuff that does nothing" somewhere between the November 1964 and March 1965 issues of *Reader's Digest* and is taken from *Science News Letter* of August 8, 1964.

I wish I had some money to invest I would sure offer it. That hole has intrigued my husband and I more than anything else we ever heard of.

If you ever locate the buried items be sure and have it published in a leading magazine so we can hear about it.

Every good wish to you and your family and may
your years of effort and concern pay off.
Sincerely …

Several other people suggested the freezing method too. They told
how it had been used successfully to retrieve potash in Saskatchewan
and had worked in keeping dynamite dry.

Several letters were written in languages other than English. One
from Vasa, Finland, required no translation; it contained a picture of a
mammoth digging bucket. Inside the bucket two men stood talking.
There is room for at least ten men side by side in the bucket, with another ten on their shoulders.

A number of the correspondents were engineers. They put considerable thought into their solutions and, clearly, much time into their
detailed drawings. Some sent resumés and offered to join the work if
their solutions were tried.

A man from Gardena, California, started by musing about unan-
swered questions: "Why, of some 300 islands, was Oak Island chosen?"
He then proffered an ingenious theory, accompanied by a detailed
sketch, suggesting the existence of a vast underground treasure chamber
with an entrance that could have been located anywhere on the surface
of the island. He concluded with, "Probably discovered by Capt.
Anderson. Another Pirate, Emanuel Wynne is the most likely one to
have engineered the hydraulic system."

The use of aqualungs to work down the Money Pit was suggested by
more than one person. Using air pressure to force the water back to the
sea was another suggestion.

A lady from New Hampshire sent a sketch to accompany her suggestion: "Dig down 200 ft. in a 100 ft. square around the treasure. Put
in a cement wall the whole 200 ft. down. Then clear everything in the
middle of the 100 sq. ft. Start on the outside and work around the
square and inward."

One gentleman from Kansas suggested that they simply walk in the
walk-in tunnel (which, if it exists, has never been found), stand directly
under the Money Pit, and pull the iron plate (which probably does not
exist) down towards them. A well-executed sketch shows the Money Pit
with a treasure chest resting on the iron plate; under this is written, "Pull
down and stand back."

Some mail was addressed to Mom.

Hegins, Pennsylvania, 17938
United States of America
Dear Mrs. Restall,

I was very interested in the article <u>Oak Island's</u> <u>Mysterious "Money Pit"</u>, appearing in the January 1965 *Reader's Digest*, pages 136 through 140; condensed from *The Rotarian*, written by David MacDonald.

I am sure that you have heard very many theories on many parts of the Money Pit. I am not going to add to the theories, I just barely finished the article, but I would like to advance some ideas that have occurred to me. Beginning with the date 1704 on the olive-colored stone, might it not be of interest to search through the records of History, for the name of a great engineer, who unaccountably disappeared, captured by a very intelligent, scheming, Pirate for a very special task? Later, he may have been killed, or, released. Then, a study should be made of this man's particular engineering genius for clues to solving the conduit's arrangements. I would notify Her Majesty's Government, explaining the case, asking for help in the research. It is quite possible that the knowledge involved in that undertaking would in the end prove even greatly more valuable than a great treasure. Tell your husband to take extremely accurate measurements of everything that can be measured accurately. It might give a Formula, which in turn would be The Clue! Get very scientific, with expert help. This could be your contribution to your husband's endeavor. And do pray. I will pray with you.

Please write to me and let me know just what you think of my idea.

Very truly yours,
[name withheld]

P.S. At one time I was an elementary teacher, later an art teacher, for a short time.

People of all ages were captivated by the Oak Island mystery:

Willowdale, Ontario
December 22, 1964
Dear Sir,

I am very interested in the treasure of Oak Island. Recently an article appeared in the *Reader's Digest* and this spurred me to writing this letter. Although I have no money to invest (I am 10 years old) I certainly would appreciate a letter, pamphlet or preferably a map showing the tunnels and layers of debris in this shaft. I have read books and from this have devised a mental picture of this island. Thank you.

Some correspondents expressed interest in investing in the venture:

Ellsworth, Maine
Dear Mr. Restall,

I read the account of the "Money Pit" in the January *Reader's Digest* and it re-aroused the curiosity awakened by previous articles and stories I have read on the same subject. Would you be so kind as to tell me what, if any, work is being done at the moment and what the possibilities of investment in the project are? I'm not yearning after buried treasure. I'm just plain curious about what is down there. I hope it is something a lot more interesting than gold! Thank you.

Several people offered to work on the island for free. One gentleman from Portugal wrote that he had experience and would like to join the operation but couldn't afford to bring his wife and eight children to Canada at this moment.

Many of the letters consisted of pages and pages of questions: "What is the distance between ..."; "What is the condition of ..."; "How long is it since..."; "What is the texture of ..."; and more. My parents were overwhelmed by this flood of mail. They gave it a mighty try, but there was no way they could deal with it all.

Bobby decided that if people wanted to work on their own theories of treasure recovery, at least they should have accurate measurements to work with. He had been working on a map, to scale, of the Money Pit end of the island. He now had the map reproduced (see Figure 2) and offered it for sale at $1.00, a few pennies of profit after mailing in a mailing tube, but at least something to keep the interest in Oak Island alive.

Around the time of his twenty-fourth birthday in April, Bobby also completed two essays. The longer of these comprises the next two chapters.

The History of the Hunt

CHAPTER 13

The History of the Hunt
by Robert K. Restall

Oak Island has been in the news for well over 150 years. There have been countless magazine articles and several books devoted to describing the treasure pit and its elusive treasure.

Most articles revolve around the more spectacular events from the island's history and tend to ignore less colourful, yet equally important, ones.

Many writers borrow from one another, condense, or expand the different events until the result is exciting, inspiring, but far from accurate. The full story is complicated to be sure, and one recorded fact often conflicts with another. But once the sequence of events is clearly understood, it is pretty obvious what has happened and why the treasure has not yet been recovered.

Our family has been working on Oak Island since 1959, and the unique situation of a family tackling the problems that have beaten many organized expeditions has brought us a lot of publicity.

With each new article that mentions our efforts to recover the treasure, we get letters from all over with ideas, plans, and suggestions. One astute reader wrote, "After reading a recent article about your operations, I have only one thought. Please tell me it isn't so. Tell me the treasure can't possibly be that easy to get!"

Don't worry my friend, it isn't!

Oak Island is forty-five miles southwest of Halifax, Nova Scotia, in Mahone Bay. Its name stems from the fact that of 365 islands in the bay it was the only one that had oak trees covering it in the late 1700s when it was named.

1795: McInnis, Smith, Vaughan

Daniel McInnis, John Smith, and Anthony Vaughan discovered a huge oak tree in a clearing while hunting on Oak Island in the summer of 1795. There was a sawed-off limb on this tree, and a tackle block hung from it. When trying to retrieve the block, one of the boys noticed a depression in the ground under the limb it was on. With tales of pirates and treasure in their minds they returned the next day and started digging.

At two feet a layer of flat stones was found, then at ten feet a platform of old oak logs was struck; the ends were well embedded in the sides of the pit the boys were now uncovering. The hole was 13 feet across, though one account says 4 feet. The hole went through clay so hard that pick marks could easily be seen on the walls. Platforms were also found at the 20-foot and 30-foot levels with loose fill in between. After weeks of working every spare minute they could, the three young men finally gave up at approximately 32 feet, until they could obtain outside help. The pit was refilled for secrecy.

Smith bought the Pit site and later built a house there. The stone basement can still be seen today.

1804: The Onslow Company

In 1804, a company called the Onslow Company was formed to explore the Pit for treasure that the three discoverers were sure lay at the bottom.

The Money Pit, as it was now called, was opened up and dug down to the 90-foot level, striking oak platforms every 10 feet. Charcoal, putty, and coconut fibre were found on various platforms. A flat stone with an inscription cut into it was found at the 90-foot level. The inscription was never satisfactorily deciphered, but one university professor who saw it claimed it read, "Ten feet below 2,000,000 pounds lie buried." Neither the stone nor a copy of the inscription has survived the years.

One evening, as workers were finishing for the day, a sounding bar, driven down at the 93-foot level, hit a platform at 98 feet; the first one not at a 10-foot spacing. This raised everyone's hopes, but next morning there was 60 feet of water in the pit. Bailing had no effect, and the company tried a crude pump, but it burst due to the pressure.

The next summer it was decided to dig a new shaft 14 feet away and tunnel under the Money Pit and get the treasure from below. At 110 feet the new shaft was completely dry and the tunnel was 12 feet long, when suddenly water burst in, flooding the new shaft to the same level as the Money Pit. Discouraged and without funds, the company abandoned the project.

1849: The Truro Company

In 1849 the Truro Company was formed and cleared the Money Pit of the mud and debris which had collected over the years. A depth of 86 feet was reached, with no sign of water, but the next afternoon the Money Pit was full to within 30 feet of the surface. Bailing proved useless.

It was decided to prove or disprove the theory of treasure with a primitive drill set just above the water's surface. The first two holes located nothing except the platform at 98 feet, which proved to be 5 inches thick and made of spruce, according the chips brought up. In the third hole the drill hit the 98 foot platform, then dropped 12 inches, pierced 4 inches of oak, 22 inches of "metal in pieces," 8 inches of oak, 22 inches of loose metal again, 4 inches of oak, 6 inches of spruce, and then 7 feet of clay. Three links of a gold chain came up stuck to the flat auger in the sticky clay. The fourth hole passed through the 98-foot platform and dropped 18 inches, where the drill revolved in an odd manner. Some oak splinters and a piece of a birch hoop were recovered, which indicated that the auger was turning on the side of a cask. The 6-inch spruce platform was at the 104-foot level.

One of the company's large shareholders, who was supervising the boring operations, said he saw the driller remove something from the bit and put it in his pocket. When questioned, the driller said he'd show it at the next shareholders meeting. That night he left the island and never returned.

It was later established he had some sort of connection with a man who then tried to purchase the Money Pit area of Oak Island. Legend says that the driller found a jewel on the auger. The piece of gold chain that was brought up is now lost.

With proof of treasure lying between 98 and 104 feet in the Money Pit, once again a shaft was sunk in an effort to tunnel under the treasure and recover it from below. This new shaft reached a depth of 109 feet and a tunnel was driven towards the Money Pit. Then, as in 1805, the water suddenly burst into the tunnel and flooded the 109-foot pit to the same level as the Money Pit. By bailing from the Money Pit and 109-foot pit, the water was reduced to 80 feet, but no more. Workmen noticed, however, that the water was salt and after allowing the pits to fill, the level rose and fell with the tide.

Up to now the water was thought to originate from a fresh water spring above the treasure. (We found since we arrived on the island that there is a layer of rainwater constantly on top of the salt, which explains why the presence of salt was not noticed before 1850.)

Since both this 1850 109-foot pit and the 1805 110-foot pit were completely dry until connected to the Money Pit, it was concluded that the sea made its way into the Pit through a man-made channel and not through general seepage. In looking for the channel, a search of the island's shores centered on Smith's Cove, about 515 feet east of the Money Pit, where water seemed to run out of the beach at low tide.

Skimming off about three feet of sand and gravel at the beach, the searchers found a layer of the same fibrous material as was found on one of the Money Pit platforms in 1804. Later analysis has identified this material to be the outer husk of coconut. It was used extensively in the past, and even recently, I am informed, as packing on ships carrying cargoes from tropical areas where coconuts are plentiful. On the beach at Smith's Cove a matting of this fibre covered an area 145 feet wide, and from low tide line to high tide line.

Since it was very unsatisfactory to work between tides, a cofferdam was built, and it successfully held the sea back so that the area could be properly excavated. Under the coconut fibre were beach rocks to a depth of about five feet. No sand had passed the coconut and the area below was clear between the rocks, forming a huge man-made reservoir. At the bottom of this deep rock work, or reservoir, were five- to eight-inch wide "box" drains made of flat stones which converged to a single larger drain at the high tide line. This single drain gently sloped downwards towards the heart of the island and was made of key-shaped stones fitted together in an arch of several tiers to prevent collapse and provide a clear, open hole for the water to flow through. This drain was covered with coconut, a layer of bluish sand, and the ditch in which it was buried was filled to the natural level with rock and clay.

Just after this discovery, a storm and a very high tide destroyed the cofferdam, filling the excavation with sand.

The next plan was to block the single drain by digging a shaft between the point where the five box drains converged and the Money Pit. It was estimated that the drain should be reached about 25 feet down at a site 140 feet inland of the converging point. The shaft went down to 75 feet without a trace of the drain or water.

After some discussion, another shaft was started on a line about 12 feet south of the 75-foot pit. At 35 feet salt water rushed in filling the shaft to tide level. Timbers were driven down, but as bailing was resumed, the sea flowed into the Money Pit as fast as ever.

It was then decided to sink a shaft about 20 feet south of the Money Pit. At 118 feet a tunnel was driven towards the Pit in an effort to use the new shaft for bailing to keep the water low enough to clear out the treasure. The 4-foot-high tunnel was 18 feet long, and all the workmen except one were at the surface for dinner when the water broke through. As this last man ran, with the water and timbers from the Money Pit crashing into the tunnel at this heels, he seized the end of a keg painted yellow that tumbled to his feet. On the surface, another man threw a line down the Money Pit and found it open to a depth of 114 feet, or ten feet *deeper* than the 104 foot platform which held the treasure in the 1849 drilling. Twelve feet of mud and debris were left in the new shaft.

Owing to the lack of funds, the company had to discontinue operations.

1863: The Oak Island Association

A company called the Oak Island Association resumed the search in 1863. The Money Pit was re-cribbed, but due to pumping operations the cribbing shifted and was declared unsafe. Two shafts were then sunk to locate the water tunnel, but it couldn't be found. Next, in an effort to hold back the sea, the drains in Smith's Cove were plugged with clay, but the clay washed away after holding back the sea for nearly two days.

A shaft was sunk at a point one hundred feet southeast of the Money Pit, which put it, the Money Pit, and the basement of Smith's house roughly in a line. The shaft went down to about 110 feet, and three tunnels, one north, one south, and one to Smith's Cove, failed to locate the water tunnel. Another tunnel entered the Money Pit at about 108 feet. The Pit was clear overhead and the cribbing completed to the new tunnel for strength. The company also ran an encircling tunnel around the Money Pit at about 95 feet deep. An effort to raise more funds wasn't successful and the company was forced to return the pits to the sea.

1866: The Eldorado Company of 1866
(a.k.a. The Halifax Company)

The Oak Island Eldorado Company of 1866, or the Halifax Company, as it was more commonly called, is often confused with the Oak Island Association, and over the last hundred years much work done by one company is attributed to, or blamed on, the other, depending on the situation. For example, the 110-foot shaft located 100 feet southeast of the Money Pit, which was dug by the Oak Island Association, has become known as the Halifax Pit, and tunnels from it called the Halifax Tunnels. In fact, nearly every tunnel causing any trouble in later years was called a Halifax Tunnel.

The Halifax Company's first order of business was the building of a wood and clay dam 375 feet long and 12 feet high to enclose all the old Smith's Cove work-ings. There seems to be some doubt as to whether the dam was built or not, but the company's foreman at the time says it was built but wouldn't hold the sea water from entering the Pit for some reason and the sea final-ly destroyed it.

The Money Pit was cleared to 108 feet and by con-tinuous pumping it was possible to keep water low enough to set a drill at the 90-foot level and probe the area below. Three holes were bored and coconut fibre, soft clay, bits of oak and spruce recovered from various levels, all indicated that the Money Pit at the time of construction was at least 150 feet deep. At 160 feet, all three holes were in the hard reddish marl of the natural island. No searchers' tunnels or shaft had reached beyond 118 feet up to this time.

The company then started tunneling from a new shaft at various levels, trying to intercept the water tunnel to turn its flow away from the Money Pit, which was about 120 feet away. One of these tunnels was aimed towards the Money Pit at about the 110-foot level, but when it was opened into the Pit it struck the end of the water tunnel at one side. The water suddenly rushing into this tunnel drove the men out once again. After hours of pumping, the men were able to return and inspect the water tunnel that those who buried the treasure had constructed. It was 30 inches wide, 4 feet high, and packed with beach rocks to prevent collapse.

As in the past with its predecessors, the company was forced to abandon the project due to lack of funding. Because the top of the Money Pit cribbing was breaking up, the Pit was decked over just above tide level and filled to the surface for safety, leaving the sea to resume its duty.

1878: Mrs. Sophia Sellers

In 1878, Mrs. Sophia Sellers was plowing a field between the Money Pit and Smith's Cove when one of her oxen fell down a hole that opened up under its feet. The hole was about 6 to 8 feet in diameter and 12 feet deep. This hole became know as the Sink Hole, or the Cave-in Pit.

1893: The Oak Island Treasure Co. (Frederick Blair)

In 1893 Frederick Blair formed the Oak Island Treasure Co. and promptly excavated the Cave-in Pit found in 1878. It was opened to 52 feet and was found to be 7 feet in diameter, and again, as in 1795, pick marks could be seen on the walls and the fill was loose, indicating that it was part of the original work.

No water was encountered, and a hole 16 feet deep was bored down from the bottom. The next morning water filled the pit to tide level and work was abandoned.

In 1894 a shaft was dug with the idea of going down past the water tunnel, tunneling under, and undermining it to divert the flow from the Money Pit. The water tunnel couldn't be located.

The company was reorganized and work wasn't resumed until late 1896 at which time the Cave-in Pit was reopened to 52 feet where salt water drove them out.

At this time the company had been working in a shaft they believed to be the Money Pit, although several people said it wasn't, because it had no buried platform, as left by the Halifax Co. in 1867. On deepening this shaft, they found a tunnel which led to the real Money Pit, complete with buried platform above tide level, and the water tunnel at 111 feet with the sea rushing in, as usual. The water tunnel was filled with sand and gravel, a bird's bone, a chip of wood, and other evidence which proved its connection to the shore.

Since it was obvious that it was foolish to pump the sea in a circle, 5 holes were drilled about 50 feet inland from the high tide line in Smith's Cove on the line of the Money Pit and Cave-in Pit. No water was found in four of the holes and dynamiting them gave no result. The centre hole, however, met with salt water at 80 feet; dynamiting it caused the water in the Money Pit and Cave-in Pit to boil and foam. It is said that determining the depth of the salt water in the centre hole created an argument among the workmen.

The water still poured into the Money Pit, so a drill was set up at the 90-foot level to try and locate the treasure that vanished from between the 98-foot and 104-foot platforms in 1850. Several holes were drilled, verifying the 1866 results of loose ground below the deepest searcher's shaft of 118 feet. Iron was struck at various depths in the different holes, as was wood, sand, coconut fibre, and putty-like material. In one hole iron was struck at 171 feet; it couldn't be penetrated and was thought to be an iron plate.

In another hole the drill casing jammed at about 120 feet, so a smaller drill was used to get down to 153 feet, where 7 inches of soft stone and 5 inches of oak were located. Below this was some sort of soft metal. Among the borings was a tiny piece of parchment with the letters "vi" written on it. A smaller casing was used to try and get a sample of the soft metal, but because the drill had been withdrawn the casing didn't follow the same path and the direction to the soft metal was lost.

Analysis of the borings by experts concluded that the soft stone was a primitive cement "worked by man." The scrap of parchment and the lettering was done with a quill pen and India ink. The parchment still exists today. Here, it was concluded, lay a wood and cement vault containing documents and bars of gold entirely separate from the treasure originally at 98 to 104 feet.

With these encouraging results behind them the company sank shaft after shaft to try to divert the water, but all were abandoned because of flooding or unsafe conditions.

Finally sanity ruled, and some tests were made with the purpose of locating the source of the water. After pumping the Money Pit full of dyed water, the dye appeared on the south shore and not in Smith's Cove.

In 1900 the Money Pit was doubled in size and opened to 113 feet, but progress was slow, help hard to get, and finally creditors forced operations to cease, and the company's assets were sold.

In 1905 Blair obtained a forty-year Mining Lease for the Money Pit site of Oak Island.

1909: The Old Gold Salvage Company
(Captain Henry Bowdoin)

Four years later, in 1909, Captain Henry Bowdoin formed a company, after making an agreement with Blair, to recover the treasure on Oak Island. Known as The Old Gold Salvage Company, it had Franklin D. Roosevelt as one of its financial backers and planned to salvage wrecked ships and other lost valuables after cleaning up Oak Island. Captain Bowdoin issued a prospectus to encourage the sale of his stock, and in it he outlined a sound plan of attack. In brief, it was his plan to use core drills to locate the treasure and water tunnels, and then drive sheet piling across the drains. Using an orange-peel bucket, he would dig through the drain and plug it off tightly. At the Money Pit the bucket would be used to quickly reach the treasure and if water interfered, powerful turbine pumps would remove it. If all this failed, air lock caissons would be sunk at the Money Pit to any depth necessary and side tubes driven out to any desired point. Success was inevitable.

When Bowdoin's expedition arrived on Oak Island, all these plans were scrapped. The Money Pit was pumped out and the platforms, ladders, and cross timbers left in the 1890s were torn out to 107 feet with the orange peel bucket. Then a diver was sent down, who reported, of all things, that the cribbing was in bad shape. The bucket reached 113 feet, where drills were used to bore 25 holes at various angles and depths. Cement was struck at different levels, and Bowdoin claimed that analysis showed it to be "limestone pitted by the action of water."

Bowdoin then asked Blair for more time and Blair in turn asked for proof of adequate finances before granting additional time. Bowdoin then published an article in *Colliers* in 1911 claiming that the whole thing was a hoax. Blair, in a published rebuttal, noted Bowdoin's senseless destruction of the island and failure to explain the Smith's Cove water intake discovered in 1850, the coconut fibre, and the parchment.

1931: William Chappell

William Chappell and his brother were next to try. It was Chappell who had run the drill in 1897 that recovered the parchment, and he later stated that he had seen the colour of gold on the drill but had said nothing at the time.

In 1931, a 12 foot by 14 foot shaft was sunk at the Money Pit site. This shaft was part on the hard and part on the soft ground, which caused considerable trouble with cribbing shifting and unlocking. At the 140-foot

level, the shaft was 6 feet farther north than at the surface and had a bad twist in it.

From time to time, the volume of water entering
the pit was checked and it averaged about 450 gallons
per minute. As the shaft was sunk, articles from earlier
treasure hunters were found, including an anchor fluke
at 116 feet. Everyone was completely surprised that
there was no trace of any treasure at 155 feet, so an
additional 8 feet was dug, but nothing was found.

Because the shaft was partly on hard ground it was
obvious that is wasn't exactly over the old Money Pit
but was centred south possibly 6 or 7 feet. Three short
tunnels were dug from the Chappell Pit towards the
soft area, to the north, but again no treasure was found.

Operations were postponed until 1932, but owing
to economic conditions at the time, the Chappell
brothers never returned.

1934: Thomas Nixon

Thomas Nixon of Victoria, British Columbia, made an
agreement with Blair and formed a company with the
plan of driving interlocking steel piling down 50–75
feet in diameter and excavating the enclosed area.

After his arrival on Oak Island in 1934, however, he
drilled 14 holes north of Chappell's pit instead. He
located bits of oak, old cribbing, and once hit a vacant
space at 136 feet that extended to 170 feet. His funds
exhausted, he left the island.

1935: Gilbert Hedden

Gilbert Hedden purchased the eastern end of Oak
Island in 1935 and, armed with an agreement from
Blair, set out to write the final chapter of Oak Island.
Electrically powered turbine pumps easily kept ahead
of the sea, and the Chappell Pit was recribbed where
necessary for safety and was deepened to 170 feet.
Some lateral boring was done, but nothing was located.

In the summer of 1937 a 12 foot by 24 foot shaft was

sunk adjacent to the east side of the Chappell Pit to allow ample room for tunneling and lateral boring. Many tools and articles lost by previous searchers were found, and at 80 feet an old oak stump was removed. The old encircling tunnel of 1863 was discovered and at about 110 feet the original water tunnel with beach rocks in it was located. It was dry at this point, but close by the water came rushing in through a cribbed tunnel, probably dug in the 1850s The water was diverted into the Chappell Pit and removed by the pump installed there. At 125 feet, work was halted for the winter, and holes were drilled down from the floor to 160 feet, but nothing was located.

Unfortunately, financial problems prevented Hedden from completing his objective.

During his attempt, Hedden made some other discoveries. He found a second white granite hand-drilled rock at Smith's Cove to match the white granite hand-drilled rock previously located near the Money Pit in 1895. The rocks each had a 1-1/4 inch diameter hole 2 inches deep. Also rediscovered was a triangle made of beach rocks, laid in rows, near the shore south of the Money Pit, just as it had been seen by Blair in 1897.

In 1937, a book about pirates and treasure was published with a map in it that had over a dozen resemblances to Oak Island. The map bore the legend which read:

18 W and by 7 E on Rock
30 SW 14 N Tree
7 by 8 by 4

A check showed that the two drilled rocks found on the island were exactly 25 rods apart. Using the legend on the map and standing so that one drilled rock was 7 rods east and the other was 18 rods west, a line 30 rods southwest arrived at the stone triangle. Then 14 rods north were the Chappell and Hedden Pits or where the oak tree and original Money Pit used to be. This map was supposed to be signed by William Kidd himself! A surveyor checked the measurements of the legend on the island and found them to be accurate.

1938: Professor Edwin Hamilton

Professor Edwin Hamilton of New York University took over Hedden's equipment in 1938 and spent the summer drilling holes in the floor of Hedden's Pit and laterally from the Chappell Pit.

Bits of timber and oak were found, but nothing of value.

A tunnel was driven from the northwest section to the southeast section of the Hedden Pit encircling the Chappell Pit at about the 115-foot level. The old 75-foot shaft at Smith's Cove and the tunnel connecting it to the 1860s tunnel were cleared out. The 1860s tunnel had wooden tracks and the remains of a pit pony and cart were still there in 1941. The tunnel ran up past the Halifax Shaft and stopped at a place that had caved in. Workers in the Hedden Pit could walk up the tunnel to the obstruction and the two groups were close enough to hear each other. The tunnels were approximately 80 feet below tide level.

The other end of this tunnel toward Smith's Cove was never explored to its end due to poor crib conditions and the amount of sand in the tunnel. In fact, at one point, Professor Hamilton's workmen took rough measurements underground and at dinner, one day, they retraced their steps on the surface. They refused to go back to work when it was discovered that the tunnel led out under the waters of Smith's Cove.

The last thing Professor Hamilton did was to extend an 8 foot by 8 foot section of the floor in Hedden's Pit to 168 feet. Some lateral boring was done there but with no results. Due to war conditions, Professor Hamilton was forced to give up, and the pits were decked over above tide level, and once again the sea dominated the pits.

1951: M.R. Chappell and Blair

In 1951, M.R. Chappell, son of William Chappell, purchased the island and, with Blair, who had the newly enacted Treasure Trove Licence, moved a clam shovel to the island and started a hole about 200 feet north of the Chappell and Hedden Pits. Actually this was the second shovel, because the first one was accidentally dropped on to the bottom of Mahone Bay, and the salvage crew was busy trying to raise it when the second arrived on the island and started digging.

The site of this hole was determined by the latest electronic metal-locating device. The ground was so hard that dynamite was used to loosen it, and at about 45 feet operations were halted because the locator indicated the deposit was now further south.

1955: George Greene

In 1955, George Greene, a Texas petroleum engineer arrived to "prove or disprove the legend of Oak Island." Four holes were drilled. In three holes oak platforms were struck every 10 feet. The fourth hole hit a cavity at 110 feet which extended for 45 feet. Water pumped into it escaped and couldn't be traced. Business commitments prevented continuation of operations.

1958: William and Victor Harman

William and Victor Harman, engineers from northern Ontario, were next, in 1958. They planned extensive drilling operations and excavating the entire Money Pit area. Four holes were drilled with no new results.

[With a history like this, is it any wonder that new groups of treasure hunters continue to materialize and give the island their best try? The next chapter of Bobby's writing is abridged. Removed from it was material that has been described in earlier sections of this book.]

The Restall Search

CHAPTER 14

The Restall Search
by Robert K. Restall

Before our arrival on Oak Island, my father decided on a plan of attack. He had gone over every scrap of information to try and determine exactly what had happened since 1795, how to stop the inflow of water, and where the two treasures actually were.

He had reached several conclusions.

In 1850, during the collapse of the Money Pit, the treasure, along with the 98- and 104-foot platforms, was swept into the 118-foot shaft and cross tunnel by the force of the water standing above the treasure in the Pit. Proof of this is the 12 feet of debris in the 118-foot shaft, and the Money Pit suddenly being open to 114 feet, which is even with the top of the 4-foot-high cross tunnel. It is said that some experienced miners working on the island at the time argued that the treasure was in the 118-foot shaft and cross tunnel, but were overruled by the bosses. No one has ever cleared this shaft since.

My father couldn't believe that the pirates, or whoever they were, would run the water tunnel almost flat as indicated by the boring and dynamiting in 1897 at Smith's Cove. It must be understood that various measurements have to be converted to depths below sea level due to the different heights of the land on Oak Island. For example, the Money Pit is on a 32-foot hill, so the 111-foot-deep water tunnel is approximately 80 feet below tide level at this point. The Cave-in Pit is about 18 feet above sea level, so it was excavated in 1893 to 34 feet and the drill went to 50 feet below tide. The 75-foot pit extends about 70 feet below the sea, and the drill hole of 1897 is about the same, so it supposedly hit the water tunnel about 75 feet below tide, giving only 5 feet of fall in 460 feet of tunnel to the Money Pit.

My father figured that the drill must have missed the drain and the water broke through to the drill hole when the bit happened to be at 80 feet. To confirm this is the fact that between this drill hole and the Money Pit is the 1850 shaft that hit salt water at 35 feet! Not only would the tunnel not be flat, but it definitely would not go up and down like a roller coaster.

It is certain that there never was any treasure in the Money Pit at 154 feet. This conclusion is supported by the drilling done in the Money Pit by the Halifax Co., Bowdoin, Hedden, and Professor Hamilton, and especially by the digging of the Chappell Pit in 1931 to a depth of 163 feet, plus short tunnels and lateral boring, all of which found no trace of any treasure. It is obvious that the obstruction that jammed the drill casing in 1897 also deflected the small drill. The location of the jammed casing at 120 feet is known within two or three feet, but where the drill wandered afterward on its 34-foot trip to the treasure is not known.

The iron struck at different levels during boring operations probably were old drill casing and other debris which is present around the Money Pit area in very large quantities. Evidence of this is the fact that later borings have reached 180–200 feet in the Money Pit and immediate area without striking iron at any consistent level. The popular story of an iron plate at 171 feet is a myth.

The results of putting dye in the water in 1898 was puzzling and couldn't be immediately explained, but later information has cleared up some of the question.

We pumped about 100 thousand gallons of water into the Hedden Pit from the shovel hole dug in 1951, and promptly learned why putting dye into the pits won't give accurate results. To create a flow you need a pressure difference, and due to the tunnels connecting the Money Pit to the pits at Smith's Cove, the highest possible pressure difference is about 2 to 4 pounds, because when 6 feet of water is put in the Hedden Pit, the Smith's Cove pits fill and the water overflows and runs across the beach. Two to four pounds is not enough difference with the sand-choked drains on Oak Island. At the time we searched the south shore but could find no trace of any excess water.

We have since been told that when the dye was seen on the south shore of the island in 1898, some of the people present claimed they saw it and others said they could not see it. Some who couldn't see it were quoted as saying they did.

In Smith's Cove we found bits of coconut fibre and evidence of earlier searchers' work that is unrecorded. It took the form of old plank walls buried under the sands of the beach, also five vertical board boxes built to protect drill holes of past years.

After studying some aerial photos of the island, we noticed that the cofferdam, as it's thought to be, was out of shape. By checking with some of Hedden's old workers, we found that the Hedden Wharf was built by removing the north one-third of the old 1850 coffer-dam remains.

Then by digging a series of holes past the vegetation layer, the deep rock work, or water, we finally located the reservoir, but it was well to the north of where all present records claim it to be. Also, it was found that completely surrounding the reservoir was a layer of vegetation below the natural gravel resting on a single layer of beach rocks.

In this single layer of stones, to one side of the reservoir, we found a small stone with the date 1704 chiseled into it. It was probably done by a workman at the time the reservoir was being completed and left under the vegetation and gravel, just as construction workers leave their names and dates inside walls on construction jobs today.

The construction of the water intake system was undoubtedly done after the treasure was hidden and the Money Pit and Cave-in Pit were filled. A cofferdam was built spanning the area selected for the reservoir. The reservoir itself was excavated to the desired depth and was 145 feet wide and extended from low tide mark to high tide mark. The five finger or box drains were placed in the bottom and converged to the single, larger drain which slopes back to the Cave-in Pit. The excavation above the box-drains was filled with beach rocks to the level of the surrounding area, as was the ditch that held the single drain, but with clay and rocks in this case. Then a final layer of beach rocks were placed over the reservoir and extended beyond it at least 50 feet to each side and over 50 feet inland. Over the deep rock work was placed the layer of coconut fibre. This acted, not as a sponge, but as an effective screen to prevent gravel from clogging the water intake system. On the area surrounding the reservoir, coconut was of no value and also probably in short supply, so weeds, bushes, beach grass, and anything handy, including the acorn-laden branches of oak, were placed over the single layer of stones. [One morning, returning to a shaft they were digging, Dad and Bobby found a perfectly preserved oak leaf and acorn floating in the water.]

The entire area was then filled to the natural level with sand and gravel so that its surface appearance gave no hint of the clever construction built below. Finally, when everything was completed on the Island, the cofferdam was removed without leaving a trace. The sea then filled the reservoir and water tunnel to guard the treasure, which it has effectively done, even to this day.

We drilled several holes at Smith's Cove. The actual water tunnel wasn't found, but the ditch filled with rock and clay discovered by the Truro Company was located. By digging a 16 foot by 4 foot hole down to 22 feet, the sides of this ditch were easily seen.

During an extremely low tide a double row of planks, driven vertically into the ground, was found just inside the old cofferdam. Toredo worms had eaten the wood off at the beach level. In the winter of 1963, a single row of vertical planking was discovered on the outside curve of the old dam, about 20 feet long. By projecting the line of the dam's curve past high tide mark, the dam would have been 375 feet long. It is apparent, then, that the cofferdam really was rebuilt in 1866, but because it was built on top of the debris of the old 1850 dam, it leaked. The water got through to the pits, not from a second tunnel, but through the holes in the base of the 1866 dam. The inner row of planks looks like a haphazard attempt to plug off the leaks.

In all, we dug five cribbed holes over 20 feet deep, at least a dozen uncribbed ones below the single rock layer into the clay of the island, or into the top three feet of the reservoir and countless small holes to the vegetation layer across the beach, to determine the size of the original beach work. The reservoir has not been opened up to the box drains, due to the daily tides. The sea has filled most of the holes, including one cribbed one.

The Pits were pumped out and we built ladders and a hoist track to the floor of the Hedden Pit at 125 feet. A blower and air duct for fresh air were also installed. We did considerable probing from the Hamilton Tunnel encircling the Chappell Pit. And we explored the Halifax Tunnel to the point where it is collapsed. We only had tractor headlights and auto batteries for light. [See Figure 11.]

Once, being late in the year, a sudden cold spell froze the water which is constantly raining down into sheets of ice, right down to the 90-foot level, which made it very tricky to get up and down the ladders and

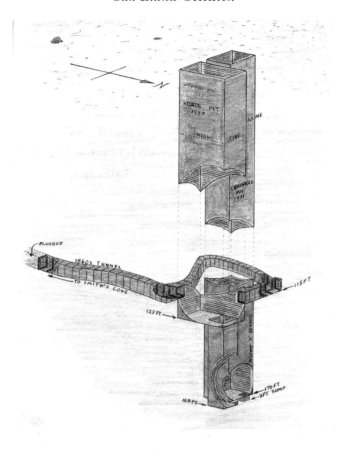

Figure 11: Sketch by Bobby Restall entitled "Oak Island's Money Pit Area, Today, 1965."

along the narrow platforms in the dark. Ice forming in the bay finally stopped operations that year.

We then got a 5-ton diesel generating plant out of a destroyer for power on the island. It was quite a wrestling match getting it on the barge at Western Shore, over to the island, then up the hill to the Money Pit area. A 440-volt, 75-HP electric motor was obtained to drive the pump, and transformers gave us 110 volts for lights and power down the pits. With this set-up we can remove 100 feet of water, or go past the 125-foot floor of the Hedden Pit in only 24 hours of pumping.

Professor Hamilton and his workers told us where they had hit a cross tunnel when digging their encircling tunnel in 1940. By cutting holes in the wall of the tunnel we found short pieces of old hewed timber, as seen by Professor Hamilton's crew. About a dozen pieces were brought to the surface.

We then planned to systematically drill holes to try and locate the treasure struck in 1897. We bored about two dozen holes at different angles from the floor of Hedden's pit and encountered soft ground, sand, and gravel at various depths. We probed the area that Nixon (1934) hit a cavity, and found it to be filled with sand and gravel with salt water rushing through it. This would have felt empty with a heavy drill such as Nixon used.

One day, on moving the pieces of hewed timber we had found outside the Hamilton Tunnel, some clay fell off one, exposing part of a drill hole along the line of the break. A check of the wood showed that some pieces were 5 inches and some 6 inches thick and made of spruce. The drilled piece and several others were apparently part of the 5-inch platform at 98 feet, and the 6-inch pieces were from the 104-foot platform located in the Money Pit during the 1849 drilling. Two or three other pieces had interlocking corner joints and these are thought to be part of the cribbing placed in the Money Pit before the collapse of 1850. The timbers were nearly all broken into short pieces about 12 inches long. The wood is still sound, indicating that tremendous force was needed to smash them.

Moving back into the Hamilton Tunnel, we probed the whole area where the broken timbers came from, but nothing as bulky as a box or cask was found. A short tunnel was dug, but it didn't locate any treasure either. Ice conditions made it too difficult to get fuel to the island, so we had to stop work in the tunnel for the winter and return to the beach area. Since then, we have managed to get a drill into a mass of loose rocks which has an unusual amount of fine sand in it. The water tunnel? We are confident of it!

The drill is into the drain between the Cave-in Pit and the Money Pit, and is much higher than we had thought only a year or so ago. We are now certain that in 1893, when the Cave-in Pit was first opened, the drill used in the bottom of the hole went right through the drain without the drillers realizing it. The drain, of course, was full of sand and the water used in drilling probably couldn't escape as fast as the drillers thought it would. We also thought the drill water would escape quickly after hitting the drain. But looking back, it is obvious that it can't. The depth of the drain, of course, brings up the results of the boring in Smith's Cove in 1897 that hit salt water at 80 feet. A long talk with Professor Hamilton has convinced us that the drill at that time hit the searchers' tunnel running to Smith's Cove dug in the 1860s. The open tunnel gave all the expected results that were recorded in history: salt water to tide level and dynamite causing the water in the Money Pit to boil. The argument over the depth of the drain, mentioned in 1897, was probably between the bosses, who knew nothing of earlier workings, and some of the men who had helped to dig that very tunnel forty years before. As in 1850, the bosses won the argument.

For final proof, Professor Hamilton and his workers point to the poor crib conditions and the unusual amount of sand that had no business being in the heart of a clay island. Professor Hamilton's measurements put the floor of the 6-foot-high tunnel at just about 80 feet below sea level.

Over the years there have been hundreds of people visit the island, or write with every idea in the book. From blowing the treasure out of the ground with dynamite to spiritual seances. Everyone has "the answer."

We tried the latest electronic metal detectors, but they proved useless in the Money Pit on Oak Island. In the first place, clay acts like a shield, as does lead with radioactivity, therefore, penetration is low. Add this to the fact that the top layer of clay is the type which has plenty of iron in it and results are false readings. Tools lost underground further confuse readings.

People today find it very difficult to believe that men could possibly dig a hole 150 feet deep 250 years ago, without modern machinery. They are surprised to learn that every single pit on Oak Island was dug by hand, with the exception of the shovel hole dug in 1951.

Who did this remarkably clever job of burying the treasure, and what is the treasure? We have some pretty good circumstantial evidence, but it cannot be revealed at this time. There are innumerable theories. Captain Kidd; Inca treasure; a pay ship from France bound for the fortress at Louisbourg in northern Nova Scotia; the French crown jewels; and even the Bacon manuscripts. But theories of who, what, and how much do not alter the problems that exist, and only after it is recovered will the "who" and the value be proven.

The water is a problem, but the pits are cribbed to 170 feet, and the water can be held at this level anytime we want to keep the diesel running.

The actual problem is locating the treasure and driving a tunnel to it. Outside the walls of the present shafts flows 450 gallons of water per minute, bringing sand, gravel, and mud with it, making it tricky stuff to tunnel through. We are sure we know just about the exact location of the treasure, based on results of our drilling from the Hedden pit. We plan to tunnel there this summer [1965] after first stopping the inflow of salt water.

The pits are real, the water still pours in a 450 gallons per minute. The oak branches, acorns, coconut fibre, and reservoir are all to be found buried at Smith's Cove. The parchment [which W.R. Chappell brought up on his drill bit in 1896] proves that there are records or documents of some sort in the Money Pit area. Some say, tear the island apart with bulldozers or draglines, but it would be almost criminal to destroy the records to gain the treasure. Do archeologists use bulldozers to excavate ancient ruins? Anthropologists use dental picks and fine brushes to uncover fossils and bones.

While Oak Island doesn't need these sensitive tech-
niques, now, after all these years, the only acceptable
way to honour the genius who buried his treasure here
is to ensure that when we raise his treasure, we can call
him by name.

1965: *The Final Push*

CHAPTER 15

D ad was not the only one swamped with letters from people energized by the *Reader's Digest* article. Chappell, in letters to Dad, told of people phoning him in the middle of the night, sending telegrams, writing letters, all offering to solve the mystery of Oak Island. Eventually, the repetitiveness of the claims and their sheer volume washed away any lingering hopes he harboured for quick solutions. Vows to be the only one who could solve this problem soon became mundane, even to Chappell. His response now, he told Dad, was to refer treasure hunters to Dad and to tell potential buyers of the island that he no was longer in a position to sell, as he had committed the island to Bob Restall for 1965.

In fact, Chappell sent my father the names of wealthy would-be treasure hunters whom he had turned away, and two of them subsequently contacted Dad and invested with him. In the midst of this melee, Chappell also wrote to Dad to inform him that one of Dad's long-time investors had inquired about obtaining the contract for himself, and Chappell had brusquely referred him back to Dad. Chappell then sent this investor a copy of his letter to Dad. The investor's hasty scrambling to explain this innocent "misunderstanding" in a letter to Dad was amusing.

On January 20, 1965, Dad wrote to Fred, "Just a quick line to let you know that we can't buy the island. Chappell has changed his mind once more and will not sell, not until the treasure is raised. It's just as well. We now have our 1965 contract signed and sealed and can concentrate on this season's financing (we don't expect much trouble with this) and getting the treasure up. It's about time. This year's end will make 6-1/4 years since we started in here. If any of the people you have talked to want to invest ..."

Among my parents' papers is a contract dated January 20, 1965, between M.R. Chappell and Robert Restall, in which Chappell agreed to pay to Dad 30 percent of the net amount he would receive of the treasure. Chappell had turned part of his percentage over to Dad so the remaining percentages from Dad's half of the treasure could be used to raise new investment capital and keep the search going.

> Feb. 20th, 1965
> Dear Fred:
>
> It has been very cold with lots of snow since I got back. Bobby blew the top off a battery while I was away. Keeping them covered with a piece of plastic while charging them and a spark caught. It wrecked the battery top but the acid missed him. Of course he was very lucky. I had told him about the danger of this plenty of times, but ... [He continued on the topic of safety.]
>
> We are doing everything possible now in the hopes that the weather will allow us to get back on the project by mid March ... [He listed their various maintenance projects.]
>
> I have written to two dozen prospects and as yet not a dime has come in. Asked most of them to write and let me know in any case, and haven't had a reply. This is a nail-biting business. Meanwhile, money goes. From [name withheld]'s $500 I paid all around and got squared away again. Since then I got the bank to up the $250 to $500, can't get them to go above this. Our cash will be done in, in about ten days. I felt that we would have no trouble with the financing but maybe I was over confident. In any case something will surely come in very soon. If not I may have to make another trip up there and I would rather stay on the job. We are making every effort to wind the job up this summer and think we can do it so long as we manage the funds. ...

[Here Dad discussed the likelihood of Chappell changing his mind again about selling the island, asked Fred to send copies of a recent *Hamilton Spectator* article so he could send them to prospective investors, and asked for a relief valve and 3/4" unions for the pump.]

We have had hundreds of letters since the article in *Reader's Digest*. All these people absolutely believe the story and picture shown are absolutely gospel and that this represents things as of today. Also that in 5 years of work we are completely baffled and only have the dated stone to show and nothing else. I am telling you we were wonderfully lucky that this story didn't come out a month or two earlier. There were phone calls, telegrams, etc. Chappell was pestered to death as well. They could all solve the problem in no time at all, for a percent and expenses, of course. Some of them phoned Chappell and us, wrote Chappell and us. You should see how different the letters are. They phoned the Chester Motel for information and several also wrote the Chester Library for information. It's got now so everyone sends the messages on to us. We couldn't possibly cope with it. It's the craziest thing I have ever heard of. Hundreds of solutions to problems that never or no longer exist. What an education.

Hope everything is going well with you. We are all keeping well except for colds. Best regards to all and remember me to your wife.

This is the year, so we had better keep moving.

Yours sincerely,

Bob

My mother was tired of life on Oak Island. The responsibility for Rick's schooling was a burden that weighed heavier each year. Rick, having turned fourteen in January, was finishing grade eight. Mom worked harder and harder to stay on top of the lessons. Here are a few fragments of her writing from that time:

Arithmetic: fractions and decimals after keeping house.

A woman after 30 yrs. (so I'm a liar) doesn't remember those things. It's impossible.

I've heard parents brag of their kids having a mind like a steel trap and now I wonder if, like mine, their kids' minds are so much like a steel trap it is nearly impossible to pry them open to poke a little bit of knowledge inside.

Her writing also took on a darker tone at this time.

[Untitled]
by Mildred Restall

By the time five summers and nearly five winters had passed with just me and three males, I was completely sick of them. Their senseless, nitpicking arguments were driving me to distraction.

My two boys argued over nothing, my husband argued with them over nothing, and I argued with all three over nothing. At times I loathed them all, and for two pins would have packed up and left, 'cept we didn't have two pins.

Besides, threatening to pack up and leave from an island loses some of its dramatic impact and presents a rather ridiculous picture of me begging someone to take me and my belongings to the mainland. I'd have to be sure the water was calm, no point in looking like a drowned rat.

My youngest is stupid and stubborn, he needs to have his ears boxed, my eldest is an arrogant snot who could do with a swift kick. And my husband is a selfish, self-centred, domineering beast who ought to be shot.

That's what I thought of them by the time my fifth spring arrived.

Karl Graeser tried to help out. He and his wife invited Mom to spend a week with them in Long Island. Mom wrote to me, "We had a letter from the Graesers last week. They invited me down to Long Island for a week and would arrange my air ticket to suit me. And me without a dress to my name. Needless to say, I can't go, I just haven't a thing to wear. And if I did have, these fellows would howl like dogs."

Early pictures of my mother show her looking glamorous in one fashionable outfit after another. Dad proudly took photo after photo. But now nothing mattered but his treasure hunt, and he begrudged every penny spent elsewhere. According to Mom, he seemed to notice her plight only once. One day he came into the shack to find her remaking one of Bobby's old work shirts into something for herself. It saddened him.

What I Miss Most
by Mildred Restall

This living all together was too much at times. There seemed to be no escape. While I missed not having another room to sneak into when I want to read or study, I missed the bathroom most of all.

When you are tired of reading, sick of TV, and don't feel like doing anything much, you can go into the bathroom, where you are sure of privacy, give yourself a manicure, a pedicure, try out a new hairdo or makeup, relax and soak for hours in a bathtub brim full of luxurious hot water.

When I was feeling low, sometimes Bob would try to cheer me with dreams of how, when the treasure came up, we would have so much that we would even have his and her yachts. That could always draw a chuckle.

But my dreams were much simpler. Just give me a bathroom with walls and floor of real ceramic tile, and a large bathtub full of steamy hot water. Now — that is luxury.

Cabin Fever
by Mildred Restall

By the fifth winter we were becoming neurotics. Speak like mad, hardly stop for breath. Gather thoughts and go like crazy. Never mind about <u>His</u> or <u>Her</u> yachts.

But despite everything, Mom retained her sharp eye and her deep appreciation for nature.

Carney
by Mildred Restall

Smart dog. She no longer dashes out to meet the visitors. She learned long ago that people were sometimes afraid when they saw a big black dog barreling along the wharf towards them. Instead, she waits under the apple tree near the beach shack and carefully looks over the "marks" as they disembark. If they have packages, her keen scent can tell, without her going close, whether they are carrying food or just bathing suits and such. If she smells food, she watches where they decide to settle for their picnics, then, shameless beggar, she minces up, plume waving, ears cocked. "Well! Fancy meeting you!"

If people say, "Go away!" she slinks back, tail drooping, looking so unhappy. Nine times out of ten, people feel ashamed. "Don't be mean to the poor dog," one will say. "It won't hurt you. Come on doggie, nice dog. Here, catch," and before long she is a member of the gang, at least until the food is gone.

If it's a family, she sidles up near the children, goes into her act as soon as she catches their eye. She sits up and begs, shakes hands. They are such pushovers.

Patience
by Mildred Restall

Waiting for spring is like waiting for the birth of a baby. Soon, not much longer, anytime now, and you wait, and wait, and wait.

Spring
by Mildred Restall

The weather was its usual freezing cold. The snow was gone and last year's dead grass lay everywhere, brown and ugly. The spruce trees were a dull green with a rusty tinge, the sea a bleak grey-blue, and the skies grey with a threat of snow. The only cheerful thing about the place was the twittering of the early arrived song birds.

The ground was still frozen as I put crumbs and anything else I thought they would eat outside on a board nailed to a fencepost. Naturally the squirrels found it and began to take the food. We took the board down and placed it on top of a twenty-gallon oil drum, figuring the squirrels couldn't climb up on the metal sides. But some of them managed to get up by taking a running jump, just touching the side of the barrel once for leverage, and they were there.

This was something I could never get used to in the Maritimes. The middle of May and the buds on the trees hadn't even begun to unfold. This goes on and on, suddenly you wake up one day in June and find that overnight the buds are open, the blossoms are on the trees, and the flowers are sprouting. Summer is here. From then on, as if to make up for lost time, everything grows like mad and in no time it is like a jungle.

By the end of June tourists are visiting, they look around, admiring the beauty of nature, "Oh! Isn't it beautiful here. How wonderful to live in a place like this", then to me, "How I envy you."

Well, here we go again.

In each letter to Fred Sparham during the spring of 1965, Dad thanked him for $50 or $100. One new investor came in for $100. Finances were critical.

In this period, Karl Graeser paid a visit to the island. He had become totally intrigued with his library research. He was developing his own interpretations and theories about measurements and the symbols found on the island, and shared his conclusions in lengthy letters to Dad.

Dad and Bobby began to put down a new shaft at the beach again. They immediately dug into oak tree roots and acorns. A good sign.

On May 20, Dad mailed a letter to Fred, jubilant at last.

Dear Fred:

Thanks very much for the telegraph money order. It was just timed right. I am pleased to be able to tell you that we have a new backer (as he calls himself) a prospector who came up with a certified cheque for $2,000. He was interested in having a go himself and phoned Chappell when that piece was in the newspaper in December that our contract expired Dec 31st and was not likely to be renewed (I agree with you now that there is no such thing as bad publicity). Anyway, he has been in touch with Chappell ever since ... and he is most concerned that we have funds so that there is no running around after money this year. This is great and with all the promises we have, only 10 percent of them will see us through. I am very pleased that we don't have to bother you about money anymore.

Best regards to all. This year so far has been a very nerve-racking experience.

Let's hope everything is sunny. I went around and paid everybody. Didn't realize some of the bills were so big (good thing I didn't or I would have worried even more). I will keep you posted.

Yours sincerely

Bob

P.S. It looks as if I will not be making any more trips to Ontario for funds.

On May 21 an investor who recently had put in $100 added another $100 to the pot. In early June, Graeser came to the island and worked side by side with Bobby and Dad. The investor who had put in $2,000 on May 18 joined them, working alongside the others. He and Graeser left on June 16.

In the second week of July Dad received a letter from Robert Dunfield, a geologist. Dunfield had contacted Chappell in hopes of getting the 1966 contract in his own name, but since that was not an option (according to Chappell, the island was committed to someone else for 1966), Dunfield was now interested in joining the Restall venture. He laid out details of the recovery operation he would have mounted had he been granted a contract with Chappell. His plan included surveying, using sheet piling to hold back the sea water, and using a two-and-a-half-yard orange-peel excavator to dig in the Money Pit area. He observed that money was not a problem but time was, and he indicated an interest in working with Dad.

Dad phoned Dunfield in California, after which he visited the island, and on July 15 a contract was signed. In it Dunfield invested $5,000, which was to be deposited to a bank trust account. His contract included the option of investing an additional $5,000.

Now it seemed the floodgates for financing were open. Dan Blankenship, a contractor from Florida, then arrived on the scene and wanted to put in $5,000, but Dad turned him away, saying he had enough money to complete the job and was within weeks of the final chapter of his search for treasure. Clearly, Blankenship was disappointed.

Less than five months of the Restall contract remained, but Dad, ever the optimist, believed that was ample. Work took on a pressured pace. Dad and Bobby were positive after all their years of sinking shafts, drilling, and putting down additional holes in the beach that they now knew precisely where to intercept the bypass sea water inlet tunnel. They dug their new shaft directly into the road they had used for years to get up to the Money Pit area. Bobby described the events in his journal.

Friday, July 16, 1965
Jim and two guys helping. Pulled old cribbing from last trench. Worked new one down. Got acorns, very thick oak, few rocks. Definitely deeper to vegetation and over 7 ft. to rocks. [All signs showed that they were in precisely the right location.]

Saturday, July 17, 1965
Got hole roughed out to about 7 ft. Deeper towards centre. Vegetation higher than normal to S.

Journal entries continued to describe work on this new shaft. They got cribbing down to thirteen feet and planned to drill down from the bottom of the shaft.

Monday, August 2, 1965
Ran drill down to just over 60 ft. Got hole and cribbing down to about 15 ft. Getting soft everywhere.

Tuesday, August 3, 1965
Got drill down through drain at <u>62 ft.</u> Got hole down and cribbed to about 17 ft.

A bulldozer was brought to the island. In his journal, Bobby drew a sketch to scale of the positioning of the white, hand-drilled rock at the beach so that it could be replaced after the bulldozer had done its job.

On August 10, in order to free up percentage for new investors, David Tobias agreed to turn back to the recovery operation the percentage he had accrued for his fuel expenditures. He retained the percentage purchased with his original investment.

Fred Sparham also agreed to reduce his percentage (which had originally been 25 percent, then 19 percent, then 12.5 percent) to 10 percent. In a note to Dad he wrote, "I always said that 10% of something is better than 25% of nothing." He still retained the 2 percent in his son's name.

In the midst of the pressures of the dig, a letter arrived from Robin Leach:

> Trans-Atlantic Features, Ltd.
> 1697 Broadway, New York 19, N.Y.
> August 10, 1965
> Dear Sir:
>
> At the early part of this year I had a long telephone conversation with your friend, Mr. Fred Sparham. He advised me to contact you later in the year to find out your progress on the treasure hunt.
>
> This letter requests from you — if you have a couple of spare moments to jot down on paper — up-to-date information as follows: —
>
> WHEN DO YOU EXPECT TO GET TO THE TREASURE?
>
> Also do you have any photographs of yourself, the work you are doing etc.
>
> Any information that you feel would be relevant to a story would be appreciated. I'm sorry that I have to write asking you this but Mr. Sparham told me you were not on a telephone linkup.
>
> Should the information you send me make for a full story at this stage I will be happy to pay you a generous sum for your co-operation with this British news agency.
>
> I wish you luck with your hunt and look forward to hearing from you shortly.
>
> My very best wishes for success
> Robin Leach
> News Editor

[P.S.] If necessary we would like to fly up a man to be with you on the final days of the treasure hunt — so we can say "Our Man was on the Spot as Bob Restall uncovers treasure."

Throughout all of his years on the island, Bobby had spent his Friday and Saturday evenings on the mainland with local youths. By now he had many friends. He built and raced his own stock cars. Over the years he had kept up a lively correspondence with his old shop teacher, Michael Farrell, from Barton Secondary School in Hamilton. Farrell, through countless letters steeped in mechanical detail, guided Bobby through heroic attempts to turn old junkers into stock cars fit for the raceway. On April 8, 1965, Bobby had turned twenty-four years old, and now, in August, leaving the island on a Sunday afternoon for the first time, he won his first race. In fact, his first two races. He must have been delighted. For the first and only time, a personal detail entered Bobby's journal.

Sunday, August 15, 1965
Dozer hitting more soft material. Down about ten feet. I went racing. Two firsts.

Monday, August 16, 1965
Dozer got down to about 13 ft. Water getting in from drill holes and beach pits. Soft in area. Found corner of shaft roughly on M.P. C-I-P line under road.

Tuesday, August 17, 1965
[In readiness, the date was written in, but there was no journal entry for August 17.]

While the bulldozer was digging a trench on the beach on August 17, Robert Dunfield watched and talked with Karl Graeser, who was there on one of his many impromptu visits to see the progress of the work. Bobby was gathering brush with three workmen. It was time for Dad to change out of his work clothes and head for the mainland before the bank closed at 3:00 p.m.

Dad took one last look down into the latest shaft to see how the pumping was coming along. Suddenly he tumbled in. Seeing him, Bobby dropped the bushes in his hands and raced to Dad's aid. As

Bobby started down the ladder inside the hole, he too fell. Karl Graeser was right behind him, rushing to help, but when he started down the ladder, he too fell victim to whatever had affected Dad and Bobby. Cyril Hiltz, one of the young men working to clear brush with Bobby, was next down the hole. His cousin Andrew Demont was right behind. Like the others before him, while descending the ladder in hopes of rescue, Demont tumbled into the shaft. Leonard Kaizer followed and fell. They must have been stacked like cordwood.

Answering calls for help, Edward White, a Buffalo, New York, fireman visiting the island with his family, tied a handkerchief around his face and was lowered down into the hole, despite his wife's begging him not to go down the shaft. Kaizer, the last to enter the shaft, had fallen across a beam that kept him out of the water. Ed White got a rope around him and rescuers at the surface pulled Kaizer out. The putrid stench emanating from the slimy water at the bottom of the shaft was overwhelming, and White found himself struggling to maintain consciousness. Nevertheless, he managed to untangle Demont from the struts bracing the cribbing and to bring him up and out of the hole. White realized it was hopeless to try to go back for more.

According to later recollections from Andrew Demont, the shaft was about ten feet by thirty feet and about twenty-seven feet deep. There was no odour at the surface of the shaft, but as Demont climbed down the ladder into the pit, an overpowering, foul rotten egg smell engulfed him. He felt himself fighting for consciousness, and fell from the ladder. A steel shaft was attached to the pump hose near the bottom of the hole, and Demont locked his arms around it. In the three to four feet of water in the bottom of the shaft, he could see only the top of Karl Graeser's head and he could see Bobby holding his father's head up. Demont placed his hand on Bobby's shoulder, then sank into unconsciousness. Apparently he remained there, unconscious, with his arms locked around the steel shaft for an hour and fifteen minutes. Later, Ed White came to visit Demont in his Halifax hospital and told him that the water had been up to his lips when White got to him. Apparently Demont, even in his unconscious state, had socked the fireman when he'd tried to get the rope harness around him.

Four men died that day: Karl Graeser, Cyril Hiltz, Bob Restall Sr., and Bob Restall Jr. It was later determined that the men were overcome by fumes and then drowned in the water at the bottom of the shaft. The Restall hunt for the treasure of Oak Island was over.

The Aftermath

CHAPTER 16

Doug and I were in our living room in Oakville when Fred Sparham phoned and broke the news. There had been an accident on the island. He'd heard it on the radio. I tried to deflect his words. The media dramatize everything. But Fred said quietly, "This might be real. They say your father and brother have been killed, along with two other men." We turned on the radio and immediately heard the announcement. A few moments later a knock came to the door. A young policeman came into the house and quietly read from his notebook. Now we knew it was true.

Doug and I flew to Nova Scotia that evening to be with Mom and Ricky. By that time, Doug was gravely ill. In fact, he was in his last two months of life.

My memory of the day of the funeral is unclear, but I do remember getting ready, then waiting for the appointed hour at Bill Sawler's house with Bill and his wife, Elva, who had been such good friends to my parents through all their years down east. Other family members of theirs were in the house too, talking quietly in the kitchen and dining room. I remember sitting alone in the living room, looking out the window and admiring the luxuriant green expanse of grass that stretched before me, when a man with dark hair and a familiar gait ambled across the lawn towards the house. Just in time I stopped myself from crying out, "There's Dad!" The reality of the deaths had not sunk in.

Though hazy, I do remember some of that day: the pews of the church filled with people who were strangers to me; the comforting words of the minister; the slow walk out of the church behind the caskets; and later, at the grave, standing between my mother and Doug with Rick at Mom's other side, watching the caskets gradually disappear into the ground. It was like watching a silent movie slowly unfold. Dad and Bobby were interred in Western Shore Cemetery, a small Anglican cemetery.

There was an outpouring of sympathy. Two women sent touching letters reminiscing about their visits on the island with Mom and Dad; they enclosed cheques to help Mom out, as did Dan Blankenship, the Florida businessman who had missed the opportunity to invest with Dad.

We were immediately pulled into a rush of activity set in motion by our investors. Legally, the estate of Robert Restall still controlled the rights to search for treasure until the end of 1965. Some of our investors decided that the Restall operation should continue immediately. That was necessary if those who had supported the project through the Restall years were to have any chance of seeing a return on their investment.

Both Mom and I moved about in a kind of slow-motion stupor, still unable to fully comprehend the horror of what had happened; Doug, ravaged by cancer, was frail and weak. Yet we three attended a meeting at Dad's lawyer's office in Halifax. Robert Dunfield and Fred Sparham were there as well as two other investors.

Our lawyer started the meeting by stating that he was unable to get a secretary to record the proceedings, so no minutes would be generated. He then announced that he was representing the interests of the estate of Bob Restall as well as the interests of Robert Dunfield. He asked if anyone objected. We were surprised, but said nothing.

A plan for action was outlined. As Dad's contract expired on the last day of December, there were only four months left before all who had been involved in the Restall search would no longer be entitled to anything. However, we were reminded, Dad had believed that the treasure was within immediate grasp, and Mom, as the chief executor of the estate, was within her rights to continue the search.

The lawyer stated that Dunfield had offered to carry on Dad's work, and since he was the only one already associated with the Restall search who showed interest in running the operation, and since time was a pressing factor, it was recommended that his offer be accepted. We were told that certain major investors and Chappell himself had already been contacted and were in agreement with all aspects of the plan.

Dunfield then stood up to speak. He began by mentioning his admiration for Dad. Then he provided details of his contract with Dad, outlined his own qualifications, and concluded by giving reasons why he was the one suitable to continue Dad's work.

The lawyer inquired as to where Mom planned to live in the future. Perhaps he thought that she might return to Ontario to live near me. The men in the meeting were visibly shaken at Mom's reply: "Oh, Rick and I will just continue living on the island." Doug and I nodded our approval. Dunfield broke the stunned silence with the opinion that the island would be a very unhappy place for Mildred and Rick now that Dad and Bobby were gone (of course he was right) and said that he had seen the perfect little house for Mom in Western Shore, on a hill over-looking Oak Island. Mom agreed to look at it. Dunfield declared that the recovery project would still support my mother. I interpreted that to mean financial support to pay her rent. But that didn't happen. My mother, however, had no such expectation, so possibly I misunderstood.

I asked Dunfield, if we did choose him to head up the operation, just how he would go about the work. He hesitated for a moment, then brightened and said, "Oh, I will continue the search in exactly the same manner as Bob Restall would have. Every effort will be made to preserve the island." That satisfied me.

According to the plan, Dunfield's $5,000 investment with Dad, which was still held in trust, would finance the start of this new phase in the recovery operation.

As 74 percent of Dad's share of the treasure had been committed to previous investors (not counting a portion to be allocated for the Restalls or the portion signed back by Chappell), and as this new phase of work on the island would undoubtedly require substantial financing, the lawyer indicated he would contact all current investors, requesting that they return a portion of their percentages to finance further explo-ration and recovery.

The contract that granted Dunfield the right to carry on the work included a clause stating that he must make every effort to obtain an extension of the existing contract in Bob Restall's name, and another clause stating that Dunfield could not seek to enter into a contract regarding the island in his own name for a period of five years.

It was patently obvious that everything under discussion in this meeting had been settled long before we entered the room. Yet permitting Dunfield to take the helm was a logical plan — likely the only viable plan, considering the short time before Dad's contract would run out. We agreed to go forward. Papers were signed.

Doug had used every ounce of energy he could draw upon to make this journey to the East Coast. By now he was so thin he was cadaverous. Weak and tired, he experienced constant dull, throbbing pain in his abdomen. He attended the meeting in the lawyer's office because we all felt it important that there be an adult male presence from the Restall side at the meeting, and Doug was it. There were no other men in the family now. His duty done, he and I returned to Ontario. Mom and Rick were left to manage for themselves.

After the deaths of my brother and father, I was totally absorbed by my own private tragedy as it slowly and painfully continued to unfold, while my mother was left to deal with hers. Neither of us was in a position to support or even stay in touch with the other for quite some time.

What I know about the Restall contracts from this point on has been gleaned mostly from letters and documents. Some of the Restall percentage in the treasure was promptly turned in to help keep the operation going. Shortly after that, Dunfield exercised his option to invest an additional $5,000 for 5 percent.

Newspapers were filled anew with reports about work on Oak Island. Dunfield immediately had a causeway built to provide a road between the mainland and Oak Island so that heavy equipment could be driven over, not brought in by barge. Newspaper reports showing the road being constructed were spectacular. It must have seemed to many that at last there was real action on Oak Island.

Despite our verbal exchange in the lawyer's office, Dunfield was under no contractual obligation with respect to how he went about his work. His contract specified, as had all the contracts between Chappell and my father, that he was free to execute the recovery in any manner he saw fit. But strangely enough, now that he was in control, Dunfield did not follow the plan he had outlined in his introductory letter to my father. A major feature of his original plan had been to use sheet piling to stop the sea water. However, this was a step he did not take once he was in charge. Nothing was done to halt the incoming sea water.

Soon heavy equipment gouged out the Money Pit area, and it was not long before the south end of the island was no longer recognizable. The beach at Smith's cove was laid bare by bulldozers. Even the huge wild rose bush that had been a landmark on the beach and a backdrop for island picnics for as long as anyone could remember was torn out.

Something significant might be buried under it. Many of the evergreen trees that comprised the southernmost tip of the island were brought down, inviting major land erosion. In the aggressive search for treasure that followed, the marker stones, shafts, pits, and tunnels that so typified the mystery of Oak Island received no special treatment. Soon the plateau that held the Money Pit became a vast, uneven, water-filled crater, more reminiscent of a saturated moonscape than the Garden of Eden it had once been.

The work was costly, and by November 29, three months after Dunfield took leadership of the operation, investors received a status report from the lawyer. It related that Dunfield had been successful in obtaining an extension of the Restall contract to August 31, 1966. Progress had not been as fast as had been anticipated; the Money Pit area had not yet been dug to the desired depth. Combined with unforeseen costs, this had led to a critical financial situation. However, now there was no more percentage to sell, so four of the major current investors had pulled together $27,223.85 to keep the search going and would be repaid "from the top" once the treasure was recovered. The report noted that since Dunfield had assumed control of the operation, some new investors had come on board (Blankenship got his chance to join the search) and $60,563.95 had gone into the recovery work. Earlier investors had been asked to turn back some percentage; many had. The rest were urged to contribute now.

It was all to no avail. Dunfield suspended operations for the winter and returned only briefly in the spring. On May 3 he issued a report accompanied by geological sketches that detailed the work that had been accomplished and what would be done next, if finances permitted. The Vertical Shaft (discovered in 1961 by Dad and Bobby) now needed to be re-excavated, but about twenty thousand yards of saturated clay (apparently excavated from the Cave-in Pit) needed to be bulldozed away before they could get into the shaft.

The last paragraph of Dunfield's report indicated that he and his family had returned to Los Angeles to wait for soil to dry on the island and to resolve tax problems and other personal matters. He quoted his foreman as stating that the island would not be workable for another one or two weeks.

To my knowledge, he never returned.

Robert Dunfield earned the everlasting enmity of my mother by not returning to her tools, equipment, and financial records that had belonged to my father. She also grieved over the destruction of her beloved island,

and she blamed Dunfield for that. Among her papers was an unfinished poem entitled "The Rape of the Island."

There was another matter. During our meeting in the lawyer's office, Dunfield had outlined the terms of his contract with Dad. For his $5,000, not only was he granted a percentage of the treasure, he was also entitled to 2.5 percent of proceeds from any Restall writings or media earnings. He sounded quite pleased with himself as he emphasized that this included writings by my mother. It was a bombshell. But we left it unremarked at the meeting.

In a subsequent meeting, Mom and Dunfield entered into a contract to turn a percentage over to the new search. In it, the item about proceeds of writings and the media was crossed out and initialed by both parties. My mother had dealt with the issue swiftly.

In the end, the clause proved to be irrelevant. The contract between Dunfield and Dad stipulated that the writings/media clause came into effect only after the discovery and recovery of the treasure under the contract between Dad and Chappell — an event, of course, that never came to pass.

Why would Dunfield have pressed for the inclusion of this clause? Any money it could have generated would have been insignificant when compared to the momentous recovery of the treasure. A person joining a search for riches beyond belief goes after pocket change earned from someone else's story? Incomprehensible.

According to my mother's notes to herself in those first days after the death, she consulted a local lawyer about the clause, and then spent "a very low day." Her grief would not have been about the money. It would have been about loyalty. My father had failed the test. After all the years that she had steadfastly stood by Dad, setting aside her own needs and wants and enduring severe hardships, in the end, my father betrayed her. Night after night, he watched her struggle for just the right word or phrase that would transform memories of life on the island into words on paper. He enjoyed seeing the pleasure she garnered from dreams of success. Yet when confronted by an investor who wanted a piece of that private domain to cinch the investment, Dad gave in. It was full surrender to his Oak Island obsession. It was Dunfield who brought this ugly test of loyalty into their lives. And my mother definitely was one who would shoot the messenger.

She investigated the possibility of suing Dunfield for the return of the tools and records, but was dissuaded by counsel in view of U.S./Canada border complications.

In time, Mom drafted a complaint to the Attorney General against Dad's lawyer, who had been the Restall lawyer for several years but who, she felt, had created a conflict of interest when he undertook to represent Dunfield as well as my mother in the continuation of the Restall recovery operation. But again, she was dissuaded by legal counsel.

There is no question that she received less than first-class legal service. It was the Restall contract that was in force throughout Dunfield's management of the search, and yet my mother received no accounting of investments, only fragments of information on expenditures, and no formal notice that Dunfield had terminated the work.

In later years this lawyer fell afoul of the law society. Need I say that my mother was jubilant?

A few other details about Oak Island need mentioning.

Shortly after Doug and I left Nova Scotia, while Mom and Rick were still living on the island, they had occasion to be away for a few hours. When they returned, they found that Dad's small tools had been stolen, as had every one of his family photograph albums. Throughout travels in Germany, the British Isles, Hawaii, and Canada, using his Zeiss Icon camera, Dad had been an avid photographer. He assembled large albums full of snapshots, which he prized highly. Now all were gone, including his carefully assembled and captioned album of Oak Island pictures. It is only because my father was such a pack rat that some duplicate photos survive, as does Bobby's own photograph album.

The autopsy performed on Dad and Bobby reported the cause of death as drowning. Nothing in the autopsy mentions what caused the unconsciousness that led to the drowning, or the foul, rotten egg smell that clung to the bodies and clothing.

My mother and I almost never spoke about the island, but on one visit I was moved to ask details of the deaths. I wondered, since it was obvious that toxic gas was present, how had the bodies been recovered? She didn't know. The Chester Volunteer Fire Department had done the job. Jimmy Kaizer, part of the Western Shore Fire Department, who had worked with Dad and Bobby on the island many times over the years, had helped. We sought him out. I think he was glad to be asked about that day at last. "We didn't know how we were going to get those bodies out. We stood around looking at the hole and talking about different things we could do. Someone suggested grappling hooks [used by fishermen to land big fish]. I said 'Nobody's going to put a grapplin' hook in Mr. Restall. No sir. Nobody's puttin' a grapplin' hook in Mr. Restall.' So I borrowed a mask, and the men lowered me down the hole, and we got them out, one by one. And, Mrs. Restall, my clothes just stunk somethin' awful," he told me. "I never smelt nothin' like it in my life. The best I can describe it is a kind of rotten egg smell. My wife washed my clothes, but the smell didn't come out. We hung the clothes outside, but it didn't help. Then we hung them downstairs by the washing machine, and every time my wife did the laundry, she put those clothes in again for another wash. But we never could get rid of that rotten egg smell. After about a year, I threw those clothes away."

Recently I spoke with Nick Gates, who, along with Allan Bremmer and Olaf Peterson, answered the call to recover the bodies. Gates related that when they arrived on the island, they tied three poles together, from which they suspended a rope so they could be lowered into the pit and bring out the bodies. The Chester fire department had no air equipment at that time, only one old gas mask that was capable of functioning somewhat as a filter. Jimmy Kaizer volunteered to go down the pit. He put on the mask and was lowered down to the bodies. He managed to get a rope around one of the dead men and to bring him to the surface. By the time the second body was retrieved, Jimmy was nauseated and unsteady. Another of the men took over, but quickly signalled to be returned to the surface. Inside the pit, the fumes were overpowering. Jimmy rallied, put on the mask again, and went down into the putrid fumes and murky waters for the last two bodies. Then began the laborious task of struggling down the hill with the bodies to the waiting boat.

I do not know what caused the noxious gas that rendered the men unconscious that day, but I am certain that it was a natural phenomenon that emanated from deep within the island and had undoubtedly been set free by digging that last shaft.

To her death in her ninety-first year, my mother had nothing but contempt for the so-called treasure of Oak Island, but she did not feel that way about the people involved. She always spoke well of David Tobias, and she considered Dan Blankenship to be a friend. Among our photos is one of Mom and Dan taken at the memorial service in August 1995 that was held in honour of the men who died on Oak Island. It was a lovely service, held on the south end of the island in a huge tent with side panels gently flapping in the breeze. It began and ended with the Chester Brass Band and included prayers by clergy and speeches by a number of dignitaries, including the Lieutenant Governor of Nova Scotia. A monument and a bronze plaque in honour of the men who lost their lives on Oak Island were unveiled. They were dedicated by the Bishop of the Anglican Diocese. After the conclusion of the service that afternoon, the Lunenberg County Fiddlers played beautiful, haunting melodies. A perfect end to a perfect day.

One last note on treasure hunting. After the deaths, Mom and Rick received countless messages of condolence. But there were also numerous letters from men who offered to work with my mother to carry on the search for treasure, or who urgently requested information on who to contact now to arrange to dig on the island themselves. And for the next ten years letters trickled in from people who had just read the *Reader's Digest* article and wanted to know how the search was going or wanted to share their solution in exchange for a percentage of the treasure.

When Mom and Rick settled on the mainland, they closed the door on Oak Island. Mom was fifty-two years old, virtually penniless, and she had a fourteen-year-old son to raise. Rick had his own challenges. After six years of near solitude on the island, he needed to learn to function in a world full of people.

Although never in her life had she held a day job or done any work not related to show business, my mother enrolled in secretarial college, obtained her diploma, and secured a job as secretary with her family doctor, George Jollymore. In no time Dr. Jollymore's practice, the Chester Medical Clinic, expanded to include two locations, several doctors, other office staff, and Mom as office manager.

In time she added two part-time jobs to her repertoire; she taught bookkeeping and typing at night school. She retired, despite Dr. Jollymore's protestations, at age seventy years.

Occasionally, in the last twenty years of her life, she gave thought to moving to Ontario to be close to Rick or I, but those notions tended to surface in winter months and to pass with the first signs of spring. She never could tear herself away from the beauty of Nova Scotia or the solid friendships she had formed.

She never discussed the past. I urged her to write her biography, even without the Oak Island part. I remember once trying to encourage her: "We had such a wonderful life in Hamilton, so many laughs, so many good times."

She was silent for a moment, then, with a touch of bitterness in her voice, she replied, "Funny. I can't remember that."

She felt responsible for Bobby's death. Near the end, he and Dad had quarrelled frequently. One day Bobby prepared to leave the island for good, but she talked him out of it. If she hadn't intervened, she reasoned, he might still be alive. Rick confided, "He very likely would have come back anyway. It was too important to him."

She and Rick came to visit us in Oakville, the first or second Christmas after the deaths. The morning after their arrival, I awakened so completely overcome by nausea that at first I was unable to move from the bed, and inside my head I heard a faint anguished cry, "Bobby. Bobby." Later, as I stumbled about in the kitchen trying to put a breakfast together, I told my mother what I had just experienced. She listened with eyes downcast, then slowly said, "It just happened this morning. You're lucky. That happens to me every morning." Her searing pain over the loss of Bobby must have invaded my consciousness that morning, in my just-waking state.

Mom and Bobby had shared a special closeness. Bobby did precisely what he wished, and when my mother objected, he would just turn to her, pat her gently on the back, and say, "There, there, Mother. Don't you worry about a thing. I'll handle it." And Mom would giggle like a schoolgirl and turn to other concerns.

Money management skills did not abandon my mother after the deaths. By her retirement she had squirreled away enough money to purchase an annuity that provided her with a modest but comfortable retirement. She stayed on in the little house with its view of Oak Island and made it into a cozy home. She bought a new car and drove it until it was ready for permanent retirement, then she bought her next new car and then the next, always for cash. "I tried financing once," she confided, "but making those payments spoiled the fun of having a new car, so I paid it off." In time, she bought herself a lovely, brand new piano, an acquisition that thrilled her. She did some travelling out of Canada, but mostly she enjoyed her spot in Western Shore and her many jaunts to Chester, Mahone Bay, Bridgewater, Lunenburg, and Halifax.

Throughout her nearly forty years after the accident, reporters continued to contact my mother for interviews about Oak Island. She seldom acquiesced, but when she did, she revealed little. She would confide to Rick or me, "I never tell them anything important. I'm saving that for the Restall story." Suggestions that she get to work on that story were met with sharp hostility. Then, from her hospital bed in her ninety-first year, just two weeks before she died, she told me that it was her wish that either Rick or I or both of us tell the Restall story.

After her death on August 2, 2003, when we cleared out her house, Rick and I found, to our amazement, that everything had been kept. Every letter, every contract, every journal, every sketch and map, even her own four-page handwritten notes jotting down events as they unfolded in those horrible days following Dad's and Bobby's deaths.

As Mom got older her mind stayed sharp, but her body betrayed her. Walking became difficult. Too proud to use a walker, at Rick's insistence she finally agreed to use a cane. Then when she was eighty-eight, she was diagnosed with cancer of the lung. She was furious. "What can you do with a message like that? What do they expect me to do? Die?!" She solved the problem by challenging the specialist for proofs and taking her care from one doctor to another. Then she ignored the entire issue. My mother reasoned that if the Queen Mother could live until she was one hundred, she was entitled to do the same.

In July of 2003, during Rick's visit, she suddenly found she couldn't swallow. Rick took her to Queen Elizabeth Hospital in Halifax. The cancer was crowding her throat. A stent was inserted to allow her to swallow.

She revelled in the attention she received on the ward. On one occasion two young nurses from another ward came up to ask for her autograph, not because of Oak Island, but because of her motorcycle days. She was delighted.

Although the stent alleviated the problem with swallowing, she was advised that it was only a stop-gap measure. The cancer would progress, and probably more aggressively now.

Four of us — Mom and I, the oncologist who headed the cancer ward, and her assistant — sat in a small room just off the ward. (Rick had returned to Ontario.) The oncologist explained that usually there are three choices. In this case the first choice, radiation, was not an option; the cancer had spread throughout Mom's lungs, and the area affected was too large for treatment by radiation. Option two, chemotherapy, might be effective, but it was extremely hard on the patient. In view of Mom's age, a milder form of the chemo could be administered, but still it most certainly would make my mother very ill and weak, with no guarantees of success. The third option, the doctor intoned, would be for my mother to say, "Well, I've had a good life, and now I'm going to relax and enjoy what time I have left." My mother listened intently as each option was presented. Then she looked at the doctor gravely and said, "Well, I've had a good life. But I want more."

So chemotherapy it was. They kept her in hospital to administer it so that she could be observed, to make sure she was healthy enough to return home to await her next course of chemotherapy in a month's time. I would live with her.

The hospital staff treated my mother as if she were a star, and she rose to the occasion. She even requested a notebook, pencil, and tape recorder. Time to get to work on that autobiography.

As promised, she felt no change during the three days of treatment. But two days after the chemotherapy ceased, she fell ill, no doubt to some minor infection. The chemo had left her body defenseless. All day long on August 2, 2003, slipping in and out of consciousness, she fought bravely. In the evening, she finally succumbed. In accordance with her wishes, she was cremated, and her ashes buried in Western Shore Cemetery, beside Dad and Bobby.

Coda

Oak Island had her way with my father. He was so in thrall to his treasure-hunting dream that he lost sight of everything else, even the welfare of his family. All that mattered was the quest. By the end, he had come to believe that his very worth as a human being could be measured only by conquering the island.

It is a tragedy that his single-minded pursuit of the treasure led to his death on the island on August 17, 1965, but it is even more tragic that other innocent lives were taken with him: Bobby, faithfully rushing to his father's aid; Karl Graeser, selfless to the end, an intelligent, capable, good man much needed by his wife and two daughters; and Cyril Hiltz, a sixteen-year-old, barely at the brink of manhood, who left behind his mother and father, his sister and brother (Gordon, who was working with him on the island that fateful day), and his fiancé, Marjorie Demont. What a terrible waste.

Acknowledgements

This book could never have come into existence had not my father, mother, and brother Bobby been such prolific writers. Only through their own words could the true Restall story emerge.

This was my mother's first attempt at writing, and I was delighted to read her account of life on the island. She told me once how much she enjoyed reading descriptive passages when she was young. It is easy to see how her eye for detail and love of description combine to make her a compelling storyteller.

My brother Bobby amazed me. The daily work details faithfully recorded in his journals provide a framework and timeline for all that lies between these covers. His essays on the work of previous searchers and of the Restalls deepened my understanding of my family's Oak Island experience. Bobby's sketches and maps are invaluable. He was eighteen years old when he arrived on Oak Island and twenty-four when he died. I am in awe of the man he became through this adventure.

My father, in his letters to his friend, put flesh on the Restall hunt for treasure. It was only when I read his letters that I fully realized the interminable delays and frustrations that typified their doomed recovery operation. And, of course, it was Dad, the shutterbug, who left behind so many photographs to illustrate life on the island.

My contribution to this book has been to gather the pieces of my family's adventure and to try to stitch them together into a comprehensible whole. In that task I had substantial assistance.

My brother Rick set aside his own preference for anonymity and encouraged me to go forward. Recalling his years on Oak Island from ages nine to fourteen, he provided me with insider information and anecdotes. His calm and reasoned counsel in the preparation of this book has been a great help.

Ann MacIntyre is the friend who tirelessly read version after version of my first draft as I struggled to find the best way to tell this story. As she and I battled, again and again, in long-distance phone calls over the value of this anecdote or that vignette, Ann wondered aloud if our friendship would endure this book. It most definitely has.

As a young man, Jim Leskewich rode motorcycle for my parents as they travelled across Canada with the Globe of Death. Jim generously advised me with respect to technical information about those carnival years. He and his wife, Joy, served as readers of the manuscript and provided unwavering encouragement for me to complete the project.

Danny Hennigar of the Oak Island Tourism Society served as an expert in a different field. When the manuscript had to be trimmed, Danny provided advice as to which material would be most valued by Oak Island aficionados. And his wife, Yvonne, stayed my hand when some family vignettes were destined for the waste bin. Danny also provided me with information and contacts regarding the fateful accident and the recovery of the bodies.

Eddie Sparham is my special hero. I hope this biography has made it clear what a wonderful friend his father, Fred Sparham, was to my father. The sixty-eight letters that Dad wrote to Fred provide insights that are available in no other form; the sketches that accompanied the letters are invaluable. Eddie Sparham saved all of the letters from my father to his father and generously made a gift of them to me. I am deeply grateful.

A special thanks must go to the folks of Nova Scotia from Chester to Lunenburg and on to Bridgewater. Throughout my family's six years on the island, and from then until my mother's death some thirty-eight years later, these were caring neighbours and stalwart friends.

For many years, misinformation has been printed about the Restall search for treasure on Oak Island. I am grateful to my editor, Tony Hawke, and to The Dundurn Group for believing in this project and ensuring that the real Restall story can finally be told.